DELIBERATE
EVIL

DELIBERATE EVIL

―

NATHANIEL HAWTHORNE,
DANIEL WEBSTER,
and the
1830 MURDER
of a
SALEM
SLAVE TRADER

―

Edward J. Renehan Jr.

CHICAGO
REVIEW
PRESS

Published by Chicago Review Press Incorporated
814 North Franklin Street
Chicago, Illinois 60610
ISBN 978-1-64160-338-6

Library of Congress Control Number: 2021944642

Typesetting: Nord Compo

Printed in the United States of America
5 4 3 2 1

For my grandchildren
Connor William
and
Annalise Marie

"Time flies over us but leaves its shadow behind."

—Nathaniel Hawthorne, *The Marble Faun*

"You see, for a while [Daniel Webster] was the biggest man in the country. He never got to be President, but he was the biggest man. There were thousands that trusted in him right next to God Almighty, and when he argued a case, he could turn on the harps of the blessed and the shaking of the earth underground."

—Stephen Vincent Benét,
"The Devil and Daniel Webster"

CONTENTS

PROLOGUE

"Murder, though it have no tongue, will speak."
—William Shakespeare, *Hamlet*

THE APRIL 1830 MURDER of wealthy eighty-two-year-old shipmaster, trader, and slaver Joseph White in Salem, Massachusetts, inspired not only national journalistic attention but also something more: notable literary contemplations by none other than Salem native Nathaniel Hawthorne, who actually knew several of the participants in the crime. Hawthorne used aspects of the murder case, and other elements of Salem history and culture, to fuel extended ruminations on dark and complex themes—most notably, the nature of guilt, both inherited and otherwise.

The White murder also served as one of America's first real-life experiments in what would become the classic tableau of that genre known as "the detective story." Writing in 1940, Edmund Pearson spoke of how the murder of Joseph White had all the fundamental elements of the great procedurals of deduction subsequently crafted by the likes of Edgar Allan Poe and Wilkie Collins. "There was hardly," he commented, "one omission of scene, of cast, or of stage property." In addition to the "morbidly respectable and extremely horrified" citizens of the Salem establishment, there was the victim of great wealth and prominence asleep in the presumed safety of his mansion, there were menacing figures observed in darkness on the night of the crime, and there was "even talk of a cave in the woods, where a gang of 'harlots, gamblers and sharpers'" gathered.[1] Indeed, in sentencing one of the main culprits in the crime, Massachusetts Supreme Court Associate Justice Samuel Putnam said, "If such events had been set forth in a work of fiction, they would have been considered as too absurd and unnatural for public endurance. The story would have been treated as a libel upon man."[2]

The byzantine, months-long investigation into the murder of Captain White was made all the more interesting to the newspaper-reading public when it was realized that some of the people involved in the affair came from several of the most prominent and prosperous families on the entire Eastern Seaboard. This interest was heightened further by the Gothic fascination with which many already viewed Salem, home to the infamous witch trials of 1692. There was also Captain White's sordid history in the slave trade at a time when Massachusetts was becoming imbued with heated antislavery sentiment, a fact that made him quite an unsympathetic victim. Add to this the participation in the trial of one of the most famous men in the country at that time: the eloquent and brilliant Daniel Webster, then a sitting senator from Massachusetts, who came aboard as a freelance prosecutor and in that capacity rendered what is, still today, considered one of the finest summations ever uttered in an American courtroom.

The overall story of the White murder is so utterly engaging from so many different angles that one *at first* wonders why the tale—as much a story of murder as it is the study of the social history related to the great maritime families of the New England coast—has remained so obscure for so very long, since the days when it dominated headlines up and down the Eastern Seaboard. But there are reasons, which form a unique and important story unto themselves.

The suppression of this story over many decades has been due to direct efforts by wealthy descendants of several Salem shipping dynasties—prime players in the drama—who wished the tale to dry up and blow away. Suppression over the course of nearly two centuries has taken many forms. It has included, but not been limited to, the recall, rewriting, and republication of an early Daniel Webster biography, this exercise financed by the White family in order to eliminate all mention of the murder and trial. In this way, they hoped to erase from memory the visage of Joseph White, who added so much to the family wealth through his lucrative but shameful career as a slaver.

Other tools of suppression were available to descendants of these same Salem clans by virtue of their roles as major benefactors of the Peabody Essex Museum—the prime holder of documents, relics, and even real estate involved in the story. Throughout many decades, these families exercised great influence over which archives were to be open or closed and how objects related to the crime—including the site of the murder itself—were to be maintained and interpreted.

Over time, various descendants of those involved with the 1830 episode married into the very highest ranks of American society, allying themselves with the Adams, Endicott, and du Pont families, to name just a few. When these scions went on to become captains of industry and presidential cabinet secretaries, they did not need the stark memory of one ancestral ghost's career as a slaver, or another ancestral ghost's propensity for murder, haunting their families, lives, and careers. But some ghosts cannot be exorcised—at least not permanently.

Thus, the case's very obscurity, and the reasons behind that, form a significant part of the tale—a tale worthy of Hawthorne. "It is not down on any map," wrote Hawthorne's close friend Herman Melville in *Moby Dick*, "true places never are." The story to be told here, though entirely true, has been largely, though not entirely, unmapped for some 190 years.

1 | OLD SALEM BY MOONLIGHT

"Murder, like talent, seems occasionally to run in families."

—George Henry Lewes,
The Physiology of Common Life (1859)

WE HAVE IT ON RECORD that there was a bright, full moon in Salem, Massachusetts, on the evening of Tuesday, April 6, 1830. If one were viewing the town of fourteen thousand from the high ground of that grim place, Gallows Hill, which according to local lore was said to have been the site of the original witch trial hangings, one would have spotted, in the distance, more than fifty wharves extending into the harbor. These wharves were the result of more than a century of the most powerful and prosperous Salem families—led at various moments by the Derbys, the Whites, the Crowninshields, and the Storys—seeking to subdue the land and waters and make both conform not to nature's plan, but to the demands of modern man and modern commerce. Not so long before 1830, Salem's prominence as the world center of the highly lucrative China trade, not to mention trade with the East Indies and other ports of the world, had stood undisputed. The city's still fairly robust waterfront was but one symbol of that status.

The wharves hummed with constant activity by day and night. Ships and crews were expensive assets not meant to rest on shore for any longer than was absolutely necessary. The spectator standing on Gallows Hill would have seen the wharves lit brightly with torches and lanterns. He or

1

she would have heard, in the distance, the incessant shouts of stevedores and the groans of tortured gangways as heavy cartons and barrels were hauled up and down. He or she would have spotted the silhouettes of men in the rigging of the tall ships, checking sheets and mending sails in the full moonlight. And the observer would have known that those members of the crews lucky enough to have a few hours away from the vessel could likely be found in the taverns, gambling dens, and whorehouses on the edge of town, abominations such as Salem's witch-killing Puritan founders could never have imagined. Many of these were owned and managed by a highly entrepreneurial free Black man of dubious reputation, John "King" Mumford, while the balance were owned by two men who shall soon become principals in this story. (Most of the vice, one contemporary report said, had popped up after the War of 1812, which, according to several observers, had caused the violent habits of war and privateering to injure public morals.)

Looking out from that same high ground of Gallows Hill, the watcher would have also seen and comprehended all the architectural landmarks of great prosperity side by side with relics of that prosperity's humble and unlikely genesis. Near the waterfront in South Salem stood the "first period" houses of the earliest settlers, dating back to the mid-1600s. These were simple frame dwellings with deep-pitched roofs: two-room, central-chimney affairs characterized by all the spartan simplicity one would expect from stern Protestant settlers intent on creating God-centered lives in a new, uncertain, and alien land.

Elsewhere, particularly along Essex, Brown, and Chestnut Streets, one could make out the elaborate Federal-style mansions of a later generation: those Puritan descendants who, over long decades, had come around to the lure of materialism, the comforts of wealth, and an understanding of the ease with which such comforts could be obtained through the practice of sometimes unscrupulous trade. Among these houses stood the looming red-brick Federal-style mansion of an eighty-two-year-old merchant, Captain Joseph White. Designed and built in 1804 by Salem's most prominent architect and builder, Samuel McIntire, the home featured high Corinthian columns framing a wide portico, just the sort of ostentation and indulgence that Salem's original inhabitants would have thought sinful.[1]

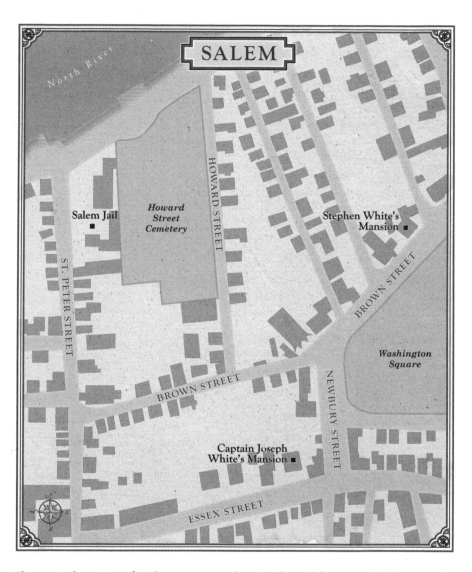

The central section of Salem, excerpted and adapted from an 1851 map of the city made by Henry McIntyre. The Salem commercial waterfront lies two blocks to the south of Essex Street. Original of the full map is in the Norman P. Leventhal Map Center of the Boston Public Library. *Chris Erichsen*

Yes, opulence had come to define the better quarters of Salem, where possessors of great fortunes dwelled in luxury not far from the waterfront where longshoremen, sailors, and shipwrights worked long hours to maintain the affluence of others. On this particular night of April 6, the minions of Salem's great families slept well—and, one would have thought, safely—in their beds, content with the world and their dominance over it.

2 | AN INCONVENIENT APPARITION

"'I am thinking,' he remarked quietly, 'whether I shall add to the disorder in this room, by scattering your brains about the fireplace.'"
—Wilkie Collins, *The Woman in White* (1859)

ACCORDING TO THE STORY he told on the morning of Wednesday, April 7, 1830, forty-year-old Benjamin White had spent the previous evening at the same place where he could be found most nights: his favorite water-front tavern. Fellow habitués of the saloon would later confirm Benjamin's presence. As usual, the impoverished Benjamin had been complaining about his employer and distant cousin, Captain Joseph White, whom he was known to despise.[1]

To the denizens of the tavern, it was a familiar rant. A drunken Benjamin could always be counted upon for vehement denunciations of White. He routinely criticized the widower's frugality when it came to wages, his swagger and commanding manner about the household, and his lasciviousness. In regard to the latter, Benjamin loudly informed anyone who would listen of White's "unnatural" relationship with his forty-year-old niece and housekeeper, Mary Beckford—an accusation that appears to have been completely fraudulent—and also the captain's frequent lewd remarks and behavior toward twenty-six-year-old chambermaid Lydia Kimball, these occurring whenever Mary was out of the house.

With each drink, Benjamin would become more and more agitated in denouncing White's many sins. The man would usually be in a pure white rage

5

by the time he headed home to his room in Captain White's mansion, which he did at around nine o'clock on the evening of April 6. The oft-repeated script was well known, an object of levity for those who made a nightly amusement of buying Benjamin drinks and urging him on.

"Mr. W. went to bed that night rather later than usual," Benjamin would recall, "about 20 minutes before ten. His usual hour was about nine. . . . I went to bed that night immediately after Captain White went. It was almost a quarter before ten." Benjamin left Lydia Kimball behind, raking up the fire. He was sure of the time because he "looked into the keeping parlor at the clock."[2] There was nothing between Benjamin's room and that of Captain White other than a short hallway and a staircase. Nevertheless, Benjamin heard nothing from the captain's room during the night.

Benjamin rose early on the seventh, as was his habit, even after a night on the town. Though his head might throb, there was still a stove to light,

Essex Street, photographed circa 1900 with the mansion of Captain Joseph White, number 128, shown at far right. Now called the Gardner-Pingree House, the mansion is owned and maintained by the Peabody Essex Museum. The house was designed and built by Salem's preeminent architect, Samuel McIntire, in 1804. *Photo by Frank Cousins from the Frank Cousins Collection of Glass Plate Negatives. Courtesy of Phillips Library, Peabody Essex Museum, Salem, MA*

water to be fetched, and a privy to be washed down—the regular daily round enacted before the rest of the household awoke. Benjamin was in the midst of these duties when he noticed a window open on the rear ground floor of the mansion and a plank leaning against the lower exterior frame. The window that had been opened went into a room that, like the entire eastern side of the house, was used very little, there being at that time only four residents of the very large place. Benjamin assumed, he said, that there had been a burglary. With this in mind, he went into the front room, where he observed nothing amiss, then upstairs to alert Lydia Kimball in her third-floor room near his own. Not long afterward, following a survey of the front parlor with Kimball, Benjamin went to wake the captain.

White's bedroom was on the second floor and had two doors, front and back. One, the front door, stood open: an uncustomary occurrence. Entering the room, Benjamin found the master of the house laying on his side, very cold, very stiff, and very dead. A pronounced wound to White's forehead looked as though it had been made with the blow of a hammer. There appeared also to be several stab wounds to the chest. The captain's face, Benjamin said, was "very pale." Benjamin saw that the bedclothes had been turned down, and "I think I saw some blood upon the side of the bed, or on his flannel."

The head of White's bed lay against the eastern wall of his chamber, near the front entry door. Therefore, anyone who might have entered that door— the door that had been left open—would have been able to come up behind Captain White as he slept, as he usually did, on his right side.

After taking a moment to digest what he was seeing, Benjamin rushed downstairs and informed Kimball as to what had happened. Once this was done, he ran to alert some near neighbors—a Mr. Mansfield and a Mr. Deland, then Captain White's physician, Dr. Samuel Johnson (who was also a neighbor), before finally trotting across Washington Square (referred to colloquially as the Salem Common), to the home of Captain Joseph White's forty-one-year-old nephew and adopted son, Stephen White. This younger White was a prominent Salem merchant, state senator, and brother-in-law to another Salem resident, Joseph Story, who at that time served both as associate justice of the US Supreme Court and dean of the Harvard Law School.

After informing Stephen White, Benjamin returned to the mansion and examined the open window. He found it raised some twenty-one or twenty-two inches. "The shutter, which opened very hard, was open some ways," Benjamin would testify. "The window was fastened by a screw, and the shutter by a bar. I found the bar standing by the right side of the window." Nothing seemed to have been forced or broken, although the window was usually secured by both the screw and the bar, and both would have had to be broken for a forced entry. Later on, examining the same spot, Dr. Johnson would note that he saw "two footprints, both directed towards the wall of the house. There was a plank set up, diagonally, the bottom of it about two feet from the sill. There were no marks of wet feet, but a little dampness on the floor."

Among the first on the scene were Captain White's twenty-year-old assistant William Ward and the aforementioned Stephen White along with physician Johnson. The elderly Dr. Johnson tried his best to judge the time of death by measuring the temperature of the corpse, saying he guessed White had been dead for something like four hours—which put the time of the murder at approximately 3:30 AM. "I went to Captain White's chamber," Johnson recalled, "and found him lying on his right side, or nearly so, and nearly diagonal to the bed. There was a mark of considerable violence on his left temple. I noticed that the bedclothes were laid slantwise, square across the body, and diagonally to the bed." The captain lay with his feet toward the left lower post of the bed, and his head toward the right headpost. "On throwing off the bedclothes, I saw that the back of his left hand was under his left hip, and there was considerable blood on the bed. He also bled a little from the nose."

White's assistant and clerk Ward surprised the others when he bent down, retrieved a large chest from under White's bed, and opened it to reveal an abundance of cash and gold coins. It was also noticed that a rouleau of Spanish doubloons, easily worth at least $1,000, had been left untouched on the captain's bureau. Thus, theft seemed eliminated as a motive for the crime. The only thing that might be missing from the chest, said Ward, was a sworn copy of Captain White's latest will—but he could be mistaken as to where the captain had kept it stored. The matter seemed unimportant. The original of the will, as both Stephen White and Ward knew, was safe in the hands of Captain White's attorney, Joseph G. Waters. In turn, Stephen White, after touring the house—with which he was very familiar—said no other valuables appeared to be missing.

As it happened, Captain White's niece and housekeeper, Mary Beckford, had been away on the night of the crime. She'd been visiting her daughter, another Mary, and Mary's husband, Joseph "Joe" Jenkins Knapp Jr., on the farm where the couple lived in Wenham, six miles to the north of Salem. (The farm was one that Beckford had purchased a year before, now managed by Beckford's son-in-law, John Davis, the husband of Mary Beckford Knapp's sister.)[3] Knapp had been to White's mansion on the sixth, at about noon, to give his mother-in-law a ride to the farm. Young Knapp had previously been the master on one of White's ships, and his Mary had once worked and lived in Captain White's mansion under the supervision of her mother.

Shortly after the discovery of the murder, Stephen White instructed one of his servants to go to Wenham, inform Mrs. Beckford of what had occurred, and bring her back to Salem. He instructed another to go to Captain White's attorney, Joseph Waters, and secure the original of the captain's latest will.

White also summoned the town coroner, Thomas Needham—a member of the city council and, by trade, a prominent cabinetmaker.[4] Needham, in turn, assembled a jury of inquest from among the curious onlookers who had already begun to gather around the house, swore them as witnesses, and led them upstairs into Captain White's bedroom. This group then witnessed a more systematic study of the body by Dr. Johnson than he had done previously, assisted by Salem's Dr. Oliver Hubbard.

Johnson explained each step to the laymen as he and Hubbard drew back Captain White's bloody bedclothes and then cut away the captain's blood-drenched nightshirt to reveal what seemed like more than a dozen knife wounds. Using a probe, Johnson identified five stabs to the heart, five to the side, and three to the chest. Johnson also pointed out the grievous wound to the skull—a profound indentation but one that, strangely, revealed no breakage of the skin.

As to the direct cause of death, Johnson said he could make no precise determination. It could have been the blow to the head. Or it could have been one or several of the knife wounds. There was no sign of a struggle, which indicated that the blow to the head had come first, knocking out the sleeping

The front door of the Joseph White mansion, photographed circa 1900.
Photo by Frank Cousins from the Frank Cousins Collection of Glass Plate Negatives.
Courtesy of Phillips Library, Peabody Essex Museum, Salem, MA

victim, and then the knife stabs. (A few illustrations for some newspaper accounts would later show, quite inaccurately, Captain White cowering with eyes open in his bed while his murderer approached. No such thing appears to have happened.)

After Johnson's examination of the corpse, the coroner supervised several men who lifted the now-shrouded body, carried it downstairs, loaded it onto a cart, and headed off in the direction of the Salem Jail, where the corpse would be stored until a more formal autopsy could be arranged. While this went on, Benjamin White and Lydia Kimball watched out the window of the mansion's front parlor.

Stephen White was to recall much later that Kimball was a frail little thing, a slight wisp of a girl both physically and, it seemed, emotionally. She'd twelve years earlier been put out to service in the White household by her parents who lived in Gloucester, her mother a seamstress and her father a fisherman. As she spoke to White on the morning after the murder, her body shivered—not from cold, but from sheer nervous agitation and exhaustion. She'd retired only a little after Captain White went up, once she'd finished cleaning the kitchen and banking the fire in the parlor. She said she'd bolted the door to her room from the inside but did not elaborate as to why. Kimball's room, on the third floor, sat immediately above and in earshot of Captain White's. "I could generally tell when he was awake," she was to recall, "if I myself was so, by a kind of cough or hem which he had when awake, which was usually in the latter part of the night." But she heard no such sounds on the night of the murder.

Of that morning she recalled Benjamin coming to her door and informing her that there had been a break-in. "I went down into the front room to see if anything had been stolen, [then told Benjamin] to go up and tell Mr. White. He came down and told me to be calm, that Mr. White had gone to the eternal world." She told Stephen White she thanked God she'd been spared, and she wondered out loud who could have transacted such a foul deed. One person whom White could not imagine doing this evil was the diminutive, delicate eggshell of a girl who sat before him. She did not seem at all the type that could swing a hammer down onto the head of a sleeping octogenarian, let alone pound his chest repeatedly with a dagger. Captain White, she said, was not always a nice man, but still it was a pity what had happened to him. Kimball impressed White as an innocent in more ways than one. As for Benjamin, Stephen White simply did not think the man, as a practical matter, capable of the deed. In the final analysis, Benjamin had neither the imagination nor the courage.

The Whites had a long history in the region of Salem. Captain White's father, Joseph White Sr., had been born there in 1724—the son of Captain John White Sr., who'd been born in Gloucester in 1698. Captain White's mother, Abigail Mutchemore, hailed from another place altogether: the southernmost island of the Isles of Shoals on the New Hampshire–Maine border, to which Joseph Sr. relocated briefly after his marriage before returning home to Salem.[5] Abigail's husband died young, in 1751, at the age of twenty-seven, leaving her with three small children: Mary (age five), Joseph (three), and Henry (a newborn). Abigail and her children were thereafter supported by Captain John White Sr. and his wife Rebecca (the children's grandparents), and Captain John White Jr. (the children's uncle). In time, Joseph and his brother Henry were brought into the family business, learning to become merchantmen and skippers. John White Sr. died in 1781, and John White Jr. in 1792. As the elder between himself and his brother Henry, Captain Joseph White inherited the business and the family wharf, the latter of which he set about expanding in 1798.

Joseph White, it was generally agreed, had been a contrary character—quick to argue, take offense, even scores, and go to war in both personal and professional life. At the time of the Revolution, he'd at first remained loyal to the Crown. Only after the British began raiding his ships did he change course. After purchasing a vessel named *Come Along Paddy* from one of the Derby clan, he had her refitted with cannon and renamed her. Then he took his newly christened *Revenge* to sea and became the first—and arguably most successful—privateer sailing out of Salem, raiding any civilian British vessel he could find.

The action highlighted a key element of his character. When punched but once, White could be counted upon to return the blow a dozen times or more. He held grudges, and he acted upon them. He was not a man to be trifled with. He made enemies easily. And apparently one of them had decided to deliver a final blow.

3 | WHARVES AND DECLINE

"He that will learn to pray, let him go to sea."
—George Herbert

SALEM'S WATERFRONT WOULD HAVE BEEN NOTHING without its wharves—massive arms of sand, gravel, and dirt projecting out into the harbor, receiving and hosting the dozens of Salem vessels that came and went every day.

The making of Salem's wharves represented Herculean efforts, staggering investments, and the most painstaking attention to engineering detail. The greatest of the wharves took years to complete, with workers laying timber walls on mud flats at periods of low tide, filling these with dirt and stone hauled from inland, then finally replacing the timber walls with enormous blocks of granite. While completed sections of a wharf were already in use for shipping, the work of extending its length might go on for another decade or more.

The most prominent of the wharves—the one built, appropriately it would seem, by a family that at one time had been the city's richest clan, the Derbys—shot a full half mile into the harbor. With its sheer size, the Derby Wharf seemed to bely any hint of frailty or impermanence. Indeed, even now in the twenty-first century, the Derby Wharf remains as one of only four such structures still evident on the Salem shoreline. But today even the substantial Derby edifice seems as if it shall eventually vanish. There is no escape from sea rise. Storm surges at high tide regularly swamp the outer reach of this vast manmade peninsula.

Ironically, the Derby Wharf has long outlasted the Derby fortune. The founding father of the short-lived Derby shipping dynasty, Elias Hasket "King"

Derby, died in 1799. By that time King Derby had made himself into America's very first millionaire. But two intransigent and improvident sons, combined with competition from the influential Crowninshield clan (some of whom had married Derby women), saw the Derbys ruined by the start of the second decade of the nineteenth century.

These days, three of Salem's four remaining quays (the Derby and Central Wharves, along with Hatch's Wharf) lay open and barren, while the Tucker Wharf, supplemented by additional landfill, accommodates stores and eateries. But at the time with which we are concerned, all four of these wharves, not to mention in excess of fifty more, hosted numerous warehouses and other buildings. In its heyday, the Derby Wharf alone incorporated no less than three warehouses (each three stories high) for the storage of imported goods from the Far East: teas, spices, silk cloth, porcelain, gold dust, ivory, and Calcutta cottons. There was also hemp from Luzon, duck and raw iron from the Baltic, and rubber and wool and molasses from South America. Outbound products included whale oil, rum, salted beef, and such iron products as nails.

In addition to its three warehouses, the Derby Wharf accommodated seventeen more buildings, one of them a large counting house. At the foot of the Derby Wharf stood (and still stands today) the ornate Salem Custom House—built 1819—with its wide front steps, its high brick walls, its cupola towering in sight of virtually every corner of the commercial waterfront, and its elaborate golden eagle perched atop the pointed roof.

The Custom House reigned as Salem's most prominent architectural landmark for a mere six years before being supplanted by the grand edifice of the East India Marine Hall, home to the East India Marine Society. Founded in 1779, at the peak of Salem's dominance as a port, the East India Marine Society existed "to assist the widows and children of deceased members, to collect such facts and observations as tended to the improvement and security of navigation, and to form a Museum of natural and artificial curiosities, particularly such as are to be found beyond the Cape of Good Hope or Cape Horn." Membership was open to any person "who shall have actually navigated seas near the Cape of Good Hope or Cape Horn, either as master or commander or as factor or supercargo in any vessel belonging to Salem."[1]

For a time, Salem native Nathaniel Bowditch—widely considered the most brilliant mathematician and astronomer anywhere in the Americas—served as

Salem Custom House, built 1819, photographed circa 1900. The Custom House sits at the foot of the Derby Wharf and is today a part of the Salem Maritime National Historic Site. *Photo by Frank Cousins from the Frank Cousins Collection of Glass Plate Negatives. Courtesy of Phillips Library, Peabody Essex Museum, Salem, MA*

president of the organization. Under his stewardship, and afterward, the collections of the society grew at a rapid rate as energetic members returned from their voyages carrying all sorts of exotic materials meant for display: stuffed tropical birds, oriental swords and armor, shrunken heads, and other oddments. The collections also included models of famed Salem clippers, paintings of same, and items as random as a coffee cup and saucer once owned by Napoleon Bonaparte and used by him during his exile on the isle of St. Helena.[2] By 1824 the collections of the society contained more than three thousand items. Thus, there arose the need for the society's new permanent home—one grand and extensive enough to match both the society's practical needs and, almost more important, Salem's dignity as a city to rival others.

Built largely with funds provided by Stephen White, the massive granite, two-story East India Marine Hall stood complete on Essex Street by October 1825. No less a personage than President John Quincy Adams spoke at the

October 14 dedication, as did Boston Mayor Josiah Quincy and Associate Justice Story.

The prominence of the speakers and the solemnity of the occasion signaled—or at least, was *meant* to signal—the prominence of Salem as a seat of commerce and culture. The event received nationwide publicity. Salem, the town fathers seemed to say, perhaps a bit too eagerly and a bit too urgently, was a city and a port to be reckoned with. Left unsaid was the fact that Salem was a port and a city on the way down, rather than up, in importance, power, and profitability. The city's best days lay behind it.

Listening to all the exuberant, bellicose speeches at the Marine Hall dedication, and gazing at the majestic structure, the uninformed observer would never have realized that Salem's status as a world-class economic center had already begun to decline. No longer was Salem a port second to none, and no more was it by far the wealthiest city in the entire country, outstripping even New York, as had been the case two decades earlier.

Yes, Salem's waterfront still buzzed with activity. Commerce continued. Accounting books showed healthy profits. The polished brass of the fine homes remained polished. And town fathers still congratulated themselves on their industry and trade. ("In all probability," wrote Caleb Foote, editor of the *Salem Gazette*, "there has never been a time in which our shipping was in so good order, or so well built and found, or our [ship] masters possessed of so much skill in navigation and trade. No insurance company has as yet suffered diminution of capital, and all, if dissolved, would return at least par.")[3]

But Boston and New York, with their much larger waterfronts and many advantages in the way of expanding railroad connections for the movement of goods, now attracted far more trade than Salem could ever hope for. Rails would not come to Salem until 1838, and even then they would only connect through to Boston. There was also another problem: Salem's harbor was simply not deep enough to accommodate the latest, largest, and most profitable vessels built in recent years. Add to this the fact that after the War of 1812, numerous other ships flying under foreign flags began to engage in the trade formerly dominated by Salem, bringing the riches of the East to ports in Italy, France, Spain, Portugal—and the United States.

Salem had 198 ships registered to its port in 1825; there would only be 119 registered in 1833. This trend was to continue. By 1830, even Salem's own ruling maritime families had begun to run some of their vessels out of Boston and New York rather than from the Salem waterfront. Many families diversified beyond maritime enterprises, among them the Crowninshields, who built an ironworks. Other manufactories sprang up—one being a pencil factory—to employ seamen who could no longer find work on ships. At the same time, a number of prosperous merchant families began to look inland, to the flowing rivers of Massachusetts, New Hampshire, and Maine, for sites to build textile mills. What could no longer be imported profitably could instead be made domestically.

An additional—but generally unspoken—reason for the shrinking of Salem's economic base was the town's loss of income from the slave trade, which had previously flooded in throughout the 1780s, '90s, and first two decades of the nineteenth century, when men like Captain White routinely dispatched ships full of worthless trinkets to the Ivory Coast, trading these for human beings that they in turn delivered to the Caribbean, making a rich profit on every head. This aspect of Salem's commerce had always been somewhat

East India Marine Hall on Essex Street, photographed circa 1900.
Photo by Frank Cousins from the Frank Cousins Collection of Glass Plate Negatives.
Courtesy of Phillips Library, Peabody Essex Museum, Salem, MA

subterranean—hardly noticeable, save for the gold it brought to the coffers of Salem's elites. Always, Salem's participation in the grim business of the "peculiar institution" remained opaque. The people of Salem were never made to directly encounter or confront the stark reality of Salem's slaving economy, even though its truth was generally known to all. Thousands of miles protected the townsmen from actually witnessing the trade as practiced.

The banning of slavery in Massachusetts in 1783, and the consequent banning of the importation of slaves to the United States in 1808, did little to curb the business between Africa and the Caribbean as conducted by the Salem moguls. What eventually *did* bring an end to that trade, however, was the declining value of each slave delivered, this due to slave populations in the Caribbean and elsewhere growing naturally through new births.

Captain White's trade in humans had been especially notorious in one particular aspect. As was well known among the roughest, meanest, and most cynical sailors who worked before the mast on Salem's ships, an added benefit of crewing on a White slaving vessel was the license White gave to his men to "enjoy" the "female cargo" while in transit. Indeed, in his younger days when he took vessels to sea, White himself often partook, without apology. But in Salem this too was a mere ghost of a fact: both known and unknown, a whisper and a rumor, albeit one all too believable.

Still, in some precincts of the community, what were whispers and rumors elsewhere echoed all too loudly—especially, it seems, among members of the clergy, who viewed White with outright skepticism and distaste. Not only had White been a slaver, but his slaving, given its particulars, seemed especially foul. Making matters worse was White's blatant refusal to show the least bit of shame or contrition about his actions. As he told William Bentley, the eminent and nationally known pastor of Salem's East Church, in 1788, "[I have no] reluctance in selling any part of the human race." Recording the statement in his journal, Bentley added that White's attitude "gives great pain to thinking men, and in consideration of [White's] easy circumstances, [betrays] the greatest moral depravity."[4]

Personally, Captain White wore this attitude proudly and loudly and therefore seemed a walking, talking anachronism, one that Salem—always nervous about its standing and reputation given the long shadow of the 1692 witch trial outrages, not to mention its subtle decline as a port—did not need in the late 1820s, just as Massachusetts began to seethe as a center of antislavery sentiment.

Unlike many other communities where civic pride demanded a strong historical memory, in Salem civic pride often demanded something else entirely: a strong willingness to hide, bury, and subdue inconvenient facts of past times, beginning but certainly not ending with the witch trials. The living ghost who was White had haunted Essex Street as the last breathing undeniable relic of yet another shameful episode in Salem's tribal memory: a most inconvenient apparition. Some commented that at least now he could sin no more. And he could be put away forever—or so it seemed.

4 | A MELANCHOLY PROCESS OF DECAY

"What other dungeon is so dark as one's own heart?
What jailor so inexorable as one's self?"

—Nathaniel Hawthorne,
The House of the Seven Gables (1851)

ONE YOUNG MAN who most certainly possessed knowledge of the town's darker maritime heritage was twenty-six-year-old Salem native Nathaniel Hawthorne. The would-be writer had graduated from Bowdoin College three years before the White murder, in 1827, as part of a class that included Henry Wadsworth Longfellow and future president Franklin Pierce. At the time of the murder, Hawthorne—who'd recently added a *w* to his ancestral name Hathorne—lived with his mother and sisters in a home that his mother's brother Robert Manning had built for them at 31 (now 26) Dearborn Street.[1] By 1830 he had already written one novel, *Fanshawe*, which he self-published anonymously through Boston's Marsh & Capen publishing house in October 1828. Although it received generally good reviews, the book did not sell well. Eventually Hawthorne gathered together the many unsold copies and burned them. He would later deny being the book's author, as he eventually came to think of it as amateurish.

At this time, Hawthorne was no stranger to Salem's lowlife. On a particular 4th of July, which also happened to be his birthday, he happily wandered the waterfront among "customers rather riotous, yet funny, calling loudly and whimsically for what they want,—young sailors & c; a young fellow and a girl coming arm in arm; perhaps two girls approaching the booth, and getting into conversation with the he-folks thereabout, while old knowing codgers wink to one another thereby indicating their opinion that these ladies are of easy virtue." He also noted "a knock-down between two half-stewed fellows in the crowd—a knock-down without a heavy blow, the receiver being scarcely able to keep his footing at any rate. Shoutings and hallooings, laughter,—oaths—generally a good-natured result."[2]

Hawthorne likely knew of Salem's slaving sins not just because of tales told in the waterfront bars that he now frequented but also because the young man already, at this early stage of life, made a morbid habit of dwelling upon Salem's many hidden shames, doing so with a dark fascination that had already influenced (in fact, come to define) his novice efforts at fiction. As one historian has noted, Hawthorne perceived in the Salem of his time "little more than a melancholy process of decay, and a dusky background for romances of a century more remote."[3] Still, Hawthorne would write in his preface to *The Scarlet Letter* that he admired the ancient Salem families

The house at 31 (now 26) Dearborn Street, where Nathaniel Hawthorne lived at the time of the murder and trials. Shown here circa 1900, the house remains today in private hands. *Photo by Frank Cousins from the Frank Cousins Collection of Glass Plate Negatives. Courtesy of Phillips Library, Peabody Essex Museum, Salem, MA*

who "from father to son, for above a hundred years, ... followed the sea; a gray-headed shipmaster in each generation retiring from the quarter-deck to the homestead, while a boy of fourteen took the hereditary place before the mast, confronting the salt spray and the gale which had blustered against his sire and grandsire."[4]

Hawthorne did indeed find in Salem "a dusky background for romances of a century more remote." In one of his earliest stories, "Alice Doane's Appeal," Hawthorne described Salem's Gallows Hill as the "field where superstition won her darkest triumph; the high place where our fathers set up their shame, to the mournful gaze of generations now remote. The dust of martyrs was beneath our feet." Although Hawthorne spoke generally here of "our fathers," he might just as well have said "*my* fathers." Hawthorne's own great-great-grandfather John Hathorne, who died in 1717, had served as a judge—and not just a judge, but a most strident and enthusiastic one—at the Salem witch trials. In the end, Hathorne caused more than twenty people to go to their deaths (nineteen hung, one crushed under heavy stones for failure to testify, and four who died of neglect in their cells while waiting to be hung).

Although ostensibly a judge, Hathorne had acted more like a prosecutor, attacking each defendant in turn and joining accusers in presuming guilt. What is more, it had been Hathorne who adopted the policy of insisting that defendants name their satanic "accomplices" in exchange for the possibility of leniency. In this way, Judge Hathorne drastically increased the number of those accused and the number sent to die. Although at least one of Hathorne's fellow judges would eventually express regret for his role in the mania of Salem's witch scare, Hathorne never did. In fact, on the very day of the very last executions, Hathorne was meeting with the bombastic Puritan preacher and pamphleteer Cotton Mather, along with others, to discuss publishing a record of the Salem proceedings that would, he hoped, encourage similar prosecutions elsewhere throughout New England.

Judge Hathorne conducted himself in a manner—and with a ferocity—practiced previously by his own father, William Hathorne, who in 1630 traveled to Massachusetts with John Winthrop aboard the *Arabella*, settling in Salem some six years later. This Hathorne—although a maker and seller of "strong waters"—was nevertheless a devout Puritan who gladly served as magistrate in his adopted community and became notorious for both the severity and ingenuity of the punishments he meted out for violations of civil and religious order.

Gossips variously had their ears cut off or holes bored into their tongues with red hot pokers. A burglar, after losing a hand, might also have his forehead branded with the letter *B*. In one particular case, a woman found "guilty" of being a Quaker was stripped naked from the waist up, bound to the tail of a cart, and dragged down Salem's main thoroughfare while being beaten from behind by a constable with a whip of knotted cords. Most murderers were—appropriately—hung. But unlucky murderers found themselves locked away to starve, all at William Hathorne's whim.

Nathaniel Hawthorne's more immediate ancestry on his father's side was maritime. Judge John Hathorne's own brother, Captain William Hathorne the younger, spent many years at sea before becoming a farmer. The judge's son Captain Joseph Hathorne (Nathaniel's great-grandfather) likewise had a long career on the oceans of the world before reverting to farming, as did Joseph's brother, another Captain William Hathorne. Joseph's son Daniel (Nathaniel's grandfather) commanded a battleship named the *True American* during the Revolutionary War. Upon the occasion of his death in 1796, his body was carried to Charter Street Burying Point in a grand procession. According to the *Salem Gazette*, "The corpse was preceded by the Marine Society. . . . The flags of the ships in port were half-mast high—and the numerous [parties who] attended on this melancholy occasion fully evinced the regret they felt at the departure of their worthy townsman."[5]

In turn, Nathaniel's father, Captain Nathaniel Hathorne Sr.—like others of the family a member of the East India Marine Society—became a ship's captain but died of yellow fever in Paramaribo, Dutch Suriname, during the year 1808, when the younger Nathaniel was just four years old. (Four years earlier, Captain Nathaniel Hathorne's brother, Daniel Hathorne Jr., had died at sea.) At the time of his death, Captain Nathaniel was in command of a vessel owned by Salem's Captain Nathaniel Silsbee: a brig of 154 tons, the *Nabby*. Perhaps because of his father's and uncle's tragedies, young Nathaniel never aspired to a nautical career. In 1825, Hawthorne wrote a poem, "The Ocean," in which he seemed to commemorate his father's burial at sea some seventeen years earlier.

> The Ocean has its silent caves,
> Deep, quiet, and alone;
> Though there be fury on the waves,
> Beneath them there is none.

> The awful spirits of the deep
> Hold their communion there;
> And there are those for whom we weep,
> The young, the bright, the fair.
>
> Calmly the wearied seamen rest
> Beneath their own blue sea.
> The ocean solitudes are blest,
> For there is purity.
>
> The earth has guilt, the earth has care,
> Unquiet are its graves;
> But peaceful sleep is ever there,
> Beneath the dark blue waves.[6]

On Nathaniel's mother's side of the family, Nathaniel's grandfather Richard Manning Jr. founded the Boston and Salem Stagecoach Line, which all of his sons save for one continued to operate after Richard's death in 1812. Manning left an estate valued in excess of $50,000, some $33,000 of this in real estate holdings. As her share of the inheritance, Elizabeth Hathorne (née Manning) received a relatively paltry sum of $200 (about $5,400 today) annually, this administered by her brother, Robert Manning, who tended to the interests and needs of Elizabeth and her family.

The odious heritage of the witch trials wore heavy with Hawthorne, as did most other aspects of traditional New England Puritanism. He was to spend a lifetime pondering what it all meant both culturally and spiritually. The ghosts of Salem's past imbued the landscape of Hawthorne's imagination, carrying with them a stain of self-righteous sin that could never be washed away, no matter how many rains fell. One critic has called this Hawthorne's "mystical blackness."[7] In his essay "New England Two Centuries Ago," James Russell Lowell commented, "I never thought it an abatement of Hawthorne's genius that he came lineally from one who sat in judgment on the witches in 1692; it was interesting rather to trace something hereditary in the somber character of his imagination, continually vexing itself to account for the origin of evil, and baffled for want of that simple solution in a personal devil."[8]

Hawthorne's Salem was a place of masks, ironies, and a multitude of never-ending blasphemies—as was the wider world that Salem, to Hawthorne's mind, represented in microcosm. Mankind by its nature was tainted, albeit beneath the skin: in hidden corners, hidden thoughts, and hidden crimes. Therefore, what happened on Essex Street on the particular moonlit night of April 6, 1830, and the complex web of deceit that was to spin off from it, probably came as no surprise to him, not in the least.

5 | GREAT THE PAIN THIS MONSTER MUST BE IN

"A man hath murdered another; why? He loved his wife or his estate; or would rob for his own livelihood; or feared to lose some such things by him; or, wronged, was on fire to be revenged. Would any commit murder upon no cause, delighted simply in murdering?"

—St. Augustine, *Confessions*

FROM THE VERY START, Stephen White seized the helm when it came to overseeing the investigation and eventual prosecution of culprits in Captain White's murder, steering the exercise around rocky hazards and toward a port that (at first consideration without any leads or even physical evidence to go on) seemed unachievable: a destination with no known coordinates.

The fact that Stephen White took the grim business of his uncle's murder quite seriously cannot be overstated. Stephen had enjoyed much good fortune in life, every bit of it the result of his uncle's efforts and concern.

Stephen lived in an elaborate mansion at 6 Brown Street on Washington Square.[1] Here he and his wife, Harriet Story, whom he'd married in 1808, raised four children, one of whom—a girl, Caroline—would one day marry Daniel Fletcher Webster, the son of White's close friend, Senator Daniel Webster of Massachusetts. White, a successful merchant, held numerous elected offices throughout the 1820s, with terms in the Massachusetts House of Representatives (1821 and 1828) and the State Senate (1825, 1826, and 1830). At his mansion, he was known to entertain many prominent visitors, among them

President James Monroe, who attended one of White's receptions on July 11, 1817. At the time of the murder, Stephen's wife Harriet had been dead some three years, and he himself was poised to leave Salem for good, relocating to Boston, which he would indeed do within a year of his uncle's death.

Stephen's older brother Joseph—born 1781 and named for their uncle—had been, like Stephen, a successful merchant, trader, and shipowner until his death in 1816. In fact, the two had been partners in a firm established for them by their uncle: the firm of Joseph White Jr. & Stephen White, Merchants of Salem. Like Stephen, Joseph had married a sister of Joseph Story: Eliza. Along this same line, the two brothers likewise inhabited nearly identical houses a stone's throw from one another, both designed and built by Salem's Joshua Upham.[2] Each brother had three daughters, and Stephen an additional son, Joseph, named for both his uncle and his great-uncle.

The brothers' numerous merchant vessels conducted business around the world. The vessels they owned included the brig *Mary & Eliza*, which Captain Nathaniel Hathorne at one point skippered. They also owned White's Wharf, passed on to them by Captain White. Joseph, the elder and leader of the duo, served in the state legislature, commanded the town militia as its colonel, held directorships in various financial institutions and at least one insurance company, and owned several vessels above and beyond those held in partnership with Stephen.

Both brothers, but Joseph in particular, were known as bon vivants. They enjoyed fine wines, collected vast libraries, supped upon the finest china, and drank from exquisite crystal glasses and silver tumblers. Unlike most merchantmen, Joseph even sailed for fun—maintaining a small yacht that he would routinely, in fair weather, pilot across Salem Harbor to Marblehead and back, sipping wine as he did so.

The two brothers had been adopted and raised by Captain White and his wife, Elizabeth Stone White, from an early age. The boys' own parents—Captain Joseph White's brother, Captain Henry, and his wife Phoebe—had a hard time supporting seven children. Henry skippered long voyages, was gone for extended periods, and, as one who owned no vessels himself, made a secure though hardly handsome living. When in 1795 Joseph (age fourteen) and Stephen (age eight) were adopted by their uncle, they found themselves instantly swept up from the sparsest of living conditions to a life of complete opulence. Suddenly there were servants. Suddenly there was a mansion of a dozen or more rooms. Suddenly there were superbly tailored suits and elegant private schools. Suddenly there were succulent dinners, with seconds and thirds readily available whenever desired. And when Joseph "went to sea" at age seventeen in 1798, after a stint clerking for a time in the counting house at White's Wharf, he did so not as a common seaman but as a supercargo in training, tasked to learn the business of the trade. Stephen was to have similar experiences.

Captain Joseph White and his wife had previously adopted and raised two nieces, Eliza Cook and Mary Ramsdell, cousins, both of whom had married and raised their own families by 1830—with the widowed Mary Beckford (née Ramsdell) having since become Captain White's manager of the household after the passing of the captain's wife. In 1805, once Stephen and his brother Joseph were well launched, Captain White and his wife adopted one more child: their grandniece, Elizabeth White Carlton, the orphaned six-year-old daughter of Eliza Cook. (In 1817, the nineteen-year-old Elizabeth White Carlton became engaged to Franklin H. Story, the brother-in-law of Stephen White, but tragically died of consumption in October 1818 before the scheduled marriage.) Captain Joseph White also saw to the safety and advancement of other relatives, including another brother of Joseph and Stephen White, John White, whose training at sea he administered and whom he eventually promoted to captain one of his vessels. All in all, Captain White's devotion to family appeared to be one of his few redeeming qualities.

Together, the brothers Joseph and Stephen White rode the ebbing but still quite high tide of Salem prosperity with their sails full and their cargo bins packed with goods destined to be turned into cash for further investment and continued growth. As an example, a typical merchant ship of some three hundred tons could easily return to port with cargo worth $50,000, or more than $1.3 million in today's currency. And the Whites—just like the Crowninshields and others of Salem's leading families—had plenty of merchant ships owned either solely or in partnership with various other clans.

With wealth came not only comforts but also influence. With Captain White's death, there came to Stephen even more of both.

The captain's namesake Joseph had for a long time been the chief heir named in his will, with other smaller bequests to various family members. Upon the 1816 death of Joseph, the captain revised his will to make Stephen the primary heir, leaving all—or at least most—of the other small bequests in place. As Joseph Story was to write to his friend Daniel Webster, "Mr. White left a will. He has given many legacies to his relatives; but the bulk of his fortune goes to Mr. Stephen White. . . . Three of my nieces will receive about $25,000 each."[3]

Of course, Stephen was already quite a wealthy man well before his uncle's murder and had already become something of a legend in both maritime and financial circles. It had been Stephen who spearheaded the building of the East India Marine Hall, which had been his conception. It had been he who raised the funds (starting with his own substantial gift), commissioned the architect's design, defined the specifics of what the building should contain and represent, and supervised every detail of the construction. And it was he who triumphantly assembled and led the parade of dignitaries who celebrated the building's completion and attended its dedication.

In recent years, Stephen, like other merchantmen, had begun to spread his holdings and business interests well beyond his family's ships and the affairs of White's Wharf. Recognizing the slow decline in Salem's seafaring trade, White had invested heavily in textile mills on the Merrimack River and in several locations throughout the interiors of Maine and New Hampshire—creating the very cloth domestically that had once been one of the staples brought into the country by Salem ships. At the same time, however, he continued to leverage the merchant trade for all that it was worth. Opium, spices, ivory, mahogany, coffee, and a range of other items continued to be imported, albeit less and less to Salem and more and more to Boston and New York.

That a civilian such as Stephen White would step in to dominate the investigation of Captain White's murder may seem strange, but Salem boasted next to no police force, per se—just a few sleepy constables charged with keeping drunkards off the streets and making sure doors were kept locked. What is more, no one in Salem, whether in law enforcement or not, had any particular expertise when it came to the formal investigation of serious crimes. The investigation of Captain White's murder was therefore first and foremost an amateurish affair, no matter how seriously approached. And approach it seriously the residents of Salem most certainly did.

Very early on, Stephen White made clear to all his belief in both Benjamin White's and Lydia Kimball's innocence. Somewhere out there, a culprit or culprits lurked: a man or men who had acted seemingly without motive, unless a motive beyond theft might be construed. The question of cui bono (who benefits) seemed not to have an answer, at least for the time being. And when the question was eventually broached, Stephen White would not care for the answer speculated by not a few Salem citizens.

Initially, White proposed that the murder was either an act of revenge by some competitor who at one time had been outsmarted or undone by Captain White or the entirely random act of a madman—an act without rationale, an act arising from a diseased mind, and therefore an act that might well be repeated, thus threatening all innocents in town. By the end of the day on the seventh, the city found itself in a state of urgent and pronounced agitation. Something must be done. Measures must be taken. Meanwhile, the very first of many printed broadside ballads began to make the rounds:

> O what a horrid tale to sound,
> Oh, what a horrid tale be sound,
> In this our land to tell,
> That Joseph White, of Salem town,
> By ruffian hands he fell!
> Perhaps for money or for gain,
> This wicked deed was done,
> But if for either, great the pain
> This monster must be in.[4]

Joseph Story, writing to Daniel Webster ten days after the killing, called the murder of Captain White "the most mysterious and dreadful affair that I have ever heard of. . . . Not the slightest trace has been found by which to trace the assassins." Story went on to say that he had never known "such a universal panic. It is not confined to Boston or Salem but seems to pervade the whole community. We are all astounded and looking to know from what quarter the next blow will come. There is a universal dread and sense of calamity, as if we lived in the midst of banditti."[5] Throughout Salem, new locks were bought. Masters of houses placed loaded pistols in their nightstands and hired armed men from the wharves to patrol their properties. People who'd never before possessed guard dogs now acquired one, or two. Blacksmiths did a good business installing bars on windows; masons bricked up basement windows.

A twenty-one-year-old Harvard student, Oliver Wendell Holmes—destined to become a noted physician, poet, and polymath—felt the same sense of general panic:

> Nothing is going on but murder and robbery; we have to look in our closets and under our beds, and strut about with sword canes and pistols. The first thing a fellow knows is that he has a rap over his head and a genteel young man fragrant with essences is fumbling with white gloved fingers in his pockets and concludes his operations with kicking him into a gully or dropping him over a bridge. Poor old Mr. White was "stabbed in the dark" and since that the very air has been redolent of assassination. The women have exhausted their intellect in epithets and exclamations, the newspapers have declared it atrocious, and worst of all the little poets have been pelting the villain or villains with verses.[6]

6 | MURDER AS ONE OF THE FINE ARTS

"This is the law: blood spilt upon the ground cries out for more."

—Aeschylus, *The Libation Bearers*

MURDER WAS HARDLY UNKNOWN in the Massachusetts of the mid-nineteenth century, especially in port towns such as Salem. The trade of the merchantmen, relying as it did on the manual labor of largely illiterate and rough-living sailors before the mast, came accompanied by grim excitement of just this type. Knives were drawn in waterfront taverns. Animosities festered among individual members of the sailor class while on board ship, where a master's discipline prevailed and could restrain things, but then were let loose (often with the aid of alcohol) upon arrival home. Whores engaged in rough trade, and sometimes had to defend themselves against would-be pimps or unruly customers. Pimps fought among themselves in territorial battles over female flesh.

Bodies were sometimes found floating beside the long wharves with throats cut or stab wounds to the heart. The same would sometimes be found up an alley or in a coal bin. Other waterfront types would simply disappear. Such cases went uncommented on in the wider world. They were generally not pursued with any diligence by such authorities as existed. And they seemed to those above the fray as simply a common phenomenon among the lower class. This view was as customary in Salem as it was anywhere else in the United States or Europe.

Writing in 1827, Thomas De Quincey in "On Murder, Considered as One of the Fine Arts" mockingly made light of the propensity for murder among the lower classes by inventing a fictional society for the study and appreciation of at least some murders as acts of great visionary stealth—elegant exercises that, if they could be painted, would be worthy to hang in the Royal Academy. De Quincey, with his tongue firmly planted in his cheek, noted that the upper class had in some way civilized murder just as they had civilized so many other matters of life (and death). "In this age," he wrote, "when masterpieces of excellence have been executed by professional men, it must be evident, that in the style of criticism applied to them, the public will look for something of a corresponding improvement" in murder. To be art, something more must go into the "composition of a fine murder than two blockheads to kill and be killed—a knife—a purse—and a dark lane." How banal, how commonplace, how very far beneath a gentleman.

The important thing, De Quincey kidded, was to approach murder "in relation to good taste." Although murder was a most foul thing, De Quincey insisted in his satire that it offered an opportunity to "make the best of a bad matter; and, as it is impossible to hammer anything out of it for moral purposes, let us treat it aesthetically, and see if it will turn to account in that way." De Quincey argued that a homicidal transaction, though "shocking and without a leg to stand on," could nevertheless turn out to be "a very meritorious performance" when "tried by principles of taste." But the finest art was not always easy, De Quincey noted. "Awkward disturbances will arise; people will not submit to have their throats cut quietly; they will run, they will kick, they will bite; and as the portrait-painter often has to complain of too much torpor in his subject, the artist in our line is generally embarrassed by too much animation."[1]

This, of course, had not been a problem encountered by the murderer or murderers of Captain Joseph White, sound asleep amidst his sheets when the first blow fell, and then even more unconscious for all the rest. There had been no fighting back. De Quincey, in his sardonic guise as an astute critic of homicide, would surely have applauded. The murder of White had been coldly brutal, carefully calculated and planned, and coolly executed: the plank, the window, the approach from behind, the head blow before the coup de grâce stabbings, the former to avoid any possibility of quarrelsome noise or attempts at self-defense.

Artful or not, the murders of prominent, prosperous individuals such as Captain Joseph White were so rare as to be thought especially horrifying, appalling, and notorious. Therefore, they drew wide attention. The drama and salacious details often associated with these events were such that the public found them riveting. They inevitably became national news stories as sensational and spellbinding as the detective fictions that would become popular in the not too distant future.

The most recent case of such notoriety had been the 1825 murder of Kentucky politician Solomon P. Sharp by attorney Jeroboam O. Beauchamp. The murder of Sharp, who had previously fathered a stillborn child by a prominent planter's daughter, Anna Cooke, and then denied paternity, had been the price Cooke demanded of the enamored Beauchamp before she would consent to marry him. The couple were wed in June 1824. In early November 1825, Beauchamp knifed Sharp to death in front of the latter's home in Frankfort.

Arrest and conviction soon followed. Anna, although acquitted in her own trial for complicity, stayed with Beauchamp in his cell until the day appointed for his hanging. At one point, the couple made a failed attempt at suicide by drinking laudanum. A short while later, on the morning of the scheduled execution, they tried again, this time using a knife. Anna died of her wound, and Beauchamp would have died of his as well had authorities not rushed him to the gallows, where he became the very first person legally executed in the state of Kentucky. A day later, per their request, the couple were buried together, embracing, in a double coffin.

The entire affair, with its clandestine sexual element, cold-bloodedness, and raw romantic ending, made engrossing reading for the increasingly voyeuristic American public. Newspapers from across the Eastern Seaboard sent correspondents to cover the trial and execution. Broadside ballads were composed and sold in all the major cities. Pundits, editorialists, and preachers in their sermons bemoaned the decline in morals and ethics among the educated classes. (In time, the notorious case would form the inspiration for an unfinished play, *Politan*, by Poe. Some 125 years later, the story—variously known as the Kentucky Tragedy or the Beauchamp-Sharp Tragedy—would still be inspiring literary works. Robert Penn Warren's bestselling 1950 novel *World Enough and Time* draws directly from the case record.)

In the wake of the Kentucky Tragedy, and the many newspapers it sold, editors nationwide waited eagerly for the next great notorious high-profile murder—the next great pot of gold.

The old original Salem Jail—the jail of ancient witch-trial days consisting of base-ment dungeon-like cells beneath a small wooden structure—was built in 1684 and retired in 1813, at which point a family home rose above the old dungeon. In 1956, when the New England Telephone Company purchased the location, excavation for the firm's new headquarters revealed the dismal cells, impeccably preserved. These wound up being destroyed, however, when the foundations for the office were laid in. Whatever ghosts had lingered there found themselves evicted right about the same time as Elvis first appeared on *The Ed Sullivan Show*.

The new Salem Jail opened not far away from the original jail in 1813, after two years of construction. Granite-faced, the imposing jail building sat adjacent to a newly built Federal-style jailer's residence of red brick. The jail's residents—local miscreants serving short sentences for such misdemeanors as drunkenness, along with those awaiting trial on more serious charges—lived in tiny cells, many of these overlooking the Howard Street Cemetery.

Opened in 1814, the Howard Street Cemetery occupies the plot of land where, in 1692, according to tradition, the accused witch Giles Corey was crushed to death under heavy stones during an exercise of torture designed to make him testify against himself and others. It has been said that Corey's ghost walks here nightly. Among some Salemites back in the day, this was all the more believable because accusations against Corey included him leav-ing his body and attacking residents during spectral visitations. (It has gone unrecorded whether any of the Salem Jail's resident drunkards, pickpockets, and debtors ever spotted through their barred windows a transparent Corey roaming about the headstones.)

Here, on the evening after his death, in a lonesome cell, the corpse of Captain Joseph White lay on a steel bed, doing time, incarcerated not just within bars but within a shroud. If his ghost rose and walked, pacing the long corridors, no one noticed. As he laid there, he was not far away from his dead wife, Elizabeth, who in an underground vault next door awaited her husband's arrival. Before that could happen, however, an official autopsy would have to be conducted. Thirty-six hours after Captain White's murder, it was.

In front of a dozen sworn witnesses, Dr. Johnson—assisted by fellow physi-cian Abel Pierson—went to work at the jail. To get a better idea of the nature of the blow to the head, Johnson cut into Captain White's scalp and peeled it back. With that done, he could see a severe oval fracture in the temple "three and three-fourth inches long, and two and one-half inches broad." A significant portion of the skull had been broken in, "some fractures extending upwards, towards the back of the head, and another down towards the face." Johnson in turn opened the chest. "Two of the knife wounds had penetrated the walls of the captain's heart. . . . The instrument which gave the blow on the head was probably some smooth instrument, like a loaded cane, that would give a heavy blow without breaking the skin, and the instrument used in giving the wounds in the side was probably a dirk."

All in all, Johnson found thirteen stab wounds, "six in front, and seven farther back, about three inches from the others, near to the spine." There were three fractured ribs. Johnson noted that the stabs were grouped, with one group of five "within the compass of three inches." Furthermore, he found no evidence of more than one single weapon being used to deliver the stab wounds. The front wounds, he observed, "gaped more than the others and were three-fourths of an inch wide."[2] The one most significant point to come out of the autopsy was that Johnson revised his estimate of the time of death. Instead of three or four hours before the initial inquest, he now said death could have occurred up to eight hours before—thus significantly widening the window of time in which the murder might have taken place.

With the indignity of the autopsy over, Captain White's body was cleaned, dressed, and casketed on the afternoon of the ninth before being carried to his mansion, there to spend one more night under his own roof. The body lay in the front parlor. Candles and oil lamps were lit as the evening came on. Neighbors, friends, and even merchantmen adversaries came to pay their respects and convey their condolences to the grieving family. Here stood a gaggle of Crowninshields, there a group of Silsbees, among other families, including members of the Knapp clan—headed by Captain Joseph Jenkins Knapp Sr., the father of Joe Knapp Jr., husband of Captain White's grandniece, Mary.

Many noted, and thought it somewhat strange, that Joe Knapp Jr., of all the mourners, seemed the most broken up—tearfully lamenting the cruel death of one of Salem's leading citizens. As not a few of those present knew, or at least as rumor had it, there had been an acre of thin ice between Joe Jr. and Captain White for quite some time. Although the captain had once quite liked Joe Jr. and even employed him as master on some of his vessels (a task that Joe Jr. carried out successfully), he had been dead set against the young man's marriage to his grandniece. Mary, he said, was quite above Joe Knapp Jr. in terms of class and needed a suitor of higher station. (He also expressed his opinion that Joe Jr. was an adventurer and gold digger.) When the couple went ahead and married in spite of Captain White's wishes, he made good on a threat to write young Mary out of his will, disinheriting his grandniece from what would have been quite a substantial sum of money.

Captain White and Joe Jr. had rarely spoken ever since, and Joe and his wife had remained for the most part on the farm in Wenham. After the marriage, Joe Jr. hardly ever came to the mansion, and then only when Captain White was not at home. There had been about a week, as Lydia Kimball would recall, between Joe Jr.'s most recent visit to the home (on an errand she did not know or remember) and April 6, when he came to pick up Mary Beckford and bring her to Wenham for her visit.

Given his histrionics, some suspected that Joe Knapp Jr. had imbibed more than a bit of wine, or perhaps some stronger spirit, before his arrival at the White mansion for the wake. While extreme emotions were expected from the captain's nearest and dearest female family members, the same was considered quite odd when displayed by men. Joe Jr., however, rocked in his seat, muttered prayers, tearfully expressed wonderment and astonishment that such a crime could have taken place, and otherwise made himself something of a spectacle. Amid his ravings, Joe Jr. went so far as to suggest out loud that Stephen White—the captain's primary heir who stood across the room—should be considered a prime suspect, given the vast wealth that would now likely be his. What offense Stephen White might have taken from these inebriated remarks, or whether he even heard them, is not on record. But many *did* hear, and not a few kept the seed of speculation in their heads.

On the next morning, April 10, the elite of Salem—the full great and mighty membership of the of the East India Marine Society—accompanied the body of Captain Joseph White on a short march from his mansion to the Howard Street Cemetery. Nearly every business in town closed for the day, or at least closed its doors for the few early hours of official town-wide mourning. The wealthy merchants walked wearing their blackest black suits and matching top hats. There were no women among them, no Blacks, no common workers—members only, the true captains of Salem shipping and industry escorting one of their own to his final rest.

Howard Street Cemetery as it is today, where Captain Joseph White and his wife rest in their underground vault. In the distance can be seen the rear of the old Salem Jail. *Photo by the author*

The niece Mary and grandniece Mary, together with other female members of the White family, remained at the residence, as was the custom at the time. Men of the working class lined the route of the entourage down Essex Street and then onward to Howard Street. Most who stood gawking were workers from the wharves and laborers from Salem's small industries, the majority of them likely mourning more for the hourly wages they were missing than for the man who rested in the box carried on six strong shoulders.

At the burial ground, the large oblong stone above the in-ground crypt of the White family had been moved away, affording those who gathered a view of the dark space below containing the caskets of Captain White's much-mourned wife Elizabeth, his brother Henry (Stephen White's father, who'd passed in 1825), and Captain White's grandniece Elizabeth White Carlton. After a few prayers, the pallbearers used ropes to lower Captain White down and lay him next to his wife. Then the crowd dispersed, leaving only the workers who would now place the great stone back where it belonged.

Not long after the burial, the small island off the New Hampshire coast upon which Captain White had been born in 1748, the southernmost of the Isles of Shoals, was renamed in his honor: Joseph White Island (now commonly referred to as White Island). Such was the prominence of the man and the widespread word of the tragic death.

While Salem mourned and buried the captain, word of the murder began to spread beyond the town limits, as in this item that appeared in the Franklin, Massachusetts, *Republican* on the thirteenth:

> An assassination of almost unexampled atrocity took place in the town of Salem, Mass. on the night of the 6th ult. Joseph White, Esq. one of the most aged and opulent citizens of that town . . . was murdered in his bed by some unknown person, who entered the house by one of the back windows, and committed the horrid deed by first striking him on the head with some heavy instrument and then inflicting 10 [*sic*] stabs near the heart with a knife. There is no way for accounting for this cold-blooded deed, as the assassin took none of the money or other valuable articles within his reach, and appears to have been entirely actuated by a wish to take the life of Mr. White, although an aged man, retired from business and inoffensive in his conduct. Great excitement was occasioned in the town by the occurrence.[3]

Other newspapers adopted the same sensational prose:

> SHOCKING AFFAIR!—On Wednesday morning last, Joseph White, Esq. was found dead in his bed, having been murdered by some person or persons yet unknown. A severe blow was given him on the left temple, which in the opinion of the physicians, caused his immediate death—and thirteen wounds in the body, with a dirk, or other sharp instrument, which several times penetrated his heart. Mr. White was upwards of 80 years of age, was a widower, and the only persons in the family at the time, were, a young man, and a woman who had lived for many years in the family. Not an article was taken from the house, and no trace of the perpetrators of this unparalleled outrage has as yet been discovered. A reward of $2500 is offered for the detection of the murderer—$500 of which is by the Selectmen of Salem,

$1000 by the heirs of Mr. White, and $1000 by the Governor, in a proclamation issued on Thursday last.[4]

In Salem, a watch was formed. Young John Francis "Frank" Knapp, the brother of Joe Knapp Jr., was quick to join.

7 | THE KNAPPS OF SALEM

"Life is made of marble and mud."
—Nathaniel Hawthorne,
The House of the Seven Gables (1851)

IT IS IMPOSSIBLE TO NAVIGATE the balance of this story without understanding two key coordinates: the histories of two additional families along with that of the Whites. These are the Knapps of Salem and the Crowninshields of Salem.

During the summer of 1812, with war against Britain having put an end to virtually all Salem shipping, leading families such as the Whites, Silsbees, and Crowninshields became heavily engaged in the business of privateering: commandeering British vessels and seizing their cargos and sometimes the vessels themselves. With regard to these operations, the Whites were particularly active. In addition to Captain White's aptly named *Revenge*, there were also nine heavily armed brig privateers owned by Joseph and Stephen White, the largest of which, the 310-ton *Grand Turk*, carried eighteen guns. Like its sister ships, the *Grand Turk* was designed not just for firepower but also for speed. Early in the spring of 1812, the brothers sent their thirty-nine-year-old associate Captain Joseph Jenkins Knapp Sr. to New York to oversee the building of an additional 172-ton privateer, the schooner *Growler*, which went to sea that autumn.

Eighteen years later, on the very evening when Captain Joseph White was to die, Captain Knapp sat in the Derby Street mansion of attorney Joseph Waters, there to sign the papers necessary to formalize his personal and business bankruptcy. With him sat his son, Nathaniel Phippen Knapp, known as Phippen, a young, twenty-three-year-old, Harvard-educated attorney.

Here now came the conclusion of the senior Knapp's twenty-five-year merchant career—which, though not as spectacular as that of others in town, had at least been respectable up until recent setbacks. Knapp's principal creditor? None other than Captain Joseph White himself. The house at 85 Essex Street to which Knapp returned that evening, the house he'd built in 1802, was now owned not by Knapp but by White, to whom Knapp would henceforth have to pay rent if he was to stay.

In previous years, Knapp had owned several vessels in whole or part, a few of them in partnerships with the Whites. "The Knapps were well thought of in Salem," wrote Bradley and Winans. "Captain Joseph Knapp, Sr., was a shipmaster and merchant. He and Captain White were frequently associated in business transactions. Knapp and his family lived for many years on the south side of Essex Street, not far east from the home of Captain White."[1]

The Knapp House, built 1802, was originally located at 85 Essex Street (as shown here, circa 1890) but in 1895 was moved around the corner to 9 Curtis Street, where it remains in private hands. *Photo by Frank Cousins from the Frank Cousins Collection of Glass Plate Negatives. Courtesy of Phillips Library, Peabody Essex Museum, Salem, MA*

Knapp's financial unraveling seems to have started as early as 1818, a year when he could boast stock-in-trade of $5,500—a worthy sum, yet still only a fraction of the amounts the Whites and other major families could claim. Tragedy struck when, in December of that year, Knapp's 178-ton brig *General Jackson*—skippered by his brother-in-law Captain John Phippen—went down with all hands during a voyage to the Caribbean. As severe as was the personal loss, even more so was the financial loss, from which Knapp would never quite recover despite robust efforts over the next twelve years.

Knapp was a direct descendant of William Knopp, a native of Suffolk, England, who settled in Watertown, Massachusetts, in 1630 on money advanced by Richard Saltonstall, to whom he was to remain indentured for a number of years. William's grandson Isaac, born 1672, moved to Salem sometime between 1703 and 1707, and became a shipwright. All the generations thereafter descending from Isaac resided in the general Salem area and were associated with the maritime trades, either as shipwrights, merchantmen, or sailors before the mast.

Joseph Knapp married Abigail Phippen, the daughter of Salem's Nathaniel Phippen and Ann Picket Phippen, in 1798. She died in July 1827 at age forty-five. Knapp and Abigail were the parents of eight children, including Joe Jr. (born 1802), Nathaniel Phippen (1808), and John Francis "Frank" Knapp (1811).

After the death of Abigail, Knapp endured a miserable time. Although some of the children were quite grown when Abigail passed, the youngest were twelve (Sarah Ann), ten (William Henry), and seven (Samuel), each of them commanding much of his attention. What is more, his grown son Frank regularly proved himself an unwelcome and unhappy distraction, engaging in various vices and criminal activities in step with his friends Richard (Dick) and George Crowninshield—sociopathic criminal scions of the venerable Salem family, both a few years older than Frank. Sometimes, though not always, Frank lured his brother, Joe Jr., into his escapades.

By all accounts, Frank was quite handsome. The reporter James Gordon Bennett was to describe him as "a well-made full-faced youth . . . 5' 7" in height [with] thick dark and straight hair, growing low, parted and combed smoothly; the nose strong and blunt, the mouth rather large and cheeks full but very pale."[2] He was known to enjoy the ladies, especially ladies of easy virtue such as could be found walking near the wharves on late evenings, looking for trade, or working in brothels. He also enjoyed gambling. But both pastimes, combined with many libations, demanded money, which Frank, allergic to honest employment, routinely found other means of getting.

In the early summer of 1827, at the same time when his mother was gravely ill with the sickness that would kill her within a matter of weeks, the sixteen-year-old stole $300 from his father and embarked for Manhattan with the Crowninshield brothers. There the three caroused, drank, whored, gambled, and quickly ran through Frank's money. Once that was gone, they engaged in petty thefts, which landed all three in a Manhattan jail for several weeks, after which Frank returned home, leaving the Crowninshields to continue frolicking in New York. At a loss for what to do with his errant son, Joe Knapp Sr. found the solution that came most easily and naturally—arranging a job before the mast on a merchant vessel, sending him off to do as well or as poorly as he could beyond the horizon.

Joe Sr. had trouble elsewhere as well. Of particular concern was Joe Jr.'s recent marriage to the grandniece of Joe Sr.'s principal creditor, Captain Joseph White. That he steadfastly relied on the generosity and patience of White in order to keep the Knapp family finances from falling off a cliff, the senior Knapp knew all too well. A key part of this delicate equation of debt had been the measure of good will Captain White had previously displayed with regard to both Joe Sr. and Joe Jr. Now, with the all-too-vindictive Captain White in a state of rage over the marriage of Joe Jr. to his favorite grandniece, tension entered into relations between White and Joe Sr. This tension went well beyond finance, but nevertheless—as Knapp feared—wound up influencing finance and inspiring White to call in Joe Sr.'s debt. This probably came as no surprise to Knapp. After all, the matrimony had already, by all accounts, resulted in Captain White rewriting his will to disinherit the grandniece he had once so favored. And she was his blood.

Joe Knapp Jr. had—like most Salem boys—gone to sea in his teens. Records show that by the time he reached age twenty in 1823 he was qualified to serve as master on one of his father's vessels, a small brig named the *Governor Winslow*. Subsequently, he skippered a far more substantial vessel owned by the Whites, the 240-ton *Caroline*. He was admitted to the prestigious East India Marine Society in 1825.

Front door to Knapp House circa 1890. *Photo by Frank Cousins from the Frank Cousins Collection of Glass Plate Negatives. Courtesy of Phillips Library, Peabody Essex Museum, Salem, MA*

He'd seemed a success. But now, after his marriage to his Mary, he found himself without an assignment on any White vessel, and as well blackballed by other merchants who were White's friends. In the absence of a post as ship's master or at least one as supercargo, he was consigned to menial tasks about the farm under the supervision of his wife's brother-in-law, John Davis. Like his forebears, he was a man of the sea, not of the land. He'd made a stiff sacrifice for love and, many thought, had become deeply embittered by the idea of having been forced to make it.

In the time leading up to his bankruptcy, Joe Knapp Sr. had shaken the trees for revenue. He took in boarders at the large home he had once shared with so many children but now shared with only three. He sold a long-held insurance policy on his life. And, for a long while, he left unpaid the bill from the undertaker for Abigail's casketing and conveyance to her grave in Salem's Harmony Grove Cemetery. Too many other demands were more urgent, and none of his older children were in a position to help him very much, if at all.

One wonders what Joe Knapp Sr.'s reaction had been when, sometime during the day of April 7, he heard of the murder of the man to whom he'd surrendered everything the evening before. Relief? Trepidation? As Knapp well knew, now it would be Stephen White who would hold the keys to his financial destiny. And what that meant remained to be seen.

8 | THE CROWNINSHIELDS OF SALEM

"Young men and young women, full of courage, originality, and genius, are everywhere to be met with."
—Frank Crowninshield,
founding editor of *Vanity Fair* (1913)

ONE OF THE MOST MYSTERIOUS, SUCCESSFUL, and odd clans in Salem was the Crowninshields, beginning with the very first member of the family to set foot on the shores of the New World.

Upon his arrival at Boston in 1684, "Dr." Johannes Kaspar Richter von Kronenscheldt claimed to be a surgeon and the descendant of Saxon nobility. In passable English, he told of how he had been educated in Britain and Ireland but said little more about his personal or family history. Others, however, rumored that Kronenscheldt had variously fled Saxony over gambling debts, killed a man in a duel, or been expelled from Saxony on account of various other misdeeds.

To these allegations the good doctor never gave a response—which only led to even more speculation, including speculation that his nobility might be pure fiction. Two centuries later, genealogical research funded by the doctor's by-then blue-blooded WASP descendants yielded no evidence that a Kronenscheldt family ever even existed in Saxony, or anyplace else on the continent. When it was suggested that further research might yield either a Catholic or Jewish connection, the funding promptly stopped—and the family roots were left undiscovered. In Boston society at the time, one was better off not knowing certain facts.

The tradition in the family remained profoundly *un*-Puritan. As David Ferguson has written:

> Kronenscheldt's descendants have always been atypical of New England; none was ever very religious, much less troubled by any Puritan conflict between piety and the desire to get ahead in the world. Except among the women, and then not always, they have cared little for the social conventions of their times. Closely knit they were not; each went his or her way without thinking very much about what the others may have thought. . . . None was ever very self-conscious; not a few were, in money matters, ostentatious in a manner quite inconsistent with that of New England peers.[1]

They were renegades, rebels, individuals, iconoclasts, winners—and losers.

After moving to the Lynn/Salem area, Kronenscheldt married and fathered five children. He died in 1711, after which his wife, the former Elizabeth Allen, soon remarried and moved away from New England, to parts unknown. Most of the children went with her. Fifteen-year-old John, born in Salem in 1696, remained behind, soon becoming a crewmember on one of the many coastal cod- and mackerel-fishing schooners. Profoundly illiterate, John sometimes signed himself *Groucell*, sometimes *Groungsell*, sometimes *Cronchel*. Unlike his pretentious father, young John was irretrievably common and rough and soon matured into a true hard-drinking and womanizing denizen of the waterfront. The one characteristic he shared with his forebear was general irreverence. His main claims to fame in the family record are that he was the first to make a living on the water, the first to own his own vessel, and—not unimportant—the first to marry money. His bride, Anstiss Williams, born in Salem in 1700, was the daughter of a successful Salem merchant.

John prospered well enough, sticking to the coast and the profession of fishing—at least officially. This trade in cod and mackerel he reportedly combined with other seagoing ventures of a less reputable nature: smuggling and, it was said, a bit of pirating on the side. On these earnings, he and Anstiss raised ten children. When he passed in 1761, he left an estate valued at £1,500, which made him "upper-middle class." The estate included a Black slave, valued at £36.

John's house, known now as the Crowninshield-Bentley House and built by John circa 1727, is today owned and maintained by the Peabody Essex

Museum. It was home to four generations of the Crowninshield family until 1832. This is generally believed to be "the old Crowninshield house" that figures so prominently in H. P. Lovecraft's story "The Thing on the Doorstep"—a tale that turns on the murder of one Edward Derby, who occupies the house.[2] Lovecraft knew Salem well and used it as the model for his oft-mentioned village of Arkham. (In other words, the choosing of the ubiquitous Salem name *Derby* was no accident.)

Of John's numerous sons, the most energetic, wily, and shrewd was the eldest: George, born 1734. It was George who finally normalized the family name, anchoring it firmly as Crowninshield. Like his father, George was crude, probably the result of having been put to work before the mast on his father's vessel at the tender age of eight. George received his education on the foredeck, but what he lacked in knowledge when it came to belles lettres he more than made up for when it came to business savvy, ruthlessness, and an eye for opportunity.

The original Crowninshield-Bentley House. The house was moved from 106 Essex to 126 Essex in 1959. This photo shows the house at its original location circa 1900. *Photo by Frank Cousins from the Frank Cousins Collection of Glass Plate Negatives. Courtesy of Phillips Library, Peabody Essex Museum, Salem, MA*

One of those opportunities turned out to be his marriage to Mary Derby, three years his junior, scion of Salem's (at that time) most prominent family and sister to Elias Hasket Derby—as mentioned previously, America's first true millionaire. (To solidify things further, George's sister Elizabeth Crowninshield married Elias.) Thus, the Crowninshield and Derby families became, to some extent, entwined, although a stiff and venomous rivalry was to rise up between various members of the two clans and last for years.

George eventually owned several vessels. He became known as a harsh taskmaster both on shore and when afloat. Helping to pioneer trade with the East Indies, he without reservation did end runs around the British Navigation Acts, which forbade colonial vessels from such trade. He did so by falsely registering his vessels as Dutch, French, Spanish, or English in origin. These false registrations were frequently found out, and George more than once wound up prosecuted and censured by British admiralty courts, found guilty of "rioting against the King's Peace," and fined for same. The Crown even confiscated some of his ships. Still, he sailed on, although by the time of the Revolution his little fleet had been made truly tiny by the actions of the admiralty judges.

George and Mary Derby Crowninshield had six sons and two daughters, all of whom they raised in the original frame house built by John: George Jr. (born 1763), Jacob (1770), John (1771), Benjamin (1772), Richard (1774), Edward (1776), Mary (1778), and Sally (1781). Of these, several turned out to be quite remarkable individuals, although Edward died young, at age seventeen. Meanwhile, John (who skippered several Crowninshield vessels) and Sally (who married a moderately successful merchant and schoolteacher, John Parker Rice, and with him raised a daughter) seem to have led fairly nondescript lives compared to their rather sensational, frequently outrageous, and sometimes troubled siblings.

Jacob was to serve as a representative from Massachusetts and in 1805 was nominated by Thomas Jefferson and approved by the Senate for the post of secretary of the navy—a position that he declined for reasons of health. He died in 1808 of tuberculosis and was succeeded in his congressional seat by Joseph Story. With his wife, Sarah Gardiner Crowninshield (whose maternal grandfather had been one of the Derbys), Jacob was the father of two daughters. One of these, Sarah, would marry affluent Salem merchant Richard Saltonstall Rogers, who was supposedly Hawthorne's model for the treacherous character Roger Chillingworth in *The Scarlet Letter*.

Jacob's most lasting claim to fame may be the fact that he was the man who brought the very first elephant to America. Jacob purchased the two-year-old female in India for $450, and in April 1796 transported her to New York City on the vessel *America*, at that time under his command. Eventually, Jacob sold the beast for $10,000 to agents who toured about the country with the curiosity. Serving on the crew of the *America* at that time was a young officer named Nathaniel Hathorne, whose destiny as the father of the writer Hawthorne has already been discussed.[3]

Benjamin Crowninshield was to serve as secretary of the navy from 1815 to 1818 under Presidents Madison and Monroe. Previous to this, he skippered several of the family's vessels on voyages to the Orient and back and served in the Massachusetts legislature. Following his tenure as secretary of the navy, he served two more terms in the Massachusetts legislature, then four in the US House of Representatives, serving from 1823 to 1831. He and his wife Mary Boardman Crowninshield were the parents of six children. A granddaughter, Frances "Fanny" Cadwalader Crowninshield, was to become the wife of John Quincy Adams II, son of Charles Francis Adams.

Mary Crowninshield married one of Salem's prosperous Silsbee clan, Nathaniel, destined to become a US senator, and bore him three children. Their daughter Mary, on whom the young Hawthorne at one point nourished a crush, married the historian, educator, and Unitarian minister Jared Sparks—a direct descendant of John Winthrop and a future president of Harvard. They had five children.

By far the most outrageous and exotic Crowninshield of his generation was George Jr.—a man truly unique. Like other young male members of the family, George Jr. began his career by going to sea on Crowninshield vessels, first as a master's clerk and eventually as a master himself, although he seems only to have made one voyage as master, this to the East Indies in 1794 (in joint command with his brother John) aboard the Crowninshield ship *Belisarius*. Thereafter, he was for the most part employed on land, overseeing the operations of Crowninshield's Wharf and the construction, maintenance, and outfitting of Crowninshield vessels. As the eldest brother, he nominally took the helm of the family firm when his father, the elder George, passed away in 1815, even though he himself would live just three more years and spend much of that time away.

Crowninshield's Wharf (also sometimes known as India Wharf), 1806, painted by George Ropes Jr. George Ropes (American, 1788–1819).

George Jr. never married. He did, however, acknowledge an illegitimate daughter, Clarissa (commonly called Clara), born 1811 of Crowninshield's mistress Elizabeth Rowell. He provided generously for both Clarissa ($16,000) and Elizabeth ($8,000) in his will. Only seven years old when her father died, Clarissa Crowninshield's affairs were looked after by her father's attorney, Benjamin Ropes Nichols of Salem. Nichols saw to it that Clarissa was properly educated for a lady of her class by sending her to a "female seminary"—actually a finishing school, in Hingham, Massachusetts. Here she studied Latin, French, literature, and decorum while also becoming close friends with the sisters Margaret Louisa and Mary Storer Potter. The latter became the first wife of Henry Wadsworth Longfellow—a classmate of Hawthorne's at Bowdoin. Longfellow in turn became a lifelong friend of Clarissa, who eventually

Crowninshield's Wharf, 1806, oil on canvas, Salem, Massachusetts, United States. Image: 32½ x 95 inches (82.55 x 241.3 cm). Gift of Nathaniel Silsbee, 1862 M3459. Courtesy of the Peabody Essex Museum. Photography by Mark Sexton.

married a German art scholar, Louis Thies, with whom she had two children and settled in Dresden, Germany, where she died at age ninety-six in 1907.

Clara's father was nothing if not flamboyant. He was, wrote a relative, "a great swell and dandy. His clothes were of the latest cut and the most advanced pattern. [He wore] Hessian boots with gold tassels. His coat was wonderful in cloth, pattern, trimmings, and buttons, and his waistcoat was a work of art. . . . He wore a pigtail, and on top of all a bell-crowned beaver hat." Day to day, it was George Jr.'s custom to drive about "in a remarkable equipage which was one of the wonders of Salem, a curricle, painted yellow." People would stop on the streets to watch him go by "and children ran from the houses to look. He was very fond of children and delighted in driving them about." He also enjoyed the spectacle of heroics. "When emergencies arose requiring a man of daring, he was often called to the front. Three times he jumped overboard to rescue persons in danger of drowning, for one of which he received the gold medal of the Massachusetts Humane Society." He was likewise a volunteer fireman "and made several brave rescues from burning buildings."[4]

All in all, George Jr. spent his adult life as an activist who did what he wanted, when he wanted, and never hesitated to take any action he thought appropriate either in the name of patriotism or in the name of self-entertainment and vanity.

One shining example of George Jr.'s patriotism on parade occurred during the War of 1812, not long after the June 1813 battle—if one can call it that—near Salem between the outgunned US warship *Chesapeake* and HMS *Shannon*. The former sailed under the command of Captain James Lawrence and Second Officer Augustus Ludlow. The "battle" consisted of a very brief exchange of fire during which both Lawrence and Ludlow were killed. Although Lawrence's last dying charge to his men of "Don't give up the ship!" has become an inspirational legend for generations of naval officers and seamen, the fact is that the crew of the *Chesapeake* surrendered immediately after their captain died. Following this, the *Shannon* and the commandeered *Chesapeake* sailed for Halifax, Nova Scotia, where both Lawrence and Ludlow were buried with full military honors.

Not long after, Captain Joseph White proposed that a vessel, which he and other Salem worthies would pay for, be dispatched to retrieve the bodies of Lawrence and Ludlow and bring the heroes home to rest on their native soil. Inspired by White's proposal, George Jr. immediately set to putting the plan into operation, adding his own funds to the project and taking on the task of orchestrating the entire affair. He volunteered a Crowninshield ship—the brig *Henry*—and recruited a crew of captains, and only captains, from the Marine Society. Upon arrival in Halifax, the delegation was received graciously by the British authorities, who assisted in disinterring the bodies and loading them on to Crowninshield's vessel. In Salem, a grand reception awaited. As Salem historian James Duncan Phillips would write:

> On August 24, the bodies which had remained on the *Henry*, which was draped in black, were removed on barges by sailors in uniform rowing minute strokes, while the *Henry* and the United States brig

Rattlesnake fired minute guns, and landed on India Wharf. All the vessels in the harbor wore their flags at half-mast. Then a procession was formed at one o'clock. . . . The two hearses, preceded by the Salem Light Infantry and accompanied by the pallbearers . . . and followed by the town officers, the Marine Societies, and other distinguished citizens of Salem, Boston, and the vicinity proceeded through densely crowded streets to the Branch Church on Howard Street while the Salem Artillery fired minute guns on the Common. The windows on the line of march and even the housetops were crowded with spectators, while the bells on most of the churches tolled.[5]

After this demonstration, the bodies were removed to New York and then interred at Manhattan's Trinity Churchyard. In turn, George Jr. became a national celebrity, quite rivaling the fame of brother Jacob and his elephant. His notoriety even surpassed that of brother Benjamin, whose future as secretary of the navy was already as good as written. Broadsides celebrated George Jr. and his project. Newspapers extolled the glory of the great patriotic act. But what to do next? Celebrity needed fertilizing and watering in order to endure. And George Jr.'s already well-cultivated ego clearly needed his celebrity not just to endure but also to grow.

Toward this end, George envisioned the building of a great pleasure yacht to rival any other on the planet: a vessel of vast luxury as opposed to the utilitarian nature of nearly all other vessels on the high seas, one that he intended to take to Europe and thereafter anyplace else on the globe that his whims dictated. To accomplish the task, he commissioned Salem's Retire ("Tyree") Beckett, one of a long line of Salem shipwrights who had built countless vessels for the Crowninshields and other families through the years, to mastermind the design and building of his pleasure craft.[6] In due course, Retire designed what was called a hermaphrodite brig—the term meaning that the vessel was square-rigged on the foremast but fore-and-aft on the main mast, thus combining sail configurations that normally did not cohabitate.

Retire created large and comfortable cabins, a gracious dining space, and other luxuries, making the vessel a true gentleman's play toy—but one that, with skilled hands, could master any waters anywhere in the world, even the treacherous Southern Ocean and its three great and dangerous capes. When George Jr. came up with a name, he made a point of making it a spectacular one to match his vessel's grace and comfort. Launched in October 1816, *Cleopatra's Barge* was complete and fitted out by early December. (When George Jr. heard that his brother John had made mock of the pretentious name, he amended his will to state that should he die during his forthcoming voyage on the yacht, John should receive only $10 from his estate.)

Reverend William Bentley was among the first to take a tour:

> By invitation I visited the Hermaph. [*sic*] Brig. . . . Built by Capt. G. Crowninshield, and now fitted for sea in a manner never before observed in this Town. Her model is excellent and her naval architecture the best. The rigging is in the highest improvement as to its form and complete & of the best materials and workmanship. The best patent horizontal windlass with two stations just aft of the foremast. A rudder fixed to move with great ease and safety upon a new patent. The belaying pins of the Mast of brass. Below is the berth for the officers. Next is the dining-room furnished of the best materials & furnished with the best carpets, elegant settees with velvet cushions, chairs with descriptive paintings, mirrors, buffets loaded with plate of every name, and the best glass and porcelain. Adjoining are the berths for the owner and passengers [and] about midship the kitchen with all the necessary furniture for its purposes. In the forepart of the vessel are the berths of the seamen. The expense must have been very great.[7]

After a succession of private tours such as Bentley enjoyed, George Jr. threw the vessel open to the public, which came from far and wide to view what some were already calling the eighth wonder of the world. George Jr. delighted in the publicity. "You would be astonished to see the multitudes that visit my brig—or yacht—as they call her," he wrote his brother Benjamin, now firmly entrenched as secretary of the navy. "I have had 1900 women and 700 men in one day, and an average of over 900 per day for the past two weeks."[8]

A reporter from the *Salem Gazette* boarded with the throngs:

> Being introduced on board, you descend into a magnificent saloon, about 20 feet long and 19 broad, finished on all sides with polished mahogany, inlaid with other ornamental wood. The settees of the saloon are of splendid workmanship; the backs are shaped like the

ancient lyre, and the seats are covered with crimson silk velvet bordered with a very wide edging of gold lace. Two splendid mirrors, standing at either end, and a magnificent chandelier, suspended in the centre [sic] of the saloon, give a richness of effect to it, not easily surpassed. Instead of berths on the sides of this hall, there are closets for the tea equipages and a suit of plate for the dinner-table, which are finished in a style of superior elegance. The after cabin contains sleeping accommodations for the under officers of the vessel. The owner's and captain's staterooms are very commodious.[9]

When George Jr. finally set off on his voyage at the end of March 1817, with the first port of call to be in the Azores of Portugal, *Cleopatra's Barge* was overseen by officers who were all Crowninshield cousins. The barge's mixed crew totaled fourteen souls, including two Black crew members—one a steward and the other a cook, William Chapman. The latter, as a much younger man, had previously sailed with Captain James Cook. Some of the sailors before the mast had histories as scallywags in Salem, but they were scallywags well known to George Jr. and in whom he placed much faith, he at times being something of a scallywag himself.

George Jr.'s tour of Europe proved, in general, to be a success both nautically and socially. Armed with more than three hundred letters of introduction from President Monroe and other worthies, Crowninshield found himself welcomed everywhere by American ambassadors and therefore also by presidents, prime ministers, and royals. Gala receptions greeted the barge at nearly every port, such was her fame. The end of May found the ship in Majorca, then Barcelona, and then Marseille by the second week of June. After being shunned in Florence by Marie Louise, the estranged second wife of one of his great heroes, Napoleon, George Jr. quit mainland Europe for a time and made for the island Elba, where Napoleon, now exiled to St. Helena and barred from guests, had suffered his first exile several years before. Midsummer found George in Rome, where he at least was able to encounter and befriend a few other Bonapartes, including Napoleon's sister Pauline; his uncle, Cardinal Fesch; and the disgraced emperor's mother. After a few weeks in this company, *Cleopatra's Barge* departed Europe, and in the first days of October hove up to Crowninshield's Wharf—home at last.

George Jr. continued to live on board. On the evening of November 9, at age fifty-one, he suffered a heart attack and died. And his grand yacht? It was eventually sold to the royal family of Hawaii, which rebuilt it slightly, renamed it the *Pride of Hawaii*, and used it until April 1824, when it was wrecked amid a storm. The majority of the furnishings from *Cleopatra's Barge* were sold in Salem before the vessel's final departure from the port. Today there is a permanent exhibit at the Peabody Essex Museum recreating two of the vessel's rooms and incorporating many of the original furnishings.[10]

And now we come to the true bad seed: George Crowninshield Sr.'s son Richard Crowninshield Sr., born 1774. Richard and his wife had ten children—two of whom the reader will have met before: Richard Jr., known as "Dick," born 1804 and named for his father, and George, born 1806, named after his grandfather and his extraordinary uncle.[11] Yes, these are the two brothers who introduced Frank Knapp to all manner of lowlife in Salem and Manhattan, two prominent blisters on the heel of the illustrious Crowninshield clan.

Richard Sr. was himself something of a rogue. Among a family of winners, Richard seems to have lost again and again, sometimes through circumstance and other times through his own lack of discipline, pragmatism, and scruples. He was also somewhat reckless in his personal life, for a long time preferring the company of whores to the cultivation of a polite marriage to some woman of sufficient rank to bear the Crowninshield name. When, finally, he did marry, it was to an illiterate Irish immigrant of the Catholic faith—an anathema to Salem's proper Protestants, including many of the Crowninshields.

In his early years, Richard, like all his brothers, had done his time as a master on Crowninshield vessels. Later, he represented the family's interests dealing full time with their bankers in New York. This is where he met his wife, Ann Sterling, then working as a chambermaid in a Manhattan hotel. After he was removed from managing the family's banking interests (seemingly due to some form of malfeasance), Richard endeavored to build a textile factory in Connecticut. Through either misfortune or misadventure, the place burned to the ground very soon after completion, leaving Richard in bankruptcy. Returning to the neighborhood of Salem, he took up residence on a Danvers farm that had belonged to his uncle, Elias Hasket Derby, who died in 1799.[12] There he raised merino sheep (imported by his cousin, Elias Hasket Derby Jr.) while still cherishing the idea of textile manufacture.

In 1814, not far from the Derby farm, Richard found just the right spot for a new mill operation. The property, now in Peabody, was at that time within the Danvers town lines. As Reverend William Bentley was to note:

> [Crowninshield] has purchased a lot upon the Lynnfield Road above the Danvers Lower Meeting House, two miles from Salem, to possess a run of water [Proctor Brook] that passes from the place of Newell's Mills, so called, on the Seading Road and empties into the brook from Spring Pond at Danvers Lower Meeting House. The mill is to stand S. W. from Buxton's Hill, a remarkable height between the Derby farm and the brook and mill. The mill is to be in a brick building of three stories, one basement story not far from the road above the meeting house. . . . The dam is to be raised between two hills not a quarter of a mile above the mill and is to give a fall of 14 feet by calculation. The brook will be low in summer, but he expects by rain and otherwise to have water.[13]

Using borrowed money and also some funds he soon inherited when his father George Sr. passed in 1815, Richard began to build the dam, the mill, and, for himself, a fine mansion. Meanwhile, Richard's sons, especially young Dick, began early on to display signs of being trouble. At age eleven, in 1815, Dick was found to have plotted to set fire to the little Danvers schoolhouse. His younger brother George had been a willing accomplice. At about this same time, Richard's eldest child—Edward, aged fifteen—began to act erratically, demonstrating the behavior that would soon see him committed to an insane asylum for the rest of his life.

A shadow continued to follow the father. Richard's factory finally stood complete in December 1817, after more than three years of building, then promptly burned just as had the facility in Connecticut. Some thought it not a coincidence. Richard salvaged what equipment he could and moved it into his large house. Then, in an effort to fend off bankruptcy, he conveyed his dead brother George's magnificent yacht, *Cleopatra's Barge*, to a consortium of his many creditors, even though he did not own it, thus triggering a court case that would go on for many months. ("There is," wrote Rev. Bentley, "the greatest complexity of ignorance, impudence, vile purpose, and exposure in this fraud ever known.")[14]

Word soon spread that both Richard and his wife were alcoholics who fought drunken battles in the streets of Danvers and hosted endless revels with the Irish workers Richard had imported to work in his factory—workers who were now officially on the list of state paupers. These received state stipends, which they spent on liquor while living in Richard's mansion and greenhouse. Compounding such tales was the fact that one of Richard's daughters was said to have eloped with not one but two of the Irishmen for parts unknown.

A grandniece of Richard Crowninshield Sr., Louisa Crowninshield Bacon (great-granddaughter of George Sr., granddaughter of Benjamin, and daughter of painter and architect Francis Boardman Crowninshield) was to recall in 1922 that her great-uncle "made an unfortunate marriage, by which he had several children, none of whom were a credit to the family, in fact, quite the reverse." She added that "the wife of Richard Crowninshield had such a bad reputation that the rest of the family had nothing to do with her, and her children were all bad and the constant terror and mortification to their grandparents and later to my father." Louisa added that "one of the sisters used to teach in a public school in Brookline, and perhaps was the best of the lot, but a great torment to my poor father."[15]

Somehow, despite his frequent indiscretions and increasing turmoil with his sons, Richard managed to rebuild his factory within two years. In time, the textile mill proved a success, slowly but surely making Richard Crowninshield of South Danvers a wealthy man, albeit a drunken one. His son Dick, in turn, demonstrated a profound attraction to easy women and drunken reveries with the Irish millworkers in his father's employ—all this by age sixteen, in 1820. Dick's brother George was not far behind him.

Flamboyant, brash, and bold, Dick Crowninshield knew no limits. In an attempt to rein in Dick and George, Richard sent both to a boarding school in New Hampshire, there to be educated, tamed (it was hoped), and ostensibly prepared for Harvard. But the formula did not work. With Dick in the lead, both boys delighted in fomenting chaos. Dick ruled in the dormitory through violence and threats of violence. He made no secret of the fact that he thought the institution of the school, like all institutions, to be a fraud and the whole of civilized society to be a sham.

There was a strange, perverse logic to Dick's antisocial attitude—a strained intellectual justification that appears in his letters. It seems as if he anticipated the philosophical nihilism of a latter age in his ponderings with regard to the absurdity and futility of the human condition. He did not believe in ethics, in subservience to rules, or in any form of civic obligation. Each man, he said, was on his own to make his way as he saw fit, without bowing to the expectations of others. And he certainly was an intellect. At the same time that he set fires and engaged in every form of subversion, he wrote poems and read Byron. In other words, he thought himself no ordinary thug, but rather a thug worthy of the name Crowninshield.

After their expulsion from the New Hampshire school, the boys' father, realizing they needed discipline, sent them to a military academy in Vermont. But this experiment met with the same unsatisfying result. By 1821 Dick and George were back in Danvers. Here Dick began to collaborate in criminal activity with his brother and a number of other young ruffians from the Danvers-Wenham area. Their forte was petty crime, such as pilfering from liquor warehouses. This activity came to a brief halt when Dick shipped out for a year on a Crowninshield vessel owned by one of his uncles, but then it commenced again once he made landfall. When local crime in Salem got to be a bore, Dick took himself to New York City where, amid the anonymity of the finer hotels, he became an adept jewel thief. When once caught and prosecuted, a bevy of Crowninshield attorneys got him off the hook.

By 1825, at age twenty-one, Dick was ostensibly making an honest living with a machine shop he'd established in South Danvers. Here he crafted tools for textile mills and other factories, as well as parts for the makers of carriages. But he and George still enjoyed their debauches. During one night at a roadhouse gambling den and whorehouse owned by the Black entrepreneur and criminal King Mumford, the brothers tore up the place in a drunken rage, beat several Mumfords (including women), and created a furor that made local headlines for several days as the "riot at Mumford's." At about this same time, Dick and George were rumored to be involved with the robbing of fresh graves and the sale of corpses to the Harvard Medical School. There were also whispers regarding the statutory rape of a local Danvers girl.

In the wake of this publicity, Dick cleared out of town for a while. He headed south to another great port—that of Charleston, South Carolina. Here he adopted a new persona. With letters of introduction to the best of high society, this nephew of a congressman, a senator, and a former secretary of the navy whose family was known to control much of Northeastern shipping, found himself welcomed warmly. He knew how to be charming, and he'd always been a smart dresser. In Dick, the elite of Charleston saw a kindred soul, a fellow aristocrat. And he was certainly handsome. One writer said his face was "aquiline ... [with] alert dark eyes [that] brood over a prominent, slight underslung jaw; the black hair is elaborately curled and, as always, he is fashionably dressed."[16]

When Dick met a young, beautiful member of this society, a virginal seventeen-year-old whom he dazzled with his polished yet manly eloquence, it was natural that she would be attracted and he attracted in return. After Dick proposed and she accepted, her generally agreeable father made a few pro forma inquiries as to the nature of his future son-in-law. Letters went to acquaintances in the North, even though the father did not suspect he'd hear anything that would put a halt to the matrimony. But when the father received his answers, Dick was promptly banned from the household of his would-be bride and, indeed, from all the polite households of Charleston.

So Dick returned north to his machine shop, to various modes of crime, to new ambitions to displace King Mumford as the ruler of Salem's vice, and to his brother George who—though not as ambitious as Dick—was always ready to follow his brother's lead, no matter to what dark places it might take him.

By 1827 the malignant but industrious Dick had reassembled his den of ruffians and thieves, using as his headquarters a rural cave in the Wenham woods. He also founded a vice neighborhood all his own to compete with that of Mumford. Not far from an abandoned shipyard on Salem's South River, Dick established a dark and lucrative enterprise. On Peabody Street, in a large storefront that was ostensibly a grocery, Dick and a couple of partners ran an establishment—mockingly named the Reading Room—where working men could find drink, gambling, good prices on goods fenced from local thieves, and (right next door, in a whorehouse owned, or at least controlled, by George) a good number of prostitutes ready to give boys a good time.

Both Joe Knapp Jr. and Frank Knapp were customers—especially Frank. But the place was not just for sailors and waterfront laborers. Being a step above Mumford's establishment when it came to congeniality and safety, Dick's Reading Room was also sought out by Harvard students and other "gentlemen," many of whom awoke after a drunken evening to find themselves having been rolled for cash.

Aside from such occurrences, Dick kept things reasonably civil by ruling with an iron hand and regularly demonstrating his willingness to wield either his fists or a dagger quite effectively. He also seems to have been willing to wield Crowninshield family influence in order to decrease his competition and increase his market share. That summer of 1827, for the first time ever after many years of activity, King Mumford found himself arrested for fostering prostitution.

9 | VIGILANCE

"There is no good on earth; and sin is but a name.
Come, devil; for to thee is this world given."
—Nathaniel Hawthorne,
"Young Goodman Brown" (1835)

ONE THING SEEMED CLEAR. The murder of Captain Joseph White had been conducted with malice aforethought. The act had been coldblooded, calculated, and methodical—a most deliberate evil. It was also, apparently, murder for its own sake—murder for the joy of murder, destruction for the sake of destruction. There had been no theft. On its face, the murder seemed utterly diabolical, devilish, ungodly, and unholy. It was as if some man or men who were possessed by Satan had risen up and made a blood sacrifice to their dark infernal lord.

But it was no longer 1692 in Salem. Stephen White thought the crime not to be one perpetuated by the possessed, but rather perhaps by the deranged. Therefore, he speculated, there had probably been only a single operator—one utterly unhinged, devoid of a moral compass and quite adrift on the sea of life—a tempestuous brute with a blood lust or perhaps even a sleepwalking somnambulist, acting without self-knowledge and thereafter truly believing himself among the innocent. But had this madman been a wandering stranger passing through, making his way down or up the coast with an agenda to kill wantonly and savagely? Or was he a familiar face, a neighbor and friend harboring a secret life—a secret persona—of maniacal evil? If so, who would be second on the lunatic's list? What local innocent was next destined to be found a pale and bloody corpse, betwixt his or her sheets? Action needed to be taken, if not to secure justice then at least to secure the safety of the respectable citizens of Salem.

If not the work of a mad man, then who else? As Stephen White well knew—and as has been previously mentioned here—after a long and often cutthroat career in the merchant trade, Captain Joseph White possessed more than a few enemies. He had raided the remnants of bankrupt men and enterprises—most recently, on the very evening of the murder, the estate of Joe Knapp Sr. He had contested fiercely with all entrepreneurs who attempted to challenge his dominance. He had enraged abolitionists with the bravado and insolence with which he bragged about his participation in the slave trade. And he had demonstrated little empathy for those who somehow found themselves in his financial debt. In all but his family life, Captain Joseph White was a man of cold-hearted business who had spent his entire career in the most merciless pursuit of the dollar. Grudges against White, though many of them be secret, abounded in Salem at the time of his death. Never mind the grand demonstration of his funeral; among the mourning faces there were not a few that secretly smiled.

Even before the murder, there had been an uptick of less serious crimes in Salem. What had previously been confined to the domain of the waterfront and Mumford's establishments had begun to trickle into quieter neighborhoods—nothing extraordinary, nothing life threatening, at least nothing life threatening so far as respectable citizens were concerned. But travelers might well be accosted and robbed on the outskirts of town, and stores and warehouses burgled. Passengers on stagecoaches (most owned by the Manning family) found themselves robbed of cash and jewelry; owners of homes found a window smashed and valuables missing. They were such busy boys, those protégés of Dick and George Crowninshield.

This activity was just another symptom of Salem's gradual decline. With less work available on the waterfront and manufacturing jobs not always available (or attractive), men of the lower classes resorted to other endeavors to make ends meet. The town's selectman and a small number of unarmed constables were overwhelmed. The uptick had become significant enough by 1825 that Stephen White founded a small organization called the Society for the Detection of Thieves and Robbers.

Few have noticed that the name White gave to his loose-knit organization was one of the first uses—and perhaps the *very* first usage—of the term *detection* with reference to the investigation of crime. The first man to ever be called a detective, Jack Whicher of London, would not even apply to become a junior uniformed member of London's Metropolitan Police until 1837, which he did at age twenty-two. A division of elite plainclothes police designated especially for the investigation and prosecution of murderers in Britain would not be launched until 1842. The idea even then was considered somewhat exotic and experimental, the stuff of fantastic and sensational fiction. The first mention of the concept of a detective did not appear in literature until 1841, with Edgar Allan Poe's amateur practitioner Monsieur C. Auguste Dupin in "The Murders in the Rue Morgue." In the profession's earliest days, newspapers struggled to define the term *detective* for the public. The first detective squad in Boston would not be commissioned until 1846.

Note that the verb *detect* comes from the Latin word *detegere*, to uncover. And to uncover the truth behind the murder of his great patron was something Stephen White meant to do no matter what, marshaling all the considerable resources at his command. Meanwhile, the town selectman, in the immediate aftermath of the crime, did little more than print up some handbills offering a $500 reward for the arrest of the culprit. The town's court, without the power of subpoena, seemed even less useful.

One day after Captain White's elaborate funeral, Stephen White assembled an ad hoc meeting, reportedly attended by some two thousand Salemites, held in the second floor of the Town Hall on Derby Square (a building that, though decommissioned as a city resource in 1837, still stands). There he announced that he was personally posting a reward of $1,000 for information leading to the capture and conviction of the culprit or culprits guilty of Captain White's murder. This reward would soon be matched by an announcement from Stephen White's friend, Massachusetts governor Levi Lincoln Jr., that the state would offer an additional $1,000. Combined with the $500 provided by the Salem selectmen, this brought the total pot to $2,500. White also proposed the formation of a Committee of Vigilance, composed of twenty-seven members to be hand-picked by him—a committee empowered (by consensus rather than law) to take charge of the investigation of the murder, to command the cooperation of citizens in that effort, to enter and search homes and businesses on their own authority, and to detain and arrest either witnesses or suspects as situations warranted. This was unanimously approved by voice vote of those at the gathering, and a suitable committee was established.

On Stephen White's recommendation, physician Gideon Barstow III was made chairman. Barstow, a forty-seven-year-old Brown University graduate, hailed originally from Mattapoisett, Massachusetts, and was married to Salem native Nancy Forrester, Nathaniel Hawthorne's first cousin. Barstow had served one term (1821–1823) as Democratic-Republican representative to the Seventeenth Congress. Subsequently, he'd served terms variously in the State House of Representative and the State Senate. He was highly regarded on both sides of the political spectrum, well known and trusted throughout Salem, and generally considered as level-headed and steady a man as could have been found to manage the proceedings of the committee. Other members of the committee were equally successful, smart, and respected.

But the bottom line is this: the investigation was to be handled by non-professionals. As shall be shown, were it not for the intervention, and greed, of parties well beyond the limits of Salem, the case may very well have never been solved. The Committee of Vigilance would indeed ultimately identify the guilty parties, but only after the facts were handed to them on a platter. Meanwhile, the committee held nightly meetings in the counting house of Stephen White, brainstorming possible scenarios and suspects in conversations well lubricated with rum and whiskey, for it seems Stephen had provided them with $1,000 for expenses. In the meantime, impatient Salem festered with rumors, accusations, and discontent.

Whispers abounded. Hushed voices spoke of Stephen White's vast inheritance as a motive for the crime—although most discounted this theory. Stephen's devotion to Captain White was and always had been plain to see. What is more, Stephen was already a man of great wealth, and Captain White a man of great age. There would have been no reason for Stephen to want to rush the inevitable, and few could imagine him doing so. It seemed only Joe Knapp Jr. thought the theory plausible. But even he, after his initial wine-drenched outburst, generally kept his musings to himself.

Others still speculated on the roles of Benjamin White and Lydia Kimball. Perhaps their sometimes-irascible boss had finally enraged one or both of them to the point where homicide became possible. Some rumors even pegged the duo as lovers, complicit in the death of their master. Dick Crowninshield, while advancing no specific theory, was heard to mutter that once the culprit was found out, he should be given a medal, for Captain White had been the worst kind of criminal: one who pretended to be honorable. (Dick made it clear that he cherished no such pretention.) Other stories rose and fell with the frequency of the Salem tides, shifting and churning as the days and nights roiled by—a nearly constant and perfect storm of conjecture, most of it uninformed.

Stephen White left Mary Beckford in charge of the house on Essex Street, with Benjamin White and Lydia Kimball retained for the time being under her authority. In collaboration with Captain White's attorney, Joseph Waters, and the captain's duly appointed executor, John White Treadwell, he distributed the captain's wealth as prescribed in the captain's latest will, assigning real estate deeds to new owners (for the most part, himself) and distributing funds to others, including Mary Beckford, who received $15,000 (just over $400,000 in today's currency).

As Captain White had vowed, Mary Beckford's daughter, Mary Knapp, received not a dime. In total, he left approximately $141,000 in legacies for various relatives and approximately $250,000 in cash, investments, and real property for Stephen White, the latter being the equivalent of nearly $7 million in today's dollars.

Through it all, despite concern and fascination with regard to the murder, the visage of Captain Joseph White nevertheless began to fade, at least within Salem. The walking ghost from the shameful days of slaving now lay in his tomb, never to rise again, ghost or not. Years later, Nathaniel Hawthorne would write in *The House of the Seven Gables,* "Of all the events which constitute a person's biography, there is scarcely one . . . to which the world so easily reconciles itself as to his death."[1]

Such was certainly the case with Captain Joseph White. While his works— his real estate and wealth—remained, people (some even in his extended family) were generally glad to see the man gone. Joe Knapp Jr., for one, although his wife be disinherited, now at least had a very wealthy mother-in-law. Perhaps also, along with Captain White's life, there would also disappear the blacklisting that had kept Knapp from mastering ships for other merchants. Now Joe Jr. might be able to escape the drudgery of farming life, which he disdained, and go back to the life he loved and had been fitted for: life on the high seas. He had been born to navigate vast oceans, not a small sea of Wenham corn.

Both Frank Knapp and Joe Jr. seemed not so broken up by the death of Captain White that they avoided Dick Crowninshield's vice den on the South River following the murder. And Dick was pleased to have them. Both Knapp brothers appeared to be happy enough with life as they found it. They also seemed to suddenly have a newfound closeness and camaraderie with Dick and George Crowninshield. A certain knowing laughter flowed between them—all four in their element here in Dick's raucous Reading Room.

Yes, it seemed that while "proper" Salem speculated and worried, improper Salem saw no reason not to continue its long-running party. The liquor flowed. The dice rolled. Stolen goods were bartered and sold. New criminal partnerships and enterprises were launched. And the whores of Salem plied their trade as if the world was no different without Captain Joseph White than it had been with him. For the most part, they were right.

10 | A DAMNED ETERNAL FORTUNE

"Murder in the murderer is no such ruinous thought as poets and romancers will have it; it does not unsettle him, or fright him from his ordinary notice of trifles: it is an act quite easy to be contemplated, but in its sequel, it turns out to be a horrible jangle and confounding of all relations."

—Ralph Waldo Emerson, *Essays*

AT ABOUT THE SAME TIME that Dick took on Charleston Society, George—for similar reasons—had found it convenient to strike out for Louisiana. He traveled with a friend, George Needham, of the Salem cabinetmaking family. Departing Salem by ship in October 1826, the two Georges worked their way to the shameless and joyously sinful streets of New Orleans, where vice flourished in all its dark glory and where the two companions found an agreeable environment in which to ply whatever trade might seem the most opportune at any given moment, whether dice or poker or theft or any variety of cons.

Amid this carnival, it was not long before they encountered a suitable partner with whom to form a trio. A nineteen-year-old sailor from Belfast, Maine, John Carr Roberts Palmer Jr. was already well versed in petty crime of all forms. A few years later, writing in an 1831 book that was one of many trying to cash in on the murder of Captain Joseph White, Palmer was to feign naïveté and innocence by expressing outrage over the sins he'd witnessed in New Orleans:

> Here, for the first time, the picture of vice was held up to my view in every form imaginable; here, for the first time, I saw the sabbath utterly disregarded; worse than that, for it was, morally speaking, blasphemed. Gambling houses of every kind, open; horse races, boat races, bull baitings, puppet shows, balls, theatres, open; and every kind of amusement on that day, afloat, that the city could produce.[1]

Nevertheless, at the time, Palmer proved quite a worthy guide for the two Georges, leading them through the very lowest depths of New Orleans nightlife on Gallatin Street in the city's French Quarter. Here he helped them explore forbidden businesses, forbidden people, and forbidden pursuits. Truth be told, what New Orleans offered in the way of dark amusements made Salem's relatively sad excuses for vice seem like Sunday school. Here were cross-dressers cooing and beckoning from dark corners, here were exotic drugs that compared to liquor as murder would to a slap in the face, here were shameless child prostitutes and the adults (sometimes their own parents) who sold them, here were voodoo blood sacrifices and rituals and curses such as would make a Salem witch's blood run cold, here were sex shows displaying the most vile perversions, including bestiality. If there was ever a place controlled by a dark master, it was New Orleans in the 1820s rather than Salem in the 1690s.

The two Georges, who had certainly thought themselves quite worldly, now received a true education. It was only after they had graduated from this perverse college that, together with their new pal Palmer, they returned north to Danvers—on the way pausing for a few nights of debauch in Manhattan and then Providence. They were in Danvers by the start of May 1827, all three installed in Richard Crowninshield's mansion, as was Dick, returned from his failed romance in Charleston.

In the course of things, Palmer was introduced to Frank Knapp, and they formed a friendship that endured even after that spring, when Palmer left to visit his hometown of Belfast, Maine, and Dick and George Crowninshield departed for Manhattan with Frank and Frank's father's $300. Soon—in fact, very soon—after his return to Belfast, Palmer found himself justly convicted of burglary and sentenced to two years. Eventually he'd be a person of great interest to the Salem Committee of Vigilance investigating the murder of Captain Joseph White.

Today, across Essex Street from the East India Marine Hall, there stands an elaborate and unique fountain first installed for the nation's Bicentennial in 1976. At that time, it was a part of the Heritage Plaza Urban Renewal Plan funded by the Salem Redevelopment Authority as an attempt to dress up East India Square and make it presentable for tourists. The fountain's two levels consist of large granite boulders resurrected from the original colonial bed of Essex Street. The centerpiece sculpture, from the top of which the water cascades, represents an archetypical example of an oriental archway. Smaller cobbles form a precarious walkway amid the pool of the fountain. Children like to play here, skipping from one cobble to another above the shallow water.

The pool itself is meant to depict two opposing things: the shorelines of old Salem and contemporary Salem, well after the days of the wharves. An upper level represents the past, the lower level today's reality: what is left now that landfills have virtually wiped out the old harbor known to the great eighteenth- and nineteenth-century merchants, an active and affluent waterfront with no need for renewal or redevelopment. In other words, the fountain—if one considers it carefully—is a gravestone commemorating the decomposed glory of old Salem. Here it stands, at the heart of East India Square, surrounded by eateries and kitschy souvenir shops. The children skipping among the stones wear faux witch's hats. The parents sit at the adjacent café, sipping gin and tonics and keeping eyes on their offspring.

Here, in 1830, stood Stephen White's counting house, where the Committee of Vigilance staged its nightly meetings in the wake of the murder. Here, Dr. Barstow ran the affairs of the Committee with the aid of legal adviser Rufus Choate and close White family associate Stephen C. Phillips. Others among the Committee members, elites one and all, included John White Treadwell, Franklin Story, and William Fettyplace.

Thirty-one-year-old, Dartmouth-educated Rufus Choate—born and raised in Ipswich—had served in the Massachusetts House of Representatives and was destined to be elected to the US Congress as a Whig that autumn of 1830. He would also eventually, in 1841, be elected to replace Daniel Webster in the Senate before serving as Massachusetts attorney general in the 1850s.

Harvard-educated, twenty-nine-year-old Stephen C. Phillips came from a Salem merchant family and was, like Choate, a veteran of the Massachusetts House of Representatives. At the time of his service on the Committee of Vigilance, Phillips sat in the State Senate. In the coming years he was to take up Choate's seat in the House of Representatives after Choate's resignation in 1834. He served as mayor of Salem for two years starting in 1838 but would fail in a subsequent bid for the governorship of Massachusetts.

John White Treadwell was a banker, a director of two merchant marine insurance companies, and a first cousin of Captain White. Franklin Story was kin to Stephen White's wife and her brother, Associate Supreme Court Justice Story. And fifty-year-old, Marblehead-born William Fettyplace was a prosperous Salem merchant, cofounder (with Stephen White) of the Oriental Insurance Company (for the insurance of cargo and vessels), and treasurer of the East India Marine Society. He would later be deeply involved with various Stephen White ventures on the waterfront of East Boston and in the timber regions of Western New York.

All the other members of the committee were equally distinguished and equally unequipped to conduct a high-profile murder investigation. Nevertheless, they carried on, often with impunity, making their own rules and laws regarding the search and seizure of evidence, the summoning of witnesses, and other matters. In effect, the committee acted as if it possessed unlimited powers—which, for all intents and purposes, it did. Despite this, however, the conclave at first produced little in the way of results. And greater Salem was nothing if not impatient. Within a week of its appointment, the committee was already fielding complaints about its ineffectiveness and enduring press editorials making the same point. There had, however, been some very quiet, unpublicized progress, all at the instigation of Stephen White.

White had for several years been involved with the so-called Prison Discipline Society, established by Rev. Louis Dwight in 1825. Although based in Boston, the scope of this somewhat ominously named group was in fact worldwide. The organization included such corresponding members as Alexis de Tocqueville. The chief agenda of the society was to gather statistics and other information on imprisonment practices and philosophies and disseminate these among interested members. Where possible, chapters were formed in various states with a view toward improving imprisonment practices and increasing efficiencies with regard to rehabilitation, reform, and efforts to counteract recidivism.

The agenda was essentially liberal and progressive, urging that prisoners be treated with respect, that spiritual guidance be readily available to them along with job skills training, that child convicts be safely insulated from older hardened criminals, that asylums for lunatics and prisons for convicts be clearly differentiated, and that there should be post-release programs to help long-term inmates acclimate to the free world. In all, this was quite a forward-looking and enlightened organization, and one wonders what it says about the state of the culture that it only survived until 1854, when it died simultaneously with Dwight.[2]

Through his connection with Dwight and the Prison Discipline Society, Stephen White was able to make a few early inroads for the investigation, which would eventually prove to be important. Within days of the murder, White used his influence to get two of his close associates from the society into the Massachusetts State Prison at Charlestown. They went there with the initial idea to simply develop a list of individuals from the Salem area with records of serious crimes who'd recently been released from the prison. While at the prison, however, they had the opportunity to speak with John Fisher, an inmate from Salem. Fisher was serving four years for burglaries that he'd conducted in partnership with Dick and George Crowninshield, but which Crowninshield attorneys had been able to pin on him alone.

Fisher had an axe to grind, a tale to tell, and a hope for early release. Stephen White's two emissaries sat across from Fisher in his cell, their notebooks out, both scribbling the story he related. This was a tale that they at first took with a veritable grain of salt because Fisher stated quite plainly that if anything came of what he said and he was called to testify, he would be looking for something substantial in return—namely, parole. Both emissaries, given their experience with the Prison Discipline Society, knew quite well that whenever there was something to gain on the part of a convict, fabrication was often more than just a possibility. Still, they scribbled.

Fisher explained that three years earlier, when he'd been a prisoner in the Salem Jail on a minor charge, he and a cellmate he knew only by the name "Hatch" had fantasized a plan to steal from the bedroom of Captain White an iron chest that was said to contain a "damned eternal fortune" in gold. The chest, it seemed, had been legend around Salem for quite some time. Not a few of Salem's thieves or would-be thieves had at times conjured thoughts of making it their own. Fisher further explained that upon their release, while drinking at Salem's Lafayette Coffee House, he and Hatch, accompanied by another con named John Quiner and a petty thief named Daniel Chase, overheard Dick Crowninshield, a man named Palmer, and one Benjamin Selman speaking along the same line, albeit half-jokingly. They were just a few more inebriates talking tough about a daring deed none would ever pull off—or so it had seemed at the time.

11 | FOREVER STAINED WITH BLOOD, BLOOD, BLOOD

"As the circumstances of the murder, gradually unravelling, took stronger and stronger possession of the public mind, I kept them away from mine by knowing as little about them as was possible in the midst of the universal excitement."
—Charles Dickens, "The Trial for Murder" (1865)

AS WORD OF CAPTAIN JOSEPH WHITE'S MURDER spread across the eastern states, many editors and readers found in White an unsympathetic victim, and an embarrassed Salem found its slaving connection on full display. There was shame, as well, that White had been prominent among Salem's citizens, despite his lack of repentance. White's history, just like the history of his town, was, as an editorial in the *Rhode Island American* put it, "forever stained with blood, blood, blood."[1]

While the country awoke to the drama of the murder, the Committee of Vigilance continued slowly with its work. The report to the committee mentioning Dick Crowninshield and the Lafayette Coffee House was duly noted—but not taken seriously, at least initially. Fisher was a known commodity in Salem, vastly distrusted and disliked, and his word was not believed to mean much. Barstow, Choate, and their colleagues sensed opportunism mixed with desperation in Fisher's statement and a willingness to say anything in return for early release. On top of that, even though they well knew Dick Crowninshield's proclivities, none of the committee were too keen to take on the Crowninshield family, who were known—at least up to now—to be highly protective of even their two blackest sheep.

And there were plenty of other suspects—in fact, far too many. The general feeling of uncertainty and fear within Salem in the wake of the murder, combined with the lure of the $2,500 in reward money, caused neighbor to eye neighbor skeptically and suspicions to grow with the abundance of weeds in the springtime. Ironically, the process of investigation took on the feel of the old witch hunts, as neighbors wrote notes to the committee naming each other as likely assassins. The results usually involved midnight raids on surprised families, whose households were then searched, and the forcible taking of men and women to Stephen White's counting house, there to answer for themselves and supply alibis.

At least in this incarnation of Salem pandemonium, unlike in 1692, those clearly not guilty of anything were quickly discharged. In the end, all those neighborly tips and leads added up to nothing. As the *Salem Gazette* noted, "In every instance in which suspicion has been excited as to any individual, investigation has made it manifest that there was no foundation for the belief of guilt."[2]

Little more than a week after the murder, Fisher's story suddenly gained credence when the committee received a communication from the warden of the New Bedford Jail offering an enticing bit of further information. It appeared that a Joseph Hatch, then in the warden's custody for the crime of shoplifting, wanted to speak to the committee. The name Hatch of course rang a bell, and the tale he told—which the warden briefly sketched in his letter—jibed with that told by Fisher. Conveniently, Hatch's story could be vouched for by another current resident of the New Bedford Jail: John Quiner, an additional name that rang a bell. Both men, in chains, were brought before the committee, and their testimonies recorded—all of these proceedings taking place in secret, lest the possible culprits become aware that they'd become suspects and flee. (As a precaution on this front, Stephen White bribed a protégé of Dick Crowninshield, Joseph Antony, to spy on Dick and keep abreast of his whereabouts.)

Despite this valuable testimony, the committee still refrained from acting and instead sought further evidence. All of the evidence so far gathered was not just hearsay but also hearsay that sprang from the mouths of loathsome criminals. Therefore, this evidence would not be enough to convict. What is more, at the time in both American and British courtrooms there was a distinct bias against all oral testimony, hearsay or not, that was not supported by additional material proof.

In *A Treatise on Judicial Evidence* (1825), philosopher and jurist Jeremy Bentham had insisted on the importance of definitive physical evidence to supplement witness—and especially eyewitness—accounts, which could be contrived, wittingly or unwittingly biased, or simply inaccurate through innocent failures of memory or misunderstandings of events. The only oral evidence that came with a near 100 percent guarantee of being accurate was a straightforward confession from a perpetrator. In the absence of physical evidence or a confession, said Bentham, only an overwhelming preponderance of oral evidence would do. (One wonders how familiar Bentham was with the witch trials, where an overwhelming preponderance of oral evidence had sent many an innocent person to his or her doom.)

For the moment, the Committee of Vigilance believed it could continue to take its time and, indeed, had no other choice given the flimsiness of the evidence on hand. However, a new feeling of urgency entered into the equation when the brothers Joe Jr. and Frank Knapp came forward with a claim of having been accosted by would-be thieves on the late evening of April 27. As they reported to the committee on the twenty-eighth, the two had been riding from Salem toward the Beckford farm in Wenham when the attack occurred. The robbers brandished what the Knapps called clubs, but Frank and Joe were also armed. They proved a match for their attackers and drove the latter off into the forest without giving chase. They said that in the dark they could not recognize the felons, but that the voices sounded familiar.

The Knapp brothers' tale of their adventure in Wenham was reported in the *Essex Register* of Monday, May 3. Their story, as told by them to the editor Warwick Palfray, was this:

> They were going on the Wednesday previous, from Salem to Wenham in a chaise; when near Wenham Pond, about half past nine in the evening, three footpads came towards them—one seized the chaise, near the boot; one of them laid hold of a trunk and was struck by one of the brothers with the butt end of his whip—the other brother having a sword cane drew it, jumped out of the chaise and pursued the person nearest to him, who ran and was followed by the others. The footpads leapt over a wall and concealed themselves in a pine

wood. It was said they were alarmed by the approach of the mail stage. The brothers continued their journey unmolested.[3]

Speaking to members of the committee, the Knapps speculated that the club-wielding brigands they'd encountered might well be the same who'd murdered Captain White. That the Knapps had entirely fabricated the story, and the reason for that fabrication, would come out soon enough. But for now, the whole of Salem became outraged that the Knapps—whom most considered extended members of the White family—should be accosted in such a manner on the heels of the murder. Calls for action mounted. Feeling itself under increasing pressure to act, even if in a manner that later on might prove unfounded, on May 2 the committee put Daniel Chase, Benjamin Selman, Richard Crowninshield Jr., and George Crowninshield under arrest. (Although George had not been explicitly mentioned by either Fisher or Hatch, he was evidently taken into custody for good measure based on the general common knowledge that he and Dick so often acted in tandem.) On the third, the committee presented Hatch to a formal grand jury. Two days later, the grand jury returned indictments, charging Dick as a principal in first-degree murder and the others as accomplices.[4]

Dick thought it all hilarious and made sure everyone knew it. Did the buffoons of the grand jury actually believe he would go to the trouble of murdering that old bastard White and then leave all the valuables behind with the corpse? What kind of brigand did they think he was?

Dick Crowninshield was a man of imagination, always capable of self-entertainment. Although he'd far rather be out contriving, whoring, gambling, and drinking, he could also be content in his cell overlooking the Howard Street Cemetery, at least for a little while. He wrote letters. He wrote poems. He told the amused guards stories of wild escapades in Salem, Boston, Charleston, and elsewhere, and he took satisfaction on the occasional looks of envy that played across their faces. Of the two of them, he told one guard, he in his cell was the only free man. As he always had, he delighted in the profile of the rebel, the renegade, the outsider and proud scofflaw.

When necessary, however, he could easily contrive a pose of eloquent self-righteous outrage—the indignation of a gentleman falsely accused. A note to his sister Sarah, probably actually meant for consumption by his accusers, put this on full display:

> But a few days since, I enjoyed contentment and liberty. I had the most flattering prospect of passing a cheerful summer with you, unconscious of the malicious and hellish schemes to blast our characters, our all in life. Now doomed to spend our youthful days in the solitary cell of a gloomy prison, I sometimes imagine it a vision. Would to God it was so! But I know too well the reality of the reverse. Had the Committee of Vigilance requested us to give an account of ourselves, we would cheerfully have done it to their entire satisfaction. The perjured State's Prison convict that they intend to bring as evidence against us will be none to their credit. What prompts him to this perjured confession? Is it anticipation of getting pardoned? Or is it wealth?[5]

He also claimed his innocence in the form of poetry such as this, composed with his upcoming twenty-sixth birthday in mind:

> Unhappy day! You'll find me in a gloomy cell,
> And thoughts of keen sensation in my bosom swell;
> In my infant years I was happy; then by friends caressed
> I'm now misfortune's deadly aim and by the world oppressed.
> There is one consolation buoyant on the wings of time
> That my soul is pure from guilt, and this most horrid crime.[6]

In point of fact, Hatch had little need of a pardon, his sentence being a brief one. What he most certainly had his eye on was the reward.

On May 14, Joe Knapp Sr. received a strange, confusing, and mysterious letter posted two days before from Belfast, Maine:

> Dear Sir,—I have taken the pen at this time to address an utter stranger, and strange as it may seem to you, it is for the purpose of

requesting a loan of three hundred and fifty dollars, for which I can give you no other security but my word, and in this case consider this to be sufficient. My call for money at this time is pressing, or I would not trouble you. . . . It is useless for me to enter into a discussion of facts which must inevitably harrow up your soul—no—I will merely tell you that I am acquainted with your brother [Frank], and also the business that he was transacting for you on the 2nd of April last; and that I think you was [sic] very extravagant in giving one thousand dollars to the person that would execute the business for you—but you know best about that—you will see such things will leak out. . . . Direct yours to Charles Grant, Jun., of Prospect, Maine.[7]

Joe Sr. did not comprehend any of the meaning of the letter, although he did infer correctly that it was not actually intended for him, but rather for Joe Jr. After consultation with his attorney son Phippen, Joe Sr. showed the note to Joe Jr. and Frank. They, in turn, expressed that they could make nothing of it. Frank suggested his father turn the note over to the Committee of Vigilance. Four or five days later, the committee received its own note from Grant, ostensibly dispatched from Maine but nevertheless postmarked as coming from Salem:

I think it is time to inform you that Stephen White came to me one night and told me that if I would remove the old gentleman he would give me $5000; he said he was afraid he would alter his will if he lived any longer. I told him I would do it, but I was afraid to go into the house, so he said he'd go with me, that he would try and get into the house in the evening and open the window, would then go home and go to bed and meet me again about 11. I found him and we both went into his chamber. I struck him on the head and then stabbed him with a dirk; he made the finishing stroke with another. He promised to send me the money next evening, and has not sent it yet, which is the reason that I mention this. Yours, &c. Grant[8]

At this juncture, the committee decided it would be best to get hold of this Grant and quiz him directly. With this as the agenda, they sent an envelope with a small amount of cash to Grant, c/o General Delivery in Prospect, Maine (the nearest post office adjacent to Belfast). At the same time, they also sent a representative of the committee, attorney Joseph G. Waters, to stake out the post office and apprehend Grant when he showed up to retrieve the mail.

While Waters was away on this mission, there arrived yet another letter, postmarked from nearby Lynn, addressed to Stephen White. The letter ordered White to pay $5,000, or part of it, by the end of the next day, or "suffer the painful consequences." The note was signed "N. Claxton, 4th."[9] White was not at this time aware of the previous two letters. Baffled by the context of the note he'd just received, he turned it over to the Committee of Vigilance.

In a matter of days—on May 24, to be specific—Waters took Grant into custody with the help of two Belfast constables who jumped him as he sought to retrieve his mail from the post office. In due course, Grant found himself delivered to Salem in chains. By that time, upon questioning by Waters while still in Maine, Grant had admitted that he was none other than Dick and George Crowninshield's old crony John Carr Palmer Jr. "He is about twenty-three years of age," Waters noted of Palmer, "has insinuating manners, and possesses an acute mind. I cannot but feel an interest in him, and sincerely hope that he will be able to convince all of his innocence."[10] In other words, Palmer had already succeeded in convincing at least Waters of his overall naïveté and goodwill—a lamb who had inadvertently found himself running with wolves.

Only after receiving assurances that he would be immunized against prosecution with regard to the extortion letter mailed to the Knapps (he denied sending the second note received by the Committee of Vigilance as well as the third note to Stephen White) did Palmer agree to speak and tell all he knew. Palmer would recall that "every word . . . I uttered was caught on the point of [Waters'] pen, and with the same movement dashed in the ink, and then on paper, for fear that it might escape his grasp. What then? All kinds of promises made, to get more!"[11]

Palmer, who'd been released from the Maine State Prison in Thomaston only a few months before, spoke of the evening three years earlier at the Lafayette Coffee House in Salem when Dick Crowninshield had joked about Captain White and the fortune under his bed. More to the point and far more relevant, however, Palmer spoke of seeing Frank Knapp at the Crowninshield home during a return visit to Danvers on April 2, 1830, four days before the evening of the murder. (At that time, for reasons that remain obscure to this day, Palmer had chosen to travel under an alias that eliminated his surname, going simply by John Carr, although George and Dick knew exactly who he was.) Palmer spoke of how Frank and a man named William H. Allen arrived on horses. Palmer insisted he'd not spoken to Frank at all but had watched from a window as George walked away with Frank into the woods, where they talked for about two hours. During that time Dick gave Allen a tour of the mill. After Knapp and Allen departed, said Palmer, Dick and George queried Palmer as to whether he'd be interested in participating in a murder for hire: the murder of Captain Joseph White.

The Crowninshields told Palmer there was to be a payday of $1,000, which would be paid by Joe Knapp Jr., and that he, Palmer, would get one-third of that amount. Dick and George explained to Palmer that all had been arranged. Joe Jr.'s mother-in-law Mary Beckford—whom, they suggested, was complicit in the plan—would be away on the night of the murder, visiting her daughter and son-in-law Joe Jr., in Wenham. Joe Jr. would see to that. He would also see to it that a window at the back of the house was left unlatched. Killing the old man would be simple enough. (An alternate plan was to kill White as he rode between Salem and a farm he owned near the Beckford place in Wenham. However, this was not acted upon.)

Although in need of cash, Palmer—a mere petty thief—evidently thought hands-on murder beyond his capacity. But one guesses it was not a case of scruples that kept him away because he did absolutely nothing to warn either authorities or the intended victim of the plot. Add to this one more salient detail: Palmer spent the night of the murder at Babb's, a halfway house in Lynn, registered as George Crowninshield—a clear attempt to give George an alibi, although as it turned out George would not need it.

While disingenuously feigning ignorance as to the reason why he'd been asked (and paid money) to use George's name, Palmer at the same time insisted that Dick and George had expressed late on the second, once it was clear Palmer had no interest, that their proposal to kill Captain White had been a joke and that he therefore "did not think them serious until after the murder."[12] His statements did not add up. He was clearly complicit. But he was more valuable to the prosecution as a witness than as a target.

According to his story, Palmer returned to the Crowninshield home on the evening of the ninth once the deed was done and the news of it had spread across the countryside. He claimed that when he encountered George that night, the latter said he'd no hand in the murder—this despite previous discussions. George said that in fact he'd spent the entire night in bed with a prostitute from his brothel. Still, he'd gone to the trouble of melting down his dirk because he knew he and his brother were among those under suspicion and it would not be good for them to be found in possession of it.

On the strength of Palmer's testimony, Joe Jr. and Frank Knapp found themselves accused as accessories to murder and placed into custody on May 26, arrested by representatives of the Committee of Vigilance at the farm in Wenham. Now they joined Dick and George Crowninshield, along with Chase and Selman, in the Salem Jail. Palmer, too, was incarcerated in Salem—held for his testimony and for further questioning as needed.

Hawthorne was not at all surprised when he learned that the accused founders of the crime included at least one apparently upstanding member of the community—Joe Jr.—whose corrupt nature had previously been known only to the Crowninshield brothers, to Frank Knapp, and to very few others. Hawthorne was to find the irony rather delectable: further evidence of Salem being a corrupt place full of false fronts and masked malice as was, he believed, the wider world.

But some still wondered: Were the right men behind bars? What of the second and third letters, which Palmer denied, that suggested Stephen White's involvement in the affair? An air of misdirection still hung about the case despite the fact that several highly likely conspirators now sat in custody. Questions stood unanswered; motives stood unresolved. The inscrutable core of the mystery remained dark and silent. A puzzle formed the throbbing heart of the crime, within which lurked all the whys, all the desires and hatreds and ambitions that had combined to send Captain Joseph White to the Howard Street Cemetery. Indeed, soon Stephen White found himself briefly called before the committee—the committee of his own devising—to give an account of his whereabouts on the night of the murder, and his associations with all of the suspects—an exercise that went nowhere and was quickly dropped. But the rumor still lingered.

12 | IN THE HANDS OF AN ANGRY GOD

"For a deadly blow let him pay with a deadly blow; it is for him who has done a deed to suffer."
—Aeschylus, *The Libation Bearers*

JOE JR. AND FRANK were brought before Justice Ezekiel Savage on May 28. In court, Savage's interrogation of the Knapp brothers yielded little. The judge accused them of complicity in the murder and of writing the two letters that had seemed to incriminate Stephen White. To this, the two Knapps—on the advice of their brother Phippen, the attorney—said nothing other than to declare their innocence. They seemed relaxed. Like the Crowninshields, the Knapps appeared quite content and comfortable in their knowledge that the only evidence against them was the testimony of thieves and convicts whose veracity and motives could easily be questioned by a capable attorney. But it wouldn't take long before a man of the cloth convinced at least one of them otherwise.

Unitarian minister Henry Colman had been in charge of Salem's Independent Congregational Church since 1825, the year of its founding. The forty-five-year-old Colman was widely believed to be "one of the ablest and most advanced in thought among the Unitarians" at that time.[1] Like William Bentley, who had died in 1819, Colman was well known and respected among the merchant class of Salem, many of these families being members of his church. In fact, the Independent Congregational Church had been explicitly founded when five of the town's most prominent merchants—Stephen Phillips, Willard Peele, Ezekiel Hersey Derby, George Nichols Sr., and Nathaniel West Jr.—funded the endeavor in response to Colman's being passed over for the job at Salem's First Church.

As a result of this affluent membership, the Independent Congregational Church was well funded and exerted a broad influence across many aspects of Salem life. Colman was considered a prominent leader in the community. He often played important roles in town affairs. Among the members of his church were Stephen White, Mary Beckford, and Joe Knapp Sr., along with Joe Knapp Jr. and his wife Mary Beckford Knapp—this despite Joe Jr.'s clandestine life of occasional debauch at Dick Crowninshield's Reading Room. In fact, it had been Colman who'd conducted the wedding ceremony between Joe Jr. and Mary. Thus, it was natural for Colman to visit the Salem Jail to minister to one of his flock who found himself in dire straits, accused as a conspirator in a successful plot of murder for hire.

Colman had a firm sense that confession and self-sacrifice led inevitably to redemption, and that it was never too late for any sinner to repent and find Grace.

> [Colman's] simple religious ideas are easily accessible in his ser-
> mons. . . . He insisted that Providence is absolute and benign, mani-
> fest . . . in the moral order which assures virtuous people of happiness
> and eternal life. [Colman believed that] God's perfect governance,
> exercised in such lawful ways, [implied] God's foreknowledge of
> events . . . [but he also believed that] Providence and freedom [had]
> equal spiritual authority, and that "it is required of us to work out
> our own salvation" . . . by choosing virtue over vice.[2]

In this spirit, Colman visited the Salem Jail within an hour of the Knapps' return from court. There he sat beside Joe Jr. on the metal bed of his cell, speaking of salvation and what must be done to attain it. Outside, beyond the barred windows and gray granite walls, spring advanced: daisies, pansies, yellow trilliums, bloodroot, poppies, and myriad other plants, flowers, and trees. All of them bloomed fresh, their lives renewing and awakening, their perennial cycles advancing. The colors of the wildflowers in the Howard Street Cemetery belied the cold reality of the bones below and looked supremely beautiful when viewed from the cells. One imagines that Colman, who would soon leave the ministry in exchange for a career as an expert in agriculture, found some peace in glimpses of the color from within the gloomy jail.

The front of Salem's grim granite-faced jail built in 1813, shown circa 1900. The building still stands, housing luxury apartments. *Photo by Frank Cousins from the Frank Cousins Collection of Glass Plate Negatives. Courtesy of Phillips Library, Peabody Essex Museum, Salem, MA*

Although Colman thought Frank a lost cause—just like the Crowninshields—the reverend sought earnestly to get Joe Jr. to speak truth. Unbeknownst to Joe Jr., Colman sought that truth not just for the sake of Joe Jr.'s eternal soul but also for the sake of the Committee of Vigilance, to whom he'd promised to reveal anything Joe Jr. might say.

The righteous man of God told Joe Jr. he must view his situation in a manner that went beyond the cold practicalities of evidence and law as weighed in *this* world. He must instead come to understand the reality of eternal damnation that awaited him if he be truly guilty, even if he somehow managed to be found innocent in a Salem court of law. Unlike the court of man, the court of God was one where obfuscation would be useless, where the eyewitness was the judge himself, and where the sentence was both final and unending. Only confession and atonement could save him in any real sense.

Fire, brimstone, an eternity of suffering. Face to face with Joe Jr., Colman became less the modern Unitarian liberal and more the Calvinistic fundamentalist of olden times: a Cotton Mather preaching to a sinner about his doom at the hands of an angry God, a God from whom there was no escape. To all of this, Colman—rather cynically, given his relationship with the committee—added a sweetener: whatever Joe Jr. might say to his minister would be sealed between them given the priest-penitent rule in law.

As Colman was to recall:

> I first heard of the arrest of the Knapps on Thursday morning, the 27th, but I did not visit . . . that day, but went on Friday. . . . I consulted previously with some of the gentlemen of the Committee of Vigilance, in regard to visiting them, and in regard to the charges alleged against them. I obtained their consent to visit the prisoners. I went first to the house of Captain Joseph J. Knapp, Sr., and saw Mrs. Knapp, the wife of Joseph J. Knapp Jr., [her mother] Mrs. Beckford . . . and Phippen, and conversed with the family. I went to the prison with the knowledge and appropriation of the family. . . . After [Joe Jr.] had been arraigned and committed, I asked permission to go into his cell and went in. I told him I was much distressed—that I was sorry for his situation, and if I could render him any service which it was proper for me to render, he might command me. He asked me if I thought they could prove it. I told him I did not know anything about it, other than what certain gentlemen, in whom I had great confidence, had told me that in their opinion the evidence was conclusive. . . . I told him I did not know what could be done; but if anything could be obtained for him, and if he saw fit, and thought he could rely upon my honor to make any disclosures to me, he might be sure they should never be divulged—I would die first.[3]

All true enough—if Colman would uphold his end of the arrangement. But Colman was the close friend of Stephen White, who among much of the public remained an object of suspicion, and of the victim, Captain Joseph White. He was also, as has been said, a comrade and friend of the Committee of Vigilance. Colman fully intended to violate Joe Jr.'s trust the moment he managed to earn it. Although Colman earnestly and truly sought Joe Jr.'s spiritual redemption, he also sought justice.

As Colman and Joe Jr. talked, Joe Jr. drew close and spoke in hushed tones, as if concerned about being overheard. "He looked up to the wall, and I looked up, and saw a crevice, from which sawdust appeared to have fallen."[4] Colman asked who was in the cell overhead, and Joe Jr. whispered that it was George Crowninshield. As Colman was about to leave, Joe Jr. asked him if he would return again later in the day, which Colman did, around 3:00 PM. During this second visit, Colman (with their permission) named Choate, Barstow, and Fettyplace as the particular members of the Committee of Vigilance who had assured him of the weight of the evidence against Joe Jr. and the others. At the end of this interview, evidently thinking himself in need of time to ponder his options, Joe Jr. asked Colman to please come back at 5:00 PM.

During the third visit, Joe finally broke down and told Colman the gist of his story. In the end he did so, it appears, not so much for theological reasons as for practical reasons. Without authorization to do so, Colman had suggested that there was quite possibly a pardon of some sort that would be made available should Joe Jr. agree to make a clean breast of things. Colman also assured the prisoner that he would keep any confession to himself unless he were able to obtain for him full immunity. Until such time, anything Joe Jr. said would be sacrosanct behind the priest-penitent shield. Colman swore to it.

Given this assurance, Joe Jr. in a nutshell admitted that he and his brother Frank had indeed engaged the Crowninshields, for the price of $1,000, to see to the death of Captain White. Their idea was to also take possession of what they believed to be the sole copy of Captain White's will, therefore leaving the impression that he had died intestate, which would cause Joe Jr.'s mother-in-law—Captain White's sole surviving adopted daughter just as Stephen White was his sole surviving adopted son—to inherit half of the sizable estate, rather than a much smaller amount. Joe Jr. said categorically that it had been Dick Crowninshield who'd personally carried out the murder. He also told Colman where the club used to strike Captain White could be found: in a rathole under the steps of the Branch Meeting House on Howard Street. Joe claimed that neither his mother-in-law nor his wife knew anything about the scheme. With Phippen Knapp present, Joe Jr. agreed to sign a full written statement once immunity from prosecution could be formally guaranteed in writing.

Phippen, however, insisted that Frank be advised of the agreement and offered the chance to forbid it. Joe Jr.'s confession, followed by his turning state's evidence, would leave Frank to stand trial. If convicted, Frank would likely face the noose, or at best a long prison sentence, as an accessory. However, according to Colman, when he and Phippen visited Frank in his cell, Phippen softened the conversation a bit by expressing hope for Frank even in light of Joe Jr.'s confession. As Colman would recall during court proceedings: "Phippen, as I understood, to reconcile Frank to Joseph's making a confession, told him that if Joseph were convicted, there would be no chance for him [i.e., Joe Jr.], but if he [Frank] were convicted there would be some chance of procuring a pardon."[5]

Whether he believed Phippen's assurance or not, Frank agreed to the plan—in essence expressing his willingness to, if it became necessary, sacrifice himself to save his brother. The other option would be for them both to be at risk of hanging. Joe Jr. was the one with a wife, even though he'd evidently also been the moving force behind the escapade to increase his mother-in-law's share of Captain White's wealth.

Early in the evening of the twenty-eighth, Phippen and Colman together set off by horse for Boston, embarked on distinctly separate missions. Phippen's mission was to find suitable representation for his brothers, since he himself had no criminal trial experience and also might well be called as a witness. Colman's mission, taken on with the permission of the Committee of Vigilance, was to get a letter from Massachusetts Attorney General Perez Morton promising immunity for Joe Jr. should he provide a written confession and agree to testify. Colman returned to Salem the next day, the twenty-ninth, with a letter from Morton saying that any *one* of the accused might be "made a witness at the trial, and that his so being made a witness will be a pledge of the Government never to be prosecuted . . . but it will be understood that this authority is not to operate in favour [*sic*] of Richard Crowningshield [*sic*], against whom sufficient evidence already appears."[6]

Shortly after his arrival back in Salem, Colman, along with two witnesses (the committee's Barstow and Fettyplace), went to the Branch Meeting House, reached down into the rathole beneath the wooden steps, and fished out the macabre tool that had been hidden there: a heavy wooden bludgeon weighted with lead inserts in the barrel and finished with a beaded grip.

Before their departures for Boston, Colman had promised Phippen that he would not again visit Joe Jr. without Phippen or some other suitable attorney being present. Despite this pledge, Colman now immediately went to Joe Jr., showed him the attorney general's letter, and proceeded to take down the prisoner's detailed explanation of all that had led up to the murder of Captain Joseph White.

Midway through the process, an annoyed Phippen Knapp arrived and pounded on the door of the cell to be allowed in. This Colman refused, promising Phippen that he would shortly show him Joe's full statement.

Circa-1900 photo of Howard Street Cemetery as seen from Howard Street, very near the spot where either Frank Knapp or Dick Crowninshield hid the bludgeon that had been used in the murder. The Salem Jail can be seen in the distance at left abutting the cemetery. The cells of the Knapp brothers and the Crowninshields overlooked the cemetery. *Photo by Frank Cousins from the Frank Cousins Collection of Glass Plate Negatives. Courtesy of Phillips Library, Peabody Essex Museum, Salem, MA*

Later that same day, the Committee of Vigilance vetoed Colman's pledge to Phippen, believing it inappropriate for Phippen to view the document since he might be called as a witness at trial. Nevertheless, they allowed a lengthy summary of the statement to be published in the next day's edition of the *Salem Gazette*.

13 | JOSEPH KNAPP JR.'S CONFESSION AS TRANSCRIBED BY HENRY COLMAN

SALEM GAOL, 29TH MAY, 1830.[1]

I mentioned to my brother, John Francis Knapp, in February last, that I would not begrudge one thousand dollars that the old gentleman, meaning Capt. Joseph White, of Salem, was dead. He asked me why. I mentioned to him that the old gentleman had a will, which if destroyed, half of the property would come on this side; that is, to my mother in law Mrs. Beckford; that with the present will, the bulk of the property would go to Stephen White; that he had injured me in the opinion of the old gentleman, and I had no doubt had also prejudiced him against all the family, and that I thought it right to get the property if I could. I mentioned to him also in a joking way, that the old gentleman had often said he wished he could go off like a flash.

We then contrived how it could be done. One way was to meet him on the road, but the old gentleman was never out at night. Another was to attack him in the house, but Frank said he had not the pluck to do it, but he knew who would. I asked him who, and he said he would see George and Dick Crowninshield. I told him, well, I did not think they would, but he could go and see. He got a chaise with Wm. H. Allen and went to their house, as he said, and proposed it to both of them. . . .

Dick said he would do it if George would back him. George would not, but Dick appointed a night to meet Frank. They met two or three different times. Once at the Universalist Meeting House . . . once in South Salem, by the South Field Bridge, as I understood my brother, and once at the Salem Theater—at the building. There was no play that night. At the meetings my brother Frank Knapp told him just what I said.

There was another meeting appointed at the Salem Common for the 2nd of April. I went on the Common that same evening and met Richard Crowninshield at eight o'clock in the very center of the Common. I told Richard Crowninshield how matters stood, and that I had taken the will of Captain White either that day or the day before. I took the will out of his iron chest; it had the key in it; I turned the key and took it out—I told him what I would give him, that it should be just as my brother had represented, meaning that I would give him a thousand dollars if he would fix him, meaning Captain White. Richard Crowninshield then showed me the tools he would do it with, which were a club and a dirk. The club was about two feet long, turned of hard wood, loaded at the end, and very heavy. I presumed it was loaded, and ornamented at the handle, that is, turned with beads at the end to keep it from slipping. I took hold of it. I think I lifted it.

The dirk was about five inches long on the blade, having a white handle, as I think—it was flat, sharp at both edges, and tapering to a point. I do not know where he got the dagger, but he said he turned the club himself. I asked him if he were going that night and told him the time the old gentleman went to bed generally, which was about ten, or a little before. He said no, he could not do it that night, that he must wait a little. He did not feel like it because he was alone, and his brother would not back him, but he said he would meet my brother another time. I do not know what evening. It got past nine, and I left and went home to Wenham. I kept the will . . . in my chaise box, wrapped up in hay. It remained there until I heard of the murder, and then I burnt it. . . .

My brother came to the farm on [Tuesday, the 6th of April, in the afternoon]. I told him that my Mother Beckford was at the farm and was to pass the night. . . . I mentioned this to my brother and told him he had better tell this to Richard Crowninshield. On the Friday preceding, I [had] unbarred and unscrewed the window of Capt. White's house, closing the shutter again. My brother said he would inform Richard Crowninshield. My brother left the farm about tea time, with the chaise in which he came up. My brother made this remark as he went off: I guess he will go tonight.

The next morning, Wednesday 7th of April, Mr. Stephen White's man came up in his chaise and informed us that the old gentleman White was dead, and Mother Beckford said she would go right down with him. My brother came to the farm about noon. He asked if we had heard the news; we told him yes and how we heard it. After dinner he told me aside how it occurred. He said Richard Crowninshield met him, I think, in Brown Street, in Salem, about 10 o'clock in the evening, and that he, Richard, left him and came round through the front yard, passed through the garden gate, pushed up the back window and got in by it; and passed through the entry, by the front stairs into Capt. White's chamber; that he struck Capt. White with the club above named, while asleep, and after striking him he used the dirk, and hit him several times with the dirk, and covered him up, and came off, and met my brother again in Brown Street, or by the Common, I think about eleven o'clock. He says Dick told him before he went in, if he saw any money there he meant to take it. When he came out my brother asked if he had got it—he told him no, but he had fixed him.

They separated and went home. This is all I know of the affair until I saw my brother again after he had seen Richard Crowninshield again. I came down to Salem on the afternoon of the 7th of April, and staid [sic] in Salem a fortnight. My brother informed me that he had seen Richard Crowninshield once or twice, and that Richard Crowninshield having seen the accounts of the number of stabs in the newspapers said he had stabbed him but four times, and Richard Crowninshield remarked that he really believed there had been another person in the chamber because he did not recollect making more than four or five stabs at the farthest.

A fortnight or three weeks after the murder Richard Crowninshield rode up with my brother Frank to the farm in Wenham. . . . While Richard was at the farm, he told me the same story which my brother had done. . . . He remarked that he was pretty short and should want some money soon. He mentioned that it was a great pity we had not got the right will. . . . Richard Crowninshield informed me that same evening, that he had put the club with which he killed Capt. White under the Branch Meeting House steps. . . .

I wrote a letter, dated I think, the 12th of May, addressed to the Hon. Stephen White . . . on Sunday Morning, the 16th of May, signed either Grant or Claxton, and another addressed to the Hon. Gideon Barstow, signed either

Grant or Claxton, . . . which letters I brought to Salem, and gave them to Wm. H. Allen, who said he would put them in the Post Office that evening. The purport of the letter addressed to the Committee was that I, the person signing the letter, went into the chamber and struck old Mr. White on the head with a piece of lead, and that I pierced him or stabbed him three or four times with a dirk, and that Stephen White gave the finishing stroke; that he offered me five thousand dollars, and had not sent any part of it.

One of the letters was dated Lynn, I do not know which. The purport of the letter to Stephen White was that he must send me the five thousand dollars or suffer the consequences. I believe that was the amount of it. There were very few words. These letters I think were put into the office in the evening. William H. Allen was at our house two or three days afterwards, and told me that he had put them in. I do not think he knew the purport of them. I told him that I had received an anonymous letter and that this would brush off the effect of it.[2]

14 | THE FIEND HAS ROBBED JUSTICE OF ITS VICTIM

"To run away from trouble is a form of cowardice and, while it is true that the suicide braves death, he does it not for some noble object but to escape some ill."

—Aristotle

PHIPPEN KNAPP RETAINED FRANKLIN DEXTER, a thirty-seven-year-old Charlestown-born attorney with whom he was friendly, to serve as chief counsel for his brothers. Dexter had a reputation in courtrooms throughout the Boston area as a formidable adversary. And he came with an impeccable pedigree. Dexter's father, Samuel Dexter—a protégé of both John Adams and Thomas Jefferson—had been the third treasury secretary of the United States, the fourth secretary of war, a senator from Massachusetts, and a congressman.[1] Dexter's wife, Salem-born Catherine Prescott, was the granddaughter of Colonel William Prescott, who'd been the commander of the American troops at Bunker Hill, in which capacity he uttered the famous phrase "Don't fire until you see the whites of their eyes!"

A conversation Dexter had with Dick Crowninshield was to have major ramifications in the court proceedings that were to come. Although the Crowninshields had at first been downright surly in their response to the accusations against them, they'd both quieted down considerably after hearing that Joe Jr. had made a full and complete confession and would be the star witness for the prosecution. Dick in particular fell into a dark mood—barely eating and seldom speaking. Even his outpouring of letters and poems ceased—having evaporated along with at least some of his bravado. He spent most of his time reading, all nonfiction: a book or two on mechanics and mathematics and a book he'd specifically requested on Massachusetts judicial procedures. A few family members visited, but most of the Crowninshields had, once the details of the crime emerged, by now backed away from both Dick and George. Dick and George's sisters Sarah and Mary remained true, however, as did their father.

Two weeks into June, as Dexter was leaving the Salem Jail after a consultation with the Knapp brothers, Dick Crowninshield motioned for the attorney to step over to his cell for a moment. There, according to informed hearsay but never documented formally in the nature of sworn court testimony, Dick briefly quizzed Dexter on Massachusetts law as it pertained to accessories and principals in crime, particularly capital crimes. If this actually happened, then Dexter would certainly have explained the fundamental governing rule in that state, which said that if there was no successful prosecution of a principal in a crime, then there could be no prosecution of accessories. In other words, if Dick were not brought to the bar as the principal, hands-on murderer of Captain White, and found guilty, then there could be no indictment or trial of the other five—George Crowninshield, Joe Knapp Jr., Frank Knapp, Daniel Chase, and Benjamin Selman—as accessories.[2]

It is doubtful Dick Crowninshield cared much for the fates of the Knapp brothers, Chase, or Selman. Besides, it seemed at the moment that Joe Jr. had already saved himself by turning witness against Dick and all the rest. Dick, however, did have genuine concern for the fate of his brother George. If the reported conversation with Dexter actually happened, then what Dick did next was almost certainly a strategy to save George while at the same time cheating the hangman.

On June 15, Dick Crowninshield carefully arranged his folded clothes and his books on the little table in his cell. Before lunch, he borrowed a razor from one of the guards and shaved. After his midday meal, he tied together several of the fine silk handkerchiefs that had long been among his trademarks, fashioning them into a noose. The great romantic who was Dick perhaps loved the drama: a hero bravely sacrificing himself so that his brother might be saved, a gesture akin to that of Frank when he said Joe Jr. should confess. Dick tied the long end of his noose to one of the horizontal bars covering his window, a bar so low that in order to asphyxiate himself Dick had to bend his knees and push the flats of his feet against the cell wall, so as not to touch the ground.

When his jailers found him, his knees hung suspended a mere two inches off the cell floor.

But how much actual romance was there to Dick's act as opposed to self-conceit? Given Joe Jr.'s damning testimony, Dick knew for sure that he could not but hang in the end. He was already a dead man. By performing an act that he believed would spare his brother George, he also spared himself the embarrassment and ignominy of a public trial and, worse, a public hanging. Through suicide—through apparent self-sacrifice—he could redeem his own image of himself and, perhaps, his image among others. He had always been a man of great vanity: imagining himself above the common herd of lawmakers and law followers. Now came one final opportunity to declare and demonstrate his independence, to take control of his life and his situation, to break one last rule, and to do it with impunity while also throwing a wrench into the wheels of justice, causing a breakdown that would result in his brother being freed. (In a carefully crafted last letter to George certainly meant for consumption by prosecutors, Dick made a point of apologizing for "what I have caused you" and offered prayers that George's "innocence" would keep him safe.)[3]

The next day's *Salem Register* carried the news to those few in town who had not already heard it by excited word of mouth:

> As soon as it was discovered that the prisoner had committed this desperate act, several physicians were sent for, and also the coroner, Thomas Needham, who immediately summoned a jury, and held an inquest over the body. The evidence produced to the jury we learn was in substance as follows: The prisoner took his dinner as usual between 12 and 1, and after 1 o'clock, the turnkey went to clear away the things, when nothing unusual was perceived. A little before 2 o'clock, Mr. [Nehemiah] Brown, the gaoler [*sic*], went to the cell to carry a note from his father, and calling him received no answer. He then looked through the hole at the top of the door, and saw the prisoner hanging to the grating of the window. He immediately called assistance, entered the cell, and had the body cut down.[4]

The jailers sent for Dick's father to collect his son's body and bring it back to Danvers for burial. Before that happened, however, dozens of townsmen assembled outside the jail, all demanding to see the corpse lest word of the suicide prove to be a hoax—a cover-up for a successful escape or some other intrigue sponsored by the powerful Crowninshields. To this Brown acceded. For the balance of the day of the fifteenth and into the evening he opened the jail. All who wished to do so paraded through and gazed down on Dick, his luxurious curls now surrounding a face that was blue from suffocation—the mouth gaping open, the arms folded across the chest, and the dark silk handkerchiefs still wrapped around the throat.

A pamphlet soon appeared. "The fiend has robbed justice of its victim," said the anonymous author.[5]

15 | AN ELABORATE GAME OF CHESS

> "Some queries have been started . . . as to the pos-
> sibility of procuring the conviction of either or both
> Knapps, now that Crowninshield is taken away. There
> does appear to be some ground for doubt. It is a rule
> of law that the conviction of the principal shall pre-
> cede that of the accessory. Can then any principal
> now be convicted?"
> —*Newburyport Herald*, June 22, 1830

MASSACHUSETTS ATTORNEY GENERAL PEREZ MORTON had been
happy enough to grant Joe Knapp Jr. immunity from prosecution in return
for assuring the conviction of Dick Crowninshield as the principal murderer
of Captain White, and the conviction of the others as accessories (although he
fully expected Selman and Chase to be discharged for lack of true participation in either the conspiracy or the act, which did indeed come to pass very
shortly). The case of the murder of Captain White already had such a high
profile with the public that Morton had looked forward to swift trials and even
swifter convictions and sentencing, with certainly at least one Crowninshield
going to the gallows. The event would be a victory for justice, a victory for
law and order in the state of Massachusetts, and, perhaps most important, a
victory for Attorney General Morton.

Although popular politically, the seventy-nine-year-old, Plymouth-born
Morton was very near the end of his public life and would retire in 1832. In
fact, he was only three years younger than the elderly Captain White. As the
most observant of his friends understood, Morton wanted—no, he *needed*—to
go out with a very high-profile success that would cement his reputation as

an attorney general of the first rank: a great administrator of justice in what promised to be the most sensational murder trial of its era. Such a role would go a long way to blot out a blemish with which his otherwise stellar public image had long been afflicted.

Years before, in 1788, there had been a great public scandal when Morton's unmarried sister-in-law gave birth to an illegitimate child of whom most everyone believed Morton to be the father. The rumor, probably true, was given wide publicity in the Boston press and, in fact, throughout New England. There was even a popular novel published in 1789, *The Power of Sympathy*, written by a Dorchester neighbor of the Morton family, that presented a thinly veiled fictional account of the episode. Morton much preferred that his legacy be that of a great soldier for justice than a great adulterer. The case of Captain Joseph White could pave the way.

On the face of it, and as Dick had believed, Dick's suicide had created a situation in which the accessories to the murder of Captain White simply could not be prosecuted since the principal of the crime had not been brought to justice. Public outrage at this idea became very heated very fast. Newspaper editorials blasted the notion that, through an untidy loophole, murderers who were just as complicit as the wielder of the bludgeon and dirk would go free to resume peaceful and profitable lives. Villainy was to go unanswered, wickedness unaccounted for. There had been a plot. The plotters needed to answer for what they had done and needed to pay for what they had done.

Within days after the suicide, Morton announced a new plan to charge and prosecute Frank as a second-degree principal in the crime. Morton's reasoning was this: According to Joe Jr.'s confession, his brother had been at the scene of the crime with Dick Crowninshield on the night of the murder. Frank had met Dick at Brown Street (to the rear of Captain White's mansion) before the deed was done, he had stood watch as Dick proceeded to the back of White's mansion and entered, and he had waited for Dick and served as a lookout while the murder was being accomplished. Conveniently, the Committee of Vigilance possessed substantiating evidence in the form of testimony from an elderly mariner, Captain Daniel Bray Jr., and a young bank clerk, Stephen Myrick, who claimed to have seen two men fitting the descriptions of Dick and Frank loitering suspiciously on Brown Street at about the time of the murder. Although the observations of the two witnesses, who could not conclusively identify the men they had seen, would have been fairly useless if left to stand on their own, taken together with Joe Jr.'s account of the night of the murder they could easily prove fatal for Frank.

Taking things a few steps further, Chief Justice Isaac Parker was to elaborate a very wide definition of what constituted being a principal during a special session of the Supreme Judicial Court held at Salem on July 10. On close inspection, Parker's interpretation put not only Frank's life at risk but the lives of others as well:

> [T]he law exacts the death penalty of any person who shall commit the crime of willful murder, or shall be present aiding and abetting in the commission of such a crime, or not being present, shall have been accessory thereto before the fact by counselling, hiring, or otherwise procuring the same to be done.
>
> It is not required that the abettor shall be actually upon the spot when the murder is committed, or even in sight of the more immediate perpetrator, or of the victim, to make him a principal. If he be at a distance, co-operating in the act, watching to prevent relief, or to give alarm, or to assist his confederate in escape, having knowledge of the purpose and object of the assassin—this, in the eye of the law, is being present, aiding and abetting, so as to make him a principal in the murder.[1]

The special session of the Supreme Judicial Court—a.k.a. grand jury—had been commenced in response to a special act of the state legislature explicitly with reference to the prosecution of the Captain White murder case. The act required that the attorney general, the solicitor general, and at least three Supreme Court justices attend. On the day, however, fully four of the justices appeared: Chief Justice Parker, Associate Justice Samuel Putnam, Associate Justice Samuel Sumner Wilde, and Associate Justice Marcus Morton (no relation to Perez Morton). The special act of the legislature was quite out of the ordinary; no murder in recent memory had caused such legislation. It signaled the importance of the victim. It also signaled, some thought, the urgent wish of his fellow legislators to exonerate their friend (and colleague in the upper house) Stephen White from any wrongdoing.

It was at the July 10 hearing that an elaborate game of chess began to play out, with attorney Franklin Dexter moving the pieces for the Knapps' defense.

At this point, the only evidence directly incriminating Frank (or, for that matter, Joe Jr. and George) was Joe Jr.'s written and signed confession. Were that confession withdrawn, all that would be left was hearsay and innuendo from highly suspicious, self-serving characters with grimly bad reputations—on the substance of which Dexter believed no jury would convict, at least not on a charge of murder. (There might, however, be brought a charge of conspiracy, Dexter warned the boys, which though serious would not carry the death penalty.)

As Dexter knew, if Joe Jr. were to withdraw his written statement and refuse to testify, the confession could not even be presented in court. State law demanded that Joe Jr. testify in person in court in order for the confession to be presented in any form. The law did not allow one man to "confess away the life and liberty of another unless he does so in open court where the accused has the right to confront the adverse witness and have his testimony subjected to cross-examination."[2] On the other hand, while such an action by Joe Jr. would certainly go a long way toward defanging the state's overall case, it would also cause the state to annul Joe Jr.'s inoculation against prosecution, a special risk given Justice Parker's exceedingly broad definition of what constituted a second-degree principal.

Another consideration was that the gist of Joe Jr.'s confession had already been published and widely disseminated. Thus, its stink would hover in the courtroom whether presented or not. Nevertheless, Dexter decided to make a bold play. Joe Jr. withdrew his confession and refused to testify for the grand jury.

The publication of details from Joe Jr.'s confession was of course no small matter. As one editorial noted even before Dick Crowninshield's death, "The morbid sensibility of the public" was roused to its "highest degree of action by the stimulants applied by the publication of every rumor which accident or cupidity could discover." What was more, "the community from which a jury is to be taken is influenced by these disclosures."[3] To say that the Salem jury pool had been contaminated would be an understatement. It would be more correct to say that, within a mere month of the murder, the jury pool of the entire Eastern Seaboard had been contaminated, so widespread was discussion of the crime and the disclosure of key revelations.

Jury selection remained a matter to be dealt with in the future when the state's grand jury returned and announced indictments on Friday, July 23. The indictments named Frank as a second-degree principal and Joe Jr. and George Crowninshield as accessories. It was at this hearing that Franklin Dexter and his associate, William Howard Gardiner, were formally appointed to represent the Knapps. The eminent (and expensive) Samuel Hoar of Concord, retained by Richard Crowninshield Sr., was in turn appointed to represent George Crowninshield. Hoar was to be assisted by two Salemites: Ebenezer Shillaber and John Walsh, although Walsh would soon drop out. The prosecution attorneys were to be Attorney General Morton as lead, assisted by Solicitor General Daniel Davis.

With this, the stage was set. Each defendant was to be tried individually, with Frank's trial to be the first, scheduled to start just four days after the handing down of the indictments: July 27. Given all that had gone before, it would have been hard for some to believe that the real drama had yet to begin. But such was the situation.

16 | BLACK DAN

"There is nothing so powerful as truth—and often nothing so strange."
—Daniel Webster, at the first trial of Frank Knapp

DANIEL WEBSTER—THE NAME ECHOES loudly even today, some seventeen decades after his death. We still hear it resonating: the fiery eloquence of Black Dan, so called because of his inexplicable dark complexion, this despite his being of prime New England ancestry. Here he stands: congressman and senator, the eloquent winner of such landmark Supreme Court cases as *Dartmouth College v. Woodward* (1819, establishing the relationship between the Contracts Clause of the US Constitution and private corporations), *McCullough v. Maryland* (1819, defining the scope of the legislative power of the US Congress with regard to the powers of state legislatures), and *Gibbons v. Ogden* (1824, establishing that the Commerce Clause of the US Constitution, empowering Congress to regulate interstate commerce, extended to navigation). Here he is, one of the most eloquent speakers ever to expound on critical issues and debate under the Capitol dome. He was forty-eight in 1830, with many conquests still to come, but already the name Daniel Webster was known in every American town and city: a legal dynamo, the so-called American Cicero, and one of the most powerful personalities and rhetoricians Massachusetts or any other state had ever sent to the Senate. Presidential timber, everyone said—only a matter of time.

But Webster was also a man. He drank excessively, though this seemed never to dull his wits. He spent lavishly—always well beyond his means. He lived in constant debt, though this never stopped him from entertaining grandly. He had another expensive habit: a strange ravenous appetite for acreage—1,800 acres adjacent to his oceanside estate in Marshfield, Massachusetts, south of Boston and some fifty miles from Salem. Also, he owned many more thousands of acres as far away as Wisconsin—speculations that went nowhere and left him in even more debt. He was as well a womanizer, an American lothario. His first wife died; he married again and then conducted a decades-long affair with Sarah Goodridge, a well-known painter of portrait miniatures, including several of Webster.

On the evening of July 27, Webster most likely read in the paper, as did so many others, that the much-anticipated trial of Frank Knapp had been unavoidably delayed. Although scheduled to start on that day, the proceedings had been interrupted by the sudden and untimely death of Chief Justice Parker. The trial therefore would not proceed until August 3.

Some friends of the prosecution believed the delay to be a blessing—no insult to Parker intended. Both Associate Justice Story and Stephen White thought the prosecution team of Morton and Davis not quite agile enough, or quite eloquent enough, to deal successfully with the core and quite thorny issue of how Frank, at first arrested as an accessory, now suddenly qualified as a principal after the death of Dick Crowninshield.

There was also the complex matter of how, and to what extent, the well-publicized and widely published Joe Knapp Jr. confession could be used in court. It would take the most articulate and persuasive arguments to navigate these treacherous legal questions, and the elderly Morton paired with Davis, nearly as old at age sixty-eight, would likely be outargued by the energetic Dexter and his equally young and ambitious partner, Gardiner.

Sometime between Parker's death and the commencement of Frank's trial on August 3, Stephen White sent a messenger to Webster with a request that he take over the prosecution. White promised $1,000 should Webster agree to do so. (Ironically, this was the same amount the Knapps had promised Dick Crowninshield for the murder of Captain White.)

The British writer and social theorist Harriet Martineau, in a memoir published a few years later, related at second hand the tale of Webster's recruitment:

> A citizen of Salem, a friend of mine, was deputed to carry the request.
> He went to Boston: Mr. Webster was not there but at his farm by the

seashore. Thither, in tremendous weather, my friend followed him. Mr. Webster was playing checkers with his boy. . . . My friend was first dried and refreshed, and then lost no time in mentioning "business." Mr. Webster writhed at the word, saying that he came hither to get out of the hearing of it. He next declared that his undertaking anything more was entirely out of the question, and pointed, in evidence, to his swollen bag of briefs lying in a corner. However, upon a little further explanation and meditation, he agreed to the request with the same good grace with which he afterward went to the task. He made himself master of all that my friend could communicate, and before daybreak was off through the woods, in the unabated storm, no doubt meditating his speech by the way. He needed all the assistance that could be given him, of course; and my friend constituted himself as Mr. Webster's fetcher and carrier of facts. . . . At the appointed hour, Mr. Webster was completely ready.[1]

Although Martineau did not give the name of the friend who found himself dispatched to recruit Webster, this was most likely Stephen C. Phillips of the Committee of Vigilance. When Martineau visited Salem in 1834, she did so as a guest of Phillips and stayed in his mansion with him and his family. Interestingly, what she saw at that time amid the dying seaport was not collapse, malaise, and a general exodus but rather great prosperity—not to mention both cultural and economic democracy. One wonders from which Salem shop she purchased her rose-colored glasses.

Or perhaps they were a gift from Phillips, who, unlike other merchants, remained in Salem as it slowly crumpled (though he eventually invested most of his personal wealth in timber interests in Canada), serving as mayor and generally working whenever possible to boost the image of the town. Martineau, seeing what she wanted to see and greatly influenced by Phillips, extolled the "state of society" in which "a dozen artisans of one town—Salem—are seen rearing each a comfortable one-story (or, as the Americans would say, two-story) house, in the place with which they have grown up! When a man who began with laying bricks criticizes, and sometimes corrects, his lawyer's composition." She lauded the idea of the "poor errand-boy" who could become "the proprietor of a flourishing store, before he is thirty; pays off the capital advanced by his friends at the rate of 2,000 dollars per month; and bids fair to be one of the most substantial citizens of the place!"[2]

Webster himself had been the son of a modest farmer. He'd worked his way through Dartmouth and could claim sole authorship of his great success in the world. Therefore, it seems likely that he exuded a certain air of self-satisfaction on the evening of August 2 as he sat in Stephen White's mansion, papers spread across the large dining room table, consulting with Morton and Davis on how best to proceed at trial.

Among the dozens of reporters who had come to town to observe the court pro-ceedings stood a thirty-five-year-old Scottish immigrant named James Gordon Bennett—a freelance journalist who also served as assistant editor of the *New York Courier & Enquirer*. In 1835 he was to found his own newspaper, the *New York Herald*, the city's first cheap, mass-circulation newspaper, which Bennett extolled as being for the working class rather than the elites. As James Crouthamel wrote, Bennett "championed the masses and created a newspaper for them," with an editorial charter to entertain as well as inform.[3] In catering to this market, Bennett took every opportunity to exploit lurid (and preferably long-running) tales of all manner of crime, from murder to prostitution—and ideally, a mix of both. This is what Karen Halttunen eloquently described as "a degraded pursuit of the thrill of sensation for its own sake, which accompanied the emergence of mass readership."[4]

One of the *Herald*'s first great successes in that realm would be its extensive coverage regarding the 1836 murder of Manhattan prostitute Helen Jewett. The twenty-three-year-old woman was found dead by the matron of the brothel in which she worked at 3:00 AM on April 10, 1836. The coroner reported that Jewett had been struck three times on the head with something sharp, perhaps a hatchet, while she slept. He detected no signs of struggle. After delivering the blows, the murderer had set fire to Jewett's bed, with her in it, charring her body on one side.

A regular customer, nineteen-year-old Richard P. Robinson, was accused and arrested based on testimony from several of Jewett's fellow prostitutes who'd seen him leaving the scene. After a much-followed trial—at which the judge instructed the jury to ignore the testimony from the eyewitnesses, given their professions—Robinson was found innocent. The *Herald's* coverage of these events was intentionally breathless and dramatic, full of dark, haunting word-images, not to mention grotesque visual renderings.

Bennett and many of those who covered the White trials with him brought this same macabre sensibility to the reporting they'd do from Salem. The more hideous the crime and the proceedings, the better. Just as had been the case with the Kentucky Beauchamp-Sharp Tragedy of 1825, the White murder could sell many, many newspapers so long as it was packaged and exhibited in the most shocking and scandalous manner possible.

James Farrell has noted that coverage of the White murder case was profuse. "More than five hundred newspaper stories appeared in New England between April 8th, 1830 and September 1st, 1830, concerning the murder of Captain White, and the trials of Frank Knapp. New England newspapers had published, on average, more than three stories per day for 116 days between the murder and the beginning of the first Knapp trial." A significant number of the stories were composed with prose meant to create outrage and spotlight beguiling intrigue—painting grisly pictures of the murder scene and the depravity of the conspirators, feeding a public famished for such engagement. "In an age when American newspapers had limited staff and covered mainly political news, the atrocious murder in Salem pivoted [national] journalistic attention toward a local criminal act."[5]

The participation of "Black Dan"—whose every utterance on any subject was considered news—would only add to the appeal of the trial coverage. In an age when true national celebrities were few, Webster brought not only a national reputation to the Salem courtroom but also an international reputation. Indeed, reportage from Salem was to travel to Britain as fast as clipper ships could carry it and be reprinted in a host of newspapers. (After a visit Webster made to Britain, Thomas Carlyle told Ralph Waldo Emerson: "No man was ever so great as Daniel Webster looks.")[6]

Throughout the coming months, the press was to be saturated with stories about the Knapp and Crowninshield court proceedings—stories that hungry readers voraciously gobbled up—until, once the drama was finally over, even Bennett would come to realize that the reading public was at last "sick of hearing of the Salem murder."[7]

17 | A MURDER OF NO ORDINARY CHARACTER

"Justice will overtake fabricators of lies and false witnesses."

—Heraclitus

THE FIRST OF WHAT WOULD BE the two trials of Frank Knapp began on Tuesday, August 3, in the scorching hot Salem Court House. Designed and built by Samuel McIntire in 1785, the building was destined to be torn down just a few years after the Knapp and Crowninshield trials, in 1839. It was a dignified red brick structure of two floors plus a large attic beneath a mansard roof and a towering cupola. The building fronted to the south, dominating Salem's Washington Street from the intersection of Washington and Federal Streets. There it stood, resolute and somber, as do the many surviving McIntire buildings in Salem, among them the mansion of Captain Joseph White. Once, forty-one years earlier in October 1789, President George Washington had stood on the courthouse's second floor balcony to receive the adulation of the citizens of Salem. Now came a spectacle to rival even that day.

The sweltering heat did not stop the throngs who lined up outside the court building, hoping to gain entrance and see the great Webster at work. With Webster a part of the program, the trial promised to be a grand show of stunning rhetoric. Webster's legend came before him. Only a few months earlier, in January, he had made headlines with his eloquence in a Senate debate with South Carolina's Robert Y. Hayne over the issue of protective tariffs. Indeed, for more than a century to come, Webster's "Second Reply to Hayne" was to be widely regarded as "the most eloquent speech ever delivered in Congress."[1]

Those who waited in a long line for a seat at the Frank Knapp trial expected at least one great oration, perhaps more. From Boston they came, and New York. Native Salemites who knew the key players and either wanted Frank to hang or go free had a hard time getting in. Constables intervened, picking familiar faces out of the crowded line. Bennett would comment on how those who entered rushed "against the railings like the tide boiling up along the rocks at Nahant" and criticized their "fierceness, levity, rudeness and roughness."[2] Journalists cued up at a separate door, their special rows in the gallery already reserved. Outside, enterprising vendors set up refreshment stands and sold paper fans. A carnival atmosphere prevailed throughout, at least at first.

Two constables delivered Frank from the prison in a simple coach. He wore handcuffs and walked into the building with great dignity, his head held high. A few reporters shouted questions, to which Frank did not respond. More coaches arrived carrying Joe Jr., George Crowninshield, and the witness Palmer—each in his own carriage lest they speak, collaborate, or in some other way taint each other's testimony. The constables walked the prisoners directly to confinement in separate basement cells, well away from each other, there to sit until called. A court deputy served tea. Crowninshield complained about being made to drink from a tin cup. Palmer asked for a lump of sugar. Joe Jr. and Frank left theirs untouched.

Attorney General Morton and Solicitor General Davis were already sitting at the prosecution table when Daniel Webster arrived just before ten—bluff, abrupt, aloof, and ready to dominate not just his team but also the entire room. He'd come in a coach with Stephen White from the latter's mansion after a hearty breakfast meant to sustain him for what promised to be a very long day. From the saddlebag he flung onto the prosecution table there spilled a large cache of papers: notes, clippings, memoranda. He also had a silver flask, containing a liquid the nature of which Webster did not volunteer to disclose.

Sweat poured down Webster's dark face as, with the eyes of an eagle, he scanned the courtroom that, upon his entry, had fallen into a pronounced hush. There he was, the great Webster, the legend suddenly made real, in the flesh. People who had previously chattered now simply gawked and stared—just as Webster's mere presence demanded. Bennett reported that Webster seemed the epitome of confidence, but the attorneys for the defense quite the opposite. "In the hands of such a man as Webster, a dozen of them are a mere mouthful."[3]

It must be noted that the rock star Webster had his groupies. During a time when women were not regular attendees at criminal trials, especially gruesome murder trials, the Knapp-Crowninshield affair became an exception to the rule, for the great Webster drew crowds of all stripes and all sexes. As one reporter noted, "a large number of ladies were admitted to the Court House. On Thursday morning, the gallery was completely filled—in the afternoon, their numbers increased, and they occupied the seats of jurors, sheriffs' boxes, &c below, and some were seen even in the midst of the dense crowd on the floor of the hall." The courtroom was "thronged by the fair auditors; they were crowded in solid masses in various parts of the hall as well as in the gallery—and some were perched upon the mantlepieces, the windows seats, &c." Even more ladies assembled in the streets, under the windows of the courthouse, eager to catch "even now and then a sentence, which the commanding voice and distinct enunciation of [Webster would enable] them to do."[4]

Given the hushed awe with which the crowded courtroom had greeted Webster, the place was already quite silent when Justices Putnam, Morton, and Wilde were announced. They'd spent the past several days eulogizing and burying their colleague Parker and seemed weary. Some thought they might be not only weary but also wary with regard to Daniel Webster. Such a powerful presence—he might well overwhelm their own authority if they were not careful.

Even though they were scheduled to be tried separately and this proceeding was to be Frank Knapp's prosecution, the three accused were nevertheless together brought before the bar. A reporter noted that Frank seemed energetic and led the other two—that he "sprang forward first with a quick and vigorous motion, more like a bound than a step." Joe Jr., on the other hand, followed behind his brother "languidly" and glumly, almost as if approaching the gallows. He looked pale and gaunt. For the past few days he'd been trying to starve himself, perhaps as an attempt to win sympathy. Crowninshield, in turn, presented a relaxed, self-confident, and "quiet easy air."[5] They were each well dressed, even dapper, especially Crowninshield, who was seen to smirk as the charge against Frank was read.

Immediately after the reading of the charge, defense attorney Gardiner requested that twenty-five-year-old attorney Robert Rantoul Jr. be added to the defense team per request of the prisoner, even though not a member of the Essex Court. This the court refused to do but pointed out that the team could still have the benefit of Rantoul's counsel and advice even though he himself would not be allowed to speak.

Rantoul hailed from Beverly. His father was well known: a veteran of terms in both the state legislature and senate and a delegate to the Massachusetts Constitutional Convention of 1820. Rantoul Jr. was wet behind the ears, having only graduated from Harvard four years earlier, but he was eager and ambitious. He was also inspired by a sense of unfairness stemming from the great publicity before the trial and—in his view—the general hysteria that publicity had caused. As Luther Hamilton would write, Rantoul "felt in every way the unjust and sickening effects of this excited state of feeling in the public; an excitement which he regarded not only as hostile to the accused, but to the calmness and the fairness of judicial proceedings, in a case of life and death."[6]

Next, just before Attorney General Morton rose to speak, Gardiner requested a delay in the proceedings due to the fact that a list of witnesses from the grand jury—the doings of which were secret while ongoing—had not been presented to himself and Dexter, thus inhibiting their efforts to prepare for the trial. In response, the court now ruled that the list be provided, but there was to be no delay in the trial.

Before jury selection commenced, Attorney General Morton formally requested that the Honorable Daniel Webster be recognized by the court as a member of the prosecution team, along with Morton and Davis. With the defense team voicing no objection—after all, how could it?—the justices readily agreed, with Putnam going so far as to say that the court was honored to have Webster as a participant in the trial. Of course, Webster was no more a member of the Essex Court than was Rantoul—but then again, Webster was Webster.

To not a few observers, it seemed as if the justices were themselves starting off in a manner almost deferential to Webster, ready to follow him wherever he might care to lead, if not persuaded by his eloquence, then by the sheer magnitude of his august presence.

After a rigorous hour or so of questioning and challenging potential jurors from an extensive pool, a group of men were chosen. There were nineteen challenges peremptorily and eleven for cause. The final list of jurors consisted of foreman Solomon Nelson of Georgetown, Ephraim Annable of Salem, John Ayre III of Haverhill, Joseph Bartlett of Newbury, Samuel Foster of Salem, Charles Foster of Newburyport (no direct relation to Samuel), William Micklefield of Salem, Ichabod B. Sargent of Amesbury, Joshua Howard of Stoughton,

John Morrill of Salisbury, and Asa Todd of Rowley. They ran the gamut of professions—Micklefield a tobacconist, the others being shop-owners, cabinetmakers, shipwrights, and farmers.[7]

Morton opened with a brief summation of the original charges on which the three men had previously been arraigned—and reiterated the new revised charge against Frank. That charge was, of course, one of second-degree murder as a principal in the killing of Captain Joseph White, Frank having materially aided Dick Crowninshield on the night of the murder. The indictment presumed and announced Dick to be guilty, even though he'd not been found so in a court of law.

To the indictment, Frank entered an immediate plea of not guilty. The court at the same time ruled (as expected, since Joe Jr. and George Crowninshield were at this time charged only as accessories) that the others need not enter a plea until the guilt or innocence of Frank had been determined. (George's main attorney, Samuel Hoar, had not even bothered to come from Concord for today's business, leaving his two Salem associates to take notes, and, if need be, advise their client.)

With Webster reserving the summation for himself, Morton gave the opening address for the prosecution. He called the murder of Captain White "a murder of no ordinary character—a murder the most cold-blooded, unprovoked, and atrocious as has ever yet stained the annals of our Commonwealth, if not any other country." Morton said the crime was one "in the commission of which every personal security and safety which the law specially guarantees to the citizen in the asylum of his dwelling house, and in the recess of his bedchamber, has been outraged and violated."[8] Of course, no reference was made to the numerous extraconstitutional actions embarked upon by the Committee of Vigilance in the course of their early investigations.

Morton addressed directly the question of Joe Jr.'s confession. Morton pointed out that in response to his offer of immunity from prosecution, Joe Jr. had willingly volunteered a detailed confession and promised to testify in court. When called to the grand jury, however, he had refused to speak. Morton intended, he said, to give Joe Jr. another chance. "As the inquiry before the grand jury may not be considered as calling him as a witness upon the trial, I shall in the course of the examination of evidence again call him as a witness, and if he again refuses to testify, everyone will acknowledge that the pledge of the government will be completely redeemed, and his promised protection will be forfeited."[9]

Morton pointed out that for many weeks the perpetrators of White's murder remained "veiled in darkness and mystery." In the absence of any other information, early suspicions had naturally focused on members of the household, given the facts that "nothing had been taken away, that no actual violence had been committed in entering the house, [and] that the iron bar, with which the window where the assassin entered was usually fastened was taken down and carefully placed against the side of the window." Thus, family members had come under scrutiny, even Stephen White, to whom "the prime instigator of the murder, to cover his own atrocity, imputed this deed of death."[10]

Turning and pointing directly at Frank, Morton cautioned:

> The Counsel for the Government do not expect that the evidence which will be given you will justify the belief that the prisoner at the bar actually gave the blow on the head, or the stabs in the heart of the deceased, for he, who, it will appear, did the deed, wretched man, like his great prototype, who betrayed the Savior of the world for thirty pieces of silver, smitten with the stings of conscience, has gone and hanged himself; though less scrupulous than Judas, he has never returned the wages of his iniquity.
>
> It is, however, altogether immaterial whether the prisoner at the bar, actually gave the mortal blows, provided he was present, aiding and abetting the person who inflicted them. He is charged both ways.[11]

The state's parade of witnesses was predictable, at least at first. Benjamin White spoke of his discovery of the intrusion, his awakening of Kimball, their survey of the household, and his discovery of the corpse. Lydia Kimball appeared and affirmed Benjamin White's testimony. Dr. Johnson reiterated his being called, his early and later examinations of the body, and his findings. Joe Knapp Jr., when called, refused to speak and was officially informed that should he continue to refuse, his immunity would be terminated. When he remained silent, Morton simply stopped his questioning and commented, "The government will prove the conspiracy by other witnesses; in a case like this, the act of one is the act of the whole."[12]

Damning evidence came from one Benjamin Leighton, a seventeen-year-old worker on the Wenham farm. Leighton had lived there since October and—like Joe Jr.—did chores for John Davis, manager of the farm and son-in-law to Mary Beckford. Leighton professed to have overheard a conversation between Joe Jr. and Frank Knapp about a week before the murder. Joe Jr. had asked Frank when Dick would kill "the old man." When Frank replied that he did not know, Joe. Jr.—evidently exasperated—responded, "If he don't kill him soon I won't pay him."[13] Upon cross-examination by Dexter, Leighton was adamant about what he'd heard and whom he'd heard speaking. There could, he said, be no doubt—a point that he made yet again upon being examined on redirect by Webster. Another farmhand, Thomas Hart, confirmed Frank's visit to the farm but nothing more.

Following the first day's proceedings, Joseph Knapp Sr. went down to the Union Wharf, where stood the warehouse to which he'd recently relinquished title. Within the warehouse he strung a noose and endeavored to hang himself. He was nearly dead when his son Phippen rushed in, cut him down, and revived him. Rumor would soon have it that Joe Jr.'s wife, Mary, had also attempted suicide, twice. But that was rumor.

On Wednesday, August 4, Henry Colman served as the day's first witness for the prosecution. The good reverend could not have been unaware of his importance to the government's case given the withdrawal of Joe Jr.'s testimony and, therefore, also his written confession. As the one man who could, by recall, present confirmatory evidence of Joe Jr.'s admission and what it contained, Colman would be critical to the state's case. Several reporters noted that Colman seemed rather in a thrall, in some way delighted to be the star witness in what was already the most prominent case in the criminal judicial record of the United States—and better yet to be examined by the great Webster. The role would make him a celebrity with nearly equal fame as that of Webster himself, if only for a brief time. Self-importance overtook the pious minister, who opted for the role of vital citizen over that of clerical confidant.

After stern objections from the defense team, the prosecution was dealt a blow when the court decided Colman would not be allowed to allude in any direct way to the contents or details of Joe Jr.'s confession. He was, however, permitted to state the process by which he had obtained the confession and to affirm that a confession had been made. He was also able to tell directly the tale of finding the bludgeon after being advised as to its location. He even—in one of the trial's highlight moments—produced the bludgeon itself from under his waist coat. And he added an embellishment to the story that Phippen would soon repudiate once he got his chance to take the stand: Colman told the court that it had been Frank, rather than Joe Jr., who had told him the location of the weapon.

When the prosecution called John Carr Palmer Jr., defense counsel Gardiner objected to his being sworn on the grounds—said Gardiner—that Palmer was an atheist and the oath would therefore mean nothing to him. How Gardiner came by this information, although likely from George Crowninshield, is not known for certain. However, the court overruled the objection, had Palmer sworn, and then allowed him to testify that he solemnly believed in Almighty God, the hereafter, and a final judgment. Under questioning from Davis, Palmer recounted and confirmed all that he'd said before to the inquisitors of the Committee of Vigilance and in the presence of the grand jury. He also confessed to writing the letter of extortion addressed to Knapp but once again denied writing the two subsequent (and contrary) letters tending to incriminate Stephen White.

On cross-examination, Dexter attempted to explore whether Palmer had been coerced or threatened during his time in Salem Jail in order to sway his testimony in favor of the government. Webster countered that such a state of affairs would have turned the witness against the government, rather than for.

Palmer's testimony naturally led to the inquisition of William H. Allen with regard to the latter two letters—which were handed to him by Webster. Did Allen recognize the envelopes? Yes, he'd mailed them on or about May 16 at the request of Joe Jr. He did not know their contents. Joe Jr. had told him that his father and Phippen had come to Wenham the day before and brought with them a letter with a "devilish lot of trash," but the two letters Allen was to post would nip "the silly affair in the bud."[14] Webster himself read the two letters out loud to the court, quite dramatically and with a tone of biting sarcasm, as if to mock Joe Knapp Jr.'s seemingly desperate and certainly loosely construed attempt to divert attention from him and his brother.

Ezra Lummis, who kept a tavern in Wenham, testified, along with several other Wenham and Danvers locals, to Dick and George Crowninshield paying for various items using French francs such as Joe Jr. was said to have given Dick after the murder as partial payment of the $1,000 due. Stephen Phillips of the Committee of Vigilance described Joe Jr.'s and Frank's false testimony to the committee about the attempted robbery on the road to Wenham: a hoax meant to suggest the same marauders might have killed Captain White. John Burnham of Salem claimed to have seen George Crowninshield walking down Essex Street at about six o'clock on the night of the murder. Several other Salemites also claimed to have seen him, everyone saying he was headed "downtown"—presumably toward the Reading Room and his whorehouse close by. John McGlue of Salem, an acquaintance of Dick Crowninshield, described seeing Dick in the vicinity of Captain White's house on the night before the murder, the fifth, and that Dick appeared to be surveilling the place. They'd exchanged a brief greeting. Joseph Antony described keeping an eye on the Crowninshields after the murder at the behest of Stephen White, who paid him $50 for his trouble, and his failure to deduce anything incriminating from his conversations with the brothers.

The prosecution continued to make its case on Thursday, the fifth.

Stephen Myrick, who had a shop and home on Brown Street, behind Captain White's mansion, discussed seeing suspicious activity on the night of the murder. Myrick said he saw a man loitering after 9:00 PM on Brown Street near the rear of Captain White's house. The man "stayed there some time, walking now and then a few steps one way or the other." Eventually the stranger met a person at the corner of Newbury and Brown, whom he eventually left, disappearing for some minutes. Myrick reported that he did not see the second loiterer's face and did not know Frank Knapp, but nevertheless believed the person he saw was Frank based upon his observations of Frank since his arrest, Frank being about the right size and height.

Another witness, loosely acquainted with Frank, said he'd seen a man he presumed to be Frank walking arm and arm with another man on Howard Street sometime between 9:00 and 10:00 PM but could not positively say it was Frank, as they'd not spoken and the witness had not gotten a direct look at the man's face. John Southwick, a young bank teller, and Captain Daniel Bray Jr., a retired ship's master, testified that together they'd seen two figures on Brown Street at, they guessed, sometime between 10:30 and 11:00 PM, one of whom Southwick presumed to be Knapp, though he'd not gotten a look at the face.

Bray testified:

> I live in Brown Street and in the lowest house on the south side. On the evening of the sixth of April, I was passing down Brown Street from St. Peter Street, and when I passed the fourth house I saw a man dressed in a dark frock coat, dark pantaloons, and a shining cap standing at a post. The frock was very full at the bottom. I was on the north side of the street and he was on the south. As I passed on, I saw another man looking or peeping down Howard Street, who I found was Mr. John Southwick. He said that when he went into his house, a man of very suspicious appearance was sitting on the ropewalk steps. I turned round and observed: "There stands the man now." I could see him very plainly up towards Shepard's house, it was so light.
>
> I walked on with him close to the ropewalk, and stood so as to get out of the wind, when the man who stood at the post passed along on the south side and took his station at the post at the northeast corner of my house, next to the bounds between my house and that of Mrs. Andrews. I asked Southwick to go with me into my house to see what he was about. We passed about twenty feet from him and entered my west door. We went up into my chamber, because the sliding shutters in the room below were closed, and we could not unclose them without noise. I looked out of the window and, by pressing my face against the glass, I could see the man at the post and never lost sight of him while he stood there, which was five or six minutes, when another man came up from the eastward, in the middle of the road and not far from the sidewalk. I saw him when he was 150 to 200 feet off. From my window I could see down Brown Street and the Common, so the man must have come through Newbury Street or we could have seen him sooner.
>
> The man that came from the east had on light clothes. He then ran as hard as he could down Howard Street. The other at the same time started off in the opposite direction and was out of sight towards the east. I have known the prisoner since he was a boy—knew him years ago. I have seen him in prison and at the bar. I can't tell whether he was one of those I saw that night. Size and appearance agree very well.[15]

Several other witnesses from Brown and neighboring streets, including Peter Webster, who was no relation to Daniel, testified just as vaguely. Not one of all these witnesses directly identified Frank Knapp or Dick Crowninshield. The range of times mentioned posed an additional problem for the prosecution. These were two points that Dexter made sure to bring out during forceful cross-examinations.

Joseph Burns, who had a business renting horses on St. Peter Street, near to the head of Brown Street, testified that a few weeks after the murder, Frank visited the stable and asked if there was someplace where they could talk in private, as Frank had something "particular" to discuss. Burns led Frank up into the stable loft. There, Frank said he'd heard a rumor that Burns had been out on Brown Street on the night of Captain White's murder. Frank told Burns that if he'd seen anything, and the committee asked, he should keep quiet. Frank also told Burns he believed that he and his brother might be under suspicion and that both he and his brother set great store by Burns's friendship. When Burns asked Frank what he thought of the Crowninshields, then in custody, Frank said they were innocent. Burns continued:

> Frank said Captain Stephen White must be the one. I said "darn it, don't you go to tell me any such thing. Don't you tell me about Captain Stephen White. I know him too well. I've known him ever since he was 18 years old." Frank put his hand under his waist-coat, where he had a dirk. I said "Damn your dirk, I don't care for you and your dirk and 20 more." Frank said he came as a friend, that I might be on my guard, and not get into trouble.[16]

On Friday morning, in wrapping up their case—and perhaps in recognition of the weakness of what they'd presented thus far—the prosecution proposed to call Henry Colman back to the stand. Webster argued that the matters that Colman had been forbidden to discuss previously should now be allowed. The jury deserved to hear any specifics of the contents of Joe Jr.'s confession that Colman could recall. At the core of Webster's argument was the question of whether Frank Knapp, in his jail-cell conversation with Colman and Phippen regarding Joe Jr.'s proposed confession, had given his assent to Joe Jr. making that confession or if he had dissented.

In the view of the court, if assent had been positively given by Frank, then Joe Jr.'s confession could not be used; but if assent had *not* been given, then it might be introduced. The reasoning here was that assent would be taken, in law, as Frank himself admitting to the validity and truthfulness of Joe Jr.'s statement, while dissent would mean that Frank challenged, disagreed with, and denied the contents of the statement, a position which he and his counsel would be able to put forth and argue in open court. In other words, ironically, in a situation where Frank agreed with the statements incriminating him, those statements could not be used. But in a situation where Frank disagreed, then the confession would be admissible.

After much argument, the judges concurred that Colman should be returned to the stand and allowed to expand upon his previous testimony, which he did, in great detail.

Of all this, the *New Hampshire Patriot and State Gazette* wryly commented:

> The "Godlike" has already forced the Supreme Court of Massachusetts to take back and revoke one solemn decision; and under him there can be little doubt the culprits will be convicted and condemned. . . . Let it no longer be considered that the case of an individual depends upon right and justice, but upon whom he has engaged for counsel, and upon the magnitude of the fee paid to some pretended giant of the law.[17]

18 | THE CRY OF THE PEOPLE IS FOR BLOOD

GARDINER MADE THE OPENING STATEMENT for the defense on Monday, August 9.[1]

Gentlemen of the Jury:

I agree with the attorney general that this murder is most atrocious, but you are not to let the enormity of the crime and the general alarm that it has excited prevent a full and free exercise of your judgment. The feeling of vengeance has gone through the whole community, and excitement has found its way into this hall of justice. Nevertheless, you must always remember that the presumption should be for, rather than against, the prisoner, particularly in view of the peculiar circumstances in which he is placed. John Francis Knapp is a very young man, about nineteen years old, brought up in the bosom of a peaceful community, and now for the first time is placed at the bar of his country to be tried for his life. . . .

The whole community has been in a great state of excitement. . . . Large rewards have been offered by the state, the town, and the family of the deceased for the detection of the murderers. A most extraordinary tribunal has been formed under the name of a committee of vigilance, consisting of twenty-seven persons selected from the most respectable portion of the community.

But that is not all. The counsel for the prisoner is now opposed by the committee of vigilance, opposed by a private prosecutor, Mr. Stephen White, opposed by public opinion, opposed by the whole bar of Essex, and opposed by the learned officers of government. But the whole bar of Essex, both of these experienced officers, together with the committee of vigilance to back them, is not enough; more strength is necessary. The most distinguished orator of our time, the high representative of the rights of Massachusetts in the Senate of the United States, with his green and fresh-gained laurels wreathed upon his brow, comes here to aid the host already pressing down the hope and life of the prisoner, to overpower the jury with his eloquence and to "nullify" the prisoner's defense. So determined seems to be the community to establish the guilt of the persons accused, that it is almost hazardous to appear in their defense. The cry of the people is for blood. . . . If public opinion is to out-weigh public justice, and a man is to be executed by acclamation, the French Revolution and the tragedy of Notre Dame are not far distant.

Newspaper hearsay or any other kind of testimony, except that which is sworn to within these walls, is worse than idle. . . . A verdict thus founded would be a verdict on suspicion, and a thousand suspicions do not amount to one proof. The fact of guilt must be proved . . . in this house and nowhere else, on the sanctity of an oath, and by the personal knowledge of the witnesses.

How many persons have been suspected of this murder—aye, and believed to be guilty? How many false hypotheses have been stated? How many persons falsely accused? . . . Mrs. Beckford has been accused of unfastening the window. [Some have even accused] Stephen White—the private prosecutor for whom it seemed the murder was committed—because he received the greatest benefit. All have been examined, and some have been imprisoned until it was found that no accusation could be sustained by the conjectural testimony upon which they had been suspected.

And now, prison birds who have just flown from their cage are brought into court to fasten the crime on the prisoner at the bar. Mr. Palmer . . . made a felonious witness to swear away the life of the prisoner.

The Constitution that governs us is not altogether form; it is substance; and it deems everyone innocent until he is proved guilty. The evidence brought against the prisoner must be conclusive. The government is bound to prove, beyond all doubt, that the prisoner is guilty in the manner and form in which they have charged him. . . .

The government wishes the jury to infer that an original conspiracy was formed, and that Richard and George Crowninshield, together with Joseph and the prisoner, were parties to it, that the murder was committed by some of them, that the weapon was found and that it was the same weapon with which the murder was committed, and that the defendant went to the place for the avowed purpose of committing the murder. They also show a combination of a great number of facts, but all of them avail nothing unless they bring you irresistibly to the conclusion that the prisoner gave the blow, or was present, aiding and abetting the murderer.

The government have attempted to prove . . . that a conspiracy existed. . . . The evidence of the plan and motive rests altogether upon Palmer. If you discredit the testimony of these two witnesses, the conspiracy falls to the ground.

The defense intends to show that these witnesses are not entitled to credit. Palmer is all but an incompetent witness. The law says that if a man is convicted of an infamous crime, he shall not be allowed to raise his voice in a court of justice. But Palmer was convicted just across the line from Massachusetts, and his evidence cannot be excluded. The jury will consider, how-ever, what credit is due him.

Their whole evidence, if it proves anything against the prisoner, shows that he was an accessory before the fact.

Evidence is brought to show that a part of those engaged in the conspiracy were seen on that night, at about that time, near the place where the murder was committed. Witnesses are called, after the lapse of a long time, to say that the persons they saw were the individuals implicated. After suspicion is directed against the defendants—after they are told that these are the persons—the witnesses remember that they saw them within about a week. The whole tendency of the evidence, if true, is to prove that the prisoner was an accessory before the fact.

Nothing is more dangerous, and nothing is more liable to error than testimony regarding the identity of persons. Identification in this case depends upon the testimony of a number of persons. Mr. Myrick saw a person at a post whom he did not know but who was about the same size as the prisoner. It is safe to say that there are three hundred persons of the same size in this courtroom right now; the prisoner's stature is common and not at all remarkable. Peter E. Webster saw two persons going down Howard Street away from the murder; he saw no face, he saw nothing but a camblet cloak, from which the jury are asked to infer that one was the prisoner. Mr. Southwick is the only person who swears positively that he saw the prisoner, yet he saw no face; he saw a man in a cloak whom he supposed to be the prisoner. The evidence will show that it was probably not the prisoner.

If, however, you believe that the prisoner was the man seen by these witnesses, you are forced to the conclusion that he was not the man who struck the blow. The question then is: Was John Francis Knapp constructively present? Even if he was in Brown Street, he was not present except by a mere fiction of law. To make a man constructively present, he must be in a capacity to render assistance, and must be there for that purpose, and must actually assist.

The defense proposes to introduce evidence to show that the man seen in Brown Street was not the prisoner at the bar, that he was in a different place during the evening, and that Brown Street was not a place in which aid and assistance could be given to the murderer.

19 | REFUTING THE TRUTH

"O villain, villain, smiling, damned villain!"
—Shakespeare, *Hamlet*

FRANK KNAPP WAS OFTEN SEEN to smile rather wryly as Dexter and Gardiner, with the help of astute advice from Rantoul, did their best to disassemble the government's case against him. The three pillars of their strategy were to undermine the testimonies of the eyewitnesses who had, albeit with some uncertainty, indicated that Frank might have been the man spotted on Brown Street; to cast into doubt the reliability of Palmer as a witness; and to provide an alternative narrative for Frank's activities on the night of the murder. This alternative narrative would be that he was seen about town socializing and having a few drinks and then was back at the Knapp home by ten at the latest. The defense intended to save its ultimate argument, that even if present on the street Frank did not materially assist, for the closing remarks.

One of Gardiner's first steps was to recall Southwick and then Bray to the stand and, through intense questioning, hammer home the fact that the two absolutely could not positively identify Frank Knapp as the man they'd seen on Brown Street. All the other "eyewitness" accounts had evidently been rebuffed to the satisfaction of the defense team upon cross-examination during the presentation of the prosecution's case.

Then Gardiner brought to the stand a tailor, Asa Wiggin, who testified about the great commonality of the camblet cloaks the figure on Brown Street, presumed to be Frank, had been wearing. They were worn all over town. In turn, a hatter named Stephen Miller testified as to the abundance of glazed leather caps. In the past year, he said, he'd sold more than two hundred of them. Upon this statement, Gardiner asserted to the jury that the man on Brown Street could have been anyone.

To knock down another pillar of the case against Frank, Gardiner engaged in a studied character assassination of John Palmer: a painfully easy task. Gardiner had Palmer brought into court. He then noted Palmer's previous conviction for breaking and entering up in Belfast and his sentence of two years hard labor. A native of Belfast, James Webster (no relation to Daniel) swore to Palmer's bad reputation:

> I live in Belfast, Maine. I have known Palmer these eight years. As to his general reputation for truth, I don't think he has any at all, I have always heard a bad character of him. I have heard perhaps a hundred people say that he would not be believed at all in any case in which he was interested. His general character is not good.[1]

Phippen Knapp appeared and sternly repudiated Colman's testimony that it had been Frank Knapp who'd told Colman—in Phippen's presence—about the location of the murder weapon. "I did not hear," he testified, "anything said in Frank's cell about [the bludgeon] by him."[2]

Several young men who had been out on the town together on the night of the murder testified to having been in the company of Frank Knapp early in the evening. One of them, John Forrester Jr., was a Harvard student whose paternal aunt, Nancy Forrester, was married to Gideon Barstow III, the physician who had chaired the Committee of Vigilance. The young man was, as well, the son of Nathaniel Hawthorne's first cousin, once removed, John Forrester Sr., who in turn was the son of Hawthorne's first cousin on his father's side, Rachel Hathorne Forrester. As has been stated earlier in this narrative, John Forrester Sr. was married to Charlotte Story Forrester, the sister-in-law of Stephen White and the late Joseph White Jr., and the sister of Associate Justice Joseph Story.[3]

Young Forrester—who at one point had found himself briefly, like so many others, in the crosshairs of the Committee of Vigilance as a potential suspect—told of encountering Frank in the bar of the Salem Hotel and then later in the evening at Remond's in Derby Square. Remond's, an establishment run by the energetic and popular Black entrepreneur John Remond, was an oyster shop where one could also imbibe and spend time smoking a choice cigar purchased on premises, which is what these young men—among them Hawthorne's lifelong friend Zachariah ("Zach") Burchmore—likely did.[4] Another member of this group also testified to the popularity of glazed leather caps and camblet cloaks with his generation.

When Captain Joseph Knapp Sr. took the stand, he seemed a weary and broken man. By all accounts he generated great sympathy among spectators and the jurors as he narrated the night of the murder from his perspective, including the grim exercise of his bankruptcy, endeavoring to establish that Frank had been at home before the hour when the murder most likely occurred:

> I saw the prisoner just after 10. He entered my front northern parlor about five minutes after 10 and asked me if he should bolt the door. I told him no, for Phippen was out and I should wait for him. I told him that I was very glad that he was at home in good season. He asked me if I wanted any assistance; I told him no. I asked him how the weather was and he said that it blew fresh from the east. I asked him if he knew the time, and he told me it was just ten. I did not go to bed till after 2 o'clock. His chamber was in the west end of the third story. There is only one staircase up to the third story. My door opens into the entry. To come out of Frank's chamber, one must pass my door. . . .
>
> No person moved in the house that night except Phippen when he came in. I saw Frank again the next morning between 7 and 8 o'clock when he came from his chamber. . . . His usual hour of coming home was about 10, as that was the strict rule of the house. He was very regular. He will be twenty years old next month.
>
> My son Phippen was with me until near 10. I left him at Mr. Waters' house. I again saw him about twenty or 25 minutes after 10 when he came in to take the key. He was assisting Mr. Waters in making an assignment of my property, and he rejoined me just after 1 o'clock. He went to bed before I did, and at about two, immediately after he came in.[5]

Via an affidavit, Frank and Joe Jr.'s brother Samuel H. Knapp swore to the presence of Frank at home by ten o'clock on the evening of the murder. This testimony was impeached, however, by friends of Samuel's who reported him telling them as early as June that he had no idea at what time Frank returned to the house that night.

Sadly, and somewhat astonishingly, we have no complete record of the summations in this, the first trial of Frank Knapp, although we have snippets of Webster's. (Bradley and Winans note that "neither of the speeches was accurately reported, and it is impossible to make a satisfactory reconstruction of them.")[6] It is said that Franklin Dexter acquitted himself brilliantly, and there's no reason to doubt this. Dexter spoke for six hours in total, over the course of one afternoon (Tuesday, August 10) and one morning (Wednesday, the eleventh). Webster, in turn, spoke for eight hours over the course of Wednesday afternoon and Thursday morning. We have at least a few of his words—words that came at the very end of his long summation.

Dexter, in his summation, had made the case not only that the evidence against Frank wasn't substantial or reliable enough for conviction as a principal in the second degree but also that no case could even be made against him as an accessory, since Dick Crowninshield had never been convicted of the first-degree crime. Webster, of course, disagreed. In the very last paragraphs of his eight-hour summation, Webster dwelled on Dick and declared that he had indeed been convicted, if not in this court, then in another, and sentenced to death by his own hand.

20 | THE CONCLUSION OF WEBSTER'S SUMMATION IN THE FIRST TRIAL: *"SUICIDE IS CONFESSION"*

IT WAS . . . WITH SOME REGRET that I heard the learned counsel for the prisoner assert that I was brought here to hurry the jury beyond the evidence and against the law. Gentlemen I am sure that no man can hurry you against the law. I am satisfied that no man in this court will be permitted to hurry you against the law.

It has been said that there exists an excitement! Gentlemen there is cause for excitement. True, you should not be excited; You must act upon the testimony and come to the consideration of this cause with minds and consciences freed, unshackled, and unprejudiced. But there is an excitement, there ought to be an excitement which should rouse the faculties and call into operation all possible assistance, even of the dullest apprehension.

It was a cool, desperate, concerted murder. It was neither the offspring of passion nor revenge. The murderer was seduced by no lionlike temptation; all was deliberation; all was skillful.

And now that all is known it appears more atrocious than was ever apprehended. The murderer was a cool, business-like man, a calculator, a resolute and determined assassin.

The object was money, the crime murder, the price blood. The tale of silver was counted out, the price fixed. Here is the money, there is the victim—grains of silver against ounces of blood.

Under our New England example, murder has received a new character. Let the painter beware how he exhibits the murderer with the grim visage of Moloch. Let him not paint the bloodshot eye beaming with malice and red with revenge, but the cool face of an infernal spirit of another stamp about his ordinary business. Let his features be smooth and unruffled—all calmness, coolness, and deliberation. Not human nature in despair nor in paroxysms—no rushing of the blood to the face, no fiendish distortions, but calm and unagitated smoothness.

At the blessed hour when of all others repose is soundest, the murderer goes to his work. In the silence and darkness he enters the house. He does not falter, there is no trembling of the limbs, his feet sustain him. He passes through the rooms, treads lightly through the entries, ascends the stairs, arrives at the door. There is no pause. He opens it. The victim is asleep, his back is towards him, his deaf ear is uppermost, his temples bare. The moonlight plays upon his silver locks.

One blow, and the task is accomplished!

Now mark his resolution, his self-possession, his deliberate coolness! He raises the aged arm, plunges the dagger to the heart—not once but many times—replaces the arm, replaces the bedclothes, feels the pulse, is satisfied that his work is perfected and retires from the chamber. He retraces his steps. No eye has seen him, no ear has heard him. He is master of his own secret, and he escapes in secret.

That was a dreadful mistake. The guilty secret of murder never can be safe. There is no place in the universe, no corner, no cavern where he can deposit it and say it is safe. Though he take the wings of the morning and fly to the uttermost part of the seas, human murder to human vision will be known. A thousand eyes, a thousand ears are marking and listening, and thousands of excited beings are watching his bloodstained step.

The proofs of a discovery will go on. The murderer carries with him a secret which he can neither carry nor discharge. He lives at war with himself; his conscience is a domiciled accuser that cannot be ejected and will not be silent. His tormentor is inappeasable, his burden is intolerable.

The secret which he possesses, possesses him, and like the evil spirit spoken of in olden times leads him whithersoever it will. It is a vulture ever gnawing at his heart; he believes his very thoughts to be heard.

His bosom's secret overmasters him, subdues him—he succumbs. His guilty soul is relieved by suicide or confession, and suicide is confession.

I can wish nothing better for you gentlemen than that you should go home with confidence in the right discharge of your duty.

It has been truly said that this will be a day long to be remembered. It will be long remembered because it is a day full of important duty to be performed or neglected. It will follow you, gentlemen, it will follow us all, as duty accomplished or as duty neglected; and if there is anything which is at all times and everywhere present, it is the consciousness that we have discharged ourselves well of every important trust. If we could take the wings of the morning and fly to the uttermost parts of the East, the sense of memory would be present there.

This recollection will follow us in life and be with us in death. It will be with us in light, and ever near us when darkness covers us. At the close of life, it will be with us; and at that solemn hour, the consciousness of duty discharged or duty neglected will be there to afflict us if disregarded, or to console us if under the will of the Almighty, it has been performed.

Webster's dramatic, romantic rendering of what he supposed to have been Dick Crowninshield's gnawing conscience was certainly creative, and it certainly played well with his listeners. But of course, whether Webster realized it or not, the portrait he painted was fraudulent, a gross misrepresentation.

Anchored in his long-held cynicism, Dick was likely not the victim of a guilty conscience so much as he was the victim of inescapable investigative and prosecutorial triangulation. At the time that he committed suicide, Dick was a man cornered by the rules, revelations, and procedures of justice; and he was a most unlikely repentant, no matter what he might have expressed in last-minute notes contrived to console his father and exonerate his brother.

Dick's taking of his own life seems to have been as deliberate a calculation as had been his taking of the life of Captain White. His ambition was evidently twofold, and entirely pragmatic. First, as has been shown, he clearly—given his research on the topic and his conversation with Dexter—sought to remove himself from prosecution as the principal in the crime, and in so doing remove the possibility for the prosecution of accessories, most importantly his brother George. Second, with his destiny at the gallows a foregone conclusion and his sense of pompous dignity all-consuming, he likely sought to deny the public the spectacle of seeing him swing. If he was to go out, it would be in his own way and at a time of his own choosing, without the indignity of a noose made from anything other than the finest silk.

Even in his very last moments he bowed to no man, and to no authority, other than himself.

21 | A CONTAGION OF UNEXAMPLED POPULAR FRENZY

"He lies like someone who was there."

—Anonymous

AFTER TEN DAYS OF TESTIMONY, the jury finally received its charge from Judge Putnam and retired in the afternoon on August 12. The next day, at around 10:00 AM, they returned to announce themselves deadlocked: a hung jury.

Reportedly, the main disagreements concerned at least a few jury members not being satisfied that Frank had been present on Brown Street, to the rear of Joseph White's mansion, on the night of the murder, directly aiding and abetting Dick Crowninshield. Judge Putnam instructed them to go back into conference and try to work it out, but toward the end of the day they returned and said there was absolutely no way they could achieve consensus. Upon this, Judge Putnam declared a mistrial and dismissed the jury. The solicitor general immediately moved that a new jury be impaneled to try the prisoner again upon the same indictment, and the court agreed.

The result of the trial was widely disapproved and the jury held in disdain. It was speculated that members of the jury from Salem, somewhat acquainted with Frank and somewhat disliking Captain White, had been the holdouts. An editorial in a local newspaper demanded that the names of those "to whom Frank Knapp is indebted for his escape" be made public. "It would be a sad joke," commented a writer in the *New Hampshire Patriot and State Gazette*, "if the immortal Daniel, who, it was said a few days since, was 'swinging a ball around his head, ready to settle it upon the forehead of his victim,' should not succeed in getting a culprit hanged who everyone knows deserves it."[1] Indeed, along with annoyance, there was also shock and surprise at the trial's outcome—or, rather, lack of outcome, lack of resolution. Besides, was the mighty Webster actually going to be denied his victory?

Webster had many other obligations calling to him. There was no time to spare. Jury selection commenced on August 14. Given the fact that the few Salemites were generally suspected of having led the first jury to a mistrial, prosecutors made sure that *all* jurors impaneled for the second trial were from other precincts. Samuel N. Baker, of Ipswich, was made foreman. The balance of the jury were Orlando Abbot (Andover), Timothy Appleton (Ipswich), Stephen Bailey (Amesbury), Jacob Brown (Hamilton), William D. S. Chase (Newbury), Stephen Caldwell (Newburyport), Phineas Elliot (Haverhill), John Ladd (Haverhill), Thomas Merrill (Topsfield), Amos Sheldon (Beverly), and Moses Towne (Andover). They represented a mix of professions, all working class: Samuel Baker was an innkeeper, Orlando Abbot a shoemaker, and Timothy Appleton a farmer. The balance were cabinetmakers, masons, shipwrights, chandlers—none of them merchants, none of them a "gentleman," none of any particular prominence. But they were all men of good reputations and varying political persuasions who sincerely professed, when examined, to being able to render independent judgments based on evidence, regardless of whatever rumors of publicity they may previously have heard or read—and despite the media saturation of the previous trial.

The trial proceeded very much as had that before it, with the exception that most of the eyewitnesses of the man on Brown Street, evidently after a stern talking to from Webster, were now astoundingly certain that the man they'd seen was Frank—no doubt about it. As well, there was no debate as to whether or not Reverend Colman would be allowed to state the contents of Joe Jr.'s confession as he best remembered it. And he remembered very well, even better than he had previously. It was almost as if the previous ten or so days had simply been a dress rehearsal for this main event—a dress rehearsal for the prosecution. This trial was to go for six days instead of ten, culminating of course with the closing summations by Dexter and Webster.

Throughout the trial, Dexter found it expressly annoying that Colman's memory for incriminating minutiae seemed to improve with every trip he made to the witness stand. As Dexter was to complain to the jury:

Whatever the Government cannot otherwise prove, Mr. Colman swears the prisoner has confessed and nothing more. Of half an hour's conversation with the prisoner, he cannot remember a word but what turns out to be indispensable to the case of the prosecution. . . . Mr. Colman has been living in [a contagion of unexampled popular frenzy] and breathing its intoxicating air for months. No man in the community has been so much excited by this horrible event as Mr. Colman. No man has taken a more active part in enquiring into its mysteries.[2]

The good minister seemed all too eager to oblige every request of the prosecution, to scratch his head and crease his brow, to appear to think hard before suddenly discovering whatever precious detail was then being earnestly sought by his examiner, most often Webster. Once again, he produced the bludgeon with a flourish, as if unveiling a relic of the True Cross or a precious diamond. Once again, he expressed his love and sympathy for the Knapp family, and his concern for them as they confronted the darkness in which they now found themselves enveloped. Once again, he reveled in the spotlight, in the questions from reporters, in his narrowly defined celebrity.

22 | FRANKLIN DEXTER'S SUMMATION AT THE SECOND TRIAL

FRANKLIN DEXTER'S SUMMATION RAN to some twenty thousand words, which have here been edited down for the sake of brevity and clarity.[1]

Gentlemen of the Jury:
You have now heard all the evidence on which you are to form your judgment of life or death to the prisoner. He stands before you for that judgment under terrible disadvantages. . . . You see around you proofs of the power against which the accused has to struggle in his defense. You see the extraordinary array of counsel, active and inactive, brought in aid of the government or withdrawn from the reach of the prisoner. You have witnessed the efforts that have been made by those who could take no other part in the prosecution, to fasten upon him the evidence of guilt; and you may anticipate the power and eloquence with which the case is to be closed against him.

Gentlemen, why is all this? . . . If there is legal evidence against the prisoner, can there be a doubt that he will be convicted? And if there is not, is a verdict of condemnation to be wrenched from you by talent and eloquence which the ordinary course of a criminal trial would fail to procure? . . .

There is, however, a more dangerous influence in this case. . . . We care less for the array of counsel than for the array of the community against him. . . . We have greatly feared the effect of this hostile atmosphere on the testimony.

We have feared, and found, that in such a state of excitement no man could take the stand an indifferent witness. He is to be esteemed a public benefactor on whose testimony the prisoner is convicted, and he who shrinks from the certainty expected of him, does it at the peril of public displeasure and reproach. If proof of this were needed, it might be found abundantly in the variance of the evidence on the two trials of this cause ... and this last reinforcement of evidence is but proof of what had been done for the conviction of the prisoner.

After all that has been said abroad we fear that it may even seem strange that we should claim for the prisoner that presumption of innocence which the law affords every man. But it is not the less your duty to extend it to him. ... You must be satisfied by the evidence in the case, beyond reasonable doubt, of the truth of the whole and of every material part of the charge as it is here laid against him.

I say this, gentlemen, because a new doctrine of the law has been advanced to meet the difficulties of this case. We have been told that the prosecution will contend that if the general guilt of the prisoner has been established, there is a presumption of law that he is a principal offender; that the burden is thrown on him to show that he is guilty in a less degree. It is enough for us to say that this is a doctrine subversive of the very foundation of all criminal law; that it strikes at the root of that humane provision that no man's guilt is presumed; and that it is unsupported by any authority which has been or can be adduced.

What then is the crime of which the prisoner stands indicted? It is that he was present, aiding and abetting in the murder. Not that he is guilty of the murderous intent or that he procured the murder to be committed, but that he was present at the perpetration of it and gave his assistance to the murderer. But we admit the law to be well settled that an actual presence is not necessary to constitute the prisoner a principal. We admit that any place from which actual physical aid can be given in the commission of the murder is presence within the meaning of the law. ...

To make a man an aider and abettor in a felony he must be in such a situation at the moment when the crime is committed that he can render actual and immediate assistance to the perpetrator, and that he must be there by agreement, and with the intent to render such assistance. ... No previous consent or inducement, no encouragement at the moment short of the hope of actual and immediate physical assistance is sufficient for that purpose. ... Was the prisoner, with such intent, under such an agreement, in such a situation that he could render actual aid at the moment when the murder was committed? . . . Sensible of the weakness of the evidence of the prisoner's presence in Brown Street (specially as it stood on the first trial), the prosecutors have relied much on the aid of the conspiracy. . . . If then, as the prosecutors contend, the evidence of Leighton is sufficient to indicate the object of the conspiracy; if the words he so ingeniously overheard can, as is said, mean nothing but that the two Knapps and Richard Crowninshield had agreed that the latter should murder Captain White, then all the remaining proof of the conspiracy is superfluous. The only object for which it could legally be used was accomplished at the first step.

The Wenham robbery, the robbery of the Knapps' house, the preceding letters of Joseph Knapp to Stephen White and to the committee, and other circumstantial stuff that has been introduced, may be used to aggravate the general appearance of the whole transaction, but they have no bearing on the case of the prisoner. The letters may be proof that Joseph Knapp was guilty, but what is that to the prisoner? He is not to stand or fall by the subsequent and independent acts of Joseph.

Why are these evidence against him, more than Joseph's confession given to Mr. Colman? They are but confessions made after the fact and without the knowledge of the prisoner. As to the robbery, it may have been real or pretended. But whether real or pretended, what has it to do with the murder of Captain White? Not a particle of extrinsic proof of its falsehood or of its connection with that event has been produced. Some other circumstances may be dispatched in the same manner.

The conspirators wore daggers; the proof is that the Crowninshields habitually wore them before the murder and that the prisoner never had one until long after. And whether he then wore it for murder or in boyish bravado, you may judge of Leighton's account of the manner in which he used it upon him. Pleased with his new weapon, "he pricked me bull calf till he roared." And how much of Leighton's testimony is to be ascribed to that is matter of no great consequence, so incredible is the whole. So of the five-franc pieces, the proof is that Joseph received five hundred on the twenty-first of April, and that George and Richard Crowninshield spent nine between that time and their arrest—nine five-franc pieces! Richard was to receive, according to Palmer, one thousand dollars for the murder, and we are called upon to account for nine of these pieces when the whole five hundred would not half of the price agreed to be paid. And why should not the whole five hundred have been paid? And if they were, why are not more than nine traced to the Crowninshields? The coin, besides, is no uncommon one; they carry no earmarks. The witnesses tell you they pass currently, commonly, here. . . . But suppose it otherwise; how does this prove Frank Knapp guilty of this murder? Is he shown to have any of this pernicious coin? All the evidence about them is of the nine spent by the Crowninshields. . . .

Besides, the proof of any communication between Joseph and Richard after the murder completely fails. . . . The whole evidence is that about the last of March, Richard Crowninshield stopped at [a] tavern with a stranger who asked if Captain Knapp had been there lately; they left their chaise and walked away together. Afterwards, about the twentieth of April, Richard and another person stouter than the prisoner, called at [the same tavern] in the evening and spent a five-franc piece.

Hart and Leighton testify that somewhere about that time Frank Knapp came in a chaise to Wenham with a stranger who sat in the chaise at the door an hour or an hour and a half. They differ very much in their accounts of the transaction; but neither pretends to know or believe that the stranger was Richard, or that any money was paid. In fact, money could not well have been paid at that time in five-franc pieces without observation. All they knew was that there was a long conversation between the two Knapps in the house and between them and the stranger at the door. . . .

One word about George Crowninshield. . . . He came to Salem with Selman and Chase on other business. It seems to be the object of the government to show that he could not be the man in Brown Street; but we think it material to show you also that neither was he anywhere in the neighborhood of Mr. White's house at the supposed time of the murder. . . .

I come now to what is called the direct evidence of the conspiracy. It rests on two witnesses, Leighton and Palmer—or rather it rests on Leighton alone, for without his testimony that of Palmer would not be admissible. Palmer pretends only to have heard a conversation between the two Crowninshields in the absence of the prisoner. Now to make this admissible against Frank Knapp, a conspiracy must first be established between him and the Crowninshields. For that purpose, Leighton overhears the two Knapps tell each other the whole story while he listens behind a stone wall.

Now it may be supposed that this very deficiency in Palmer's story is proof of its truth. Not so. Palmer's story was first told and put in writing to convict Richard Crowninshield, and it would well enough stand alone on that. But when

Richard was out of the way and Frank became the principal, a connecting link was wanting; and to furnish this is Leighton's office.

And what is Leighton's story? Of all the gross improbabilities that ever were laid at the foundation of a cause, this is the most gross. It is just the clumsiest contrivance of a play, where the audience is informed of what has taken place behind the scenes by the actors telling each other what they have been doing together. If it were told with the utmost consistency, could you believe it for a moment?

Why, gentlemen, do but listen to it. He tells you that Frank Knapp came to Wenham about ten o'clock [and] that he and Joseph were together all morning in the fields, and that after dinner he left them together talking at the gate by the house while the witness went down the avenue to his work. There was abundant opportunity, then, for them to talk in private about what most concerned them. But after the witness had passed through the gate at the end of the avenue and taken his place behind the wall, he heard voices in the avenue.

Without rising he peeped through the gate and saw the two Knapps about twenty-five rods off coming towards him; that they ceased talking until they arrived within three feet of the wall and then began this dialogue: Said Joseph, "When did you see Dick?" "This morning." "When is he going to kill the old man?" "I don't know." "If he don't do it soon I won't pay him." And they then turned up the avenue and walked away, and this is all the witness heard.

Now is anything more than a bare statement of this story necessary to show its falsehood? For what purpose, under Heaven, could the Knapps have postponed all conversation on this most interesting subject till that very time? They had been together all morning; they were plotting a murder, and Frank had been that very day to see the perpetrator; and yet neither Joseph had the curiosity to ask, nor Frank the disposition to speak of the matter until just as they reached the place of Leighton's ambuscade. And there, in an abrupt dialogue of one minute's duration, they disclose the whole secret and walk back again.

Not a word more is heard by the witness. The conversation evidently began and ended with these words. Really it is too miserable a contrivance to deserve much comment. But there is a remarkable mistake about this story which stamps it with falsehood. Leighton fixes the conversation on Friday, the second of April. And why on that day? Because he knew, as well as every person who had read the newspapers, that on that day Frank did see Richard. But unluckily he fixes him at Wenham at the very hour in which it now appears, from the testimony of Allen and Palmer, that he was at Danvers.

Leighton says that Frank came to Wenham at ten, and said he had seen Dick that morning; but it now appears that Frank did not go to Danvers until two o'clock, and at that very hour Leighton pretends to have heard this conversation at Wenham. Again, Palmer tells you that at that interview at Danvers, the plan was first proposed to the Crowninshields, that George spoke of it to Richard and himself as what he had just heard from Frank; and yet from this dialogue at Wenham it seems that Joseph was impatient at the long delay of Richard.

"When is Dick going to kill the old man?" "If he don't soon I won't pay him." How are these things to be reconciled? Leighton tells you, too, that he never mentioned this conversation until after the murder. And why not? . . . He had heard a plan, [a] palpable plot of murder contrived by his own master, and yet he did not think [to tell it]! He did not tell it to Mr. Davis when he joined him at his work, nor to [his fellow worker on the Beckford farm] Thomas Hart who slept in the same room with him. He is directly contradicted by Hart, both as to time when he told of it and as to the circumstances of Richard's supposed visit to Wenham. . . .

Hart says he never heard of this conversation until after Leighton's examination at Salem and that Leighton told him the committee brought out a warrant to commit him to jail if he did not tell what he knew—facts both of which Leighton denied on the stand. Now what account does he give of the manner in which his evidence was brought out? He says he was summoned to attend court, taken out of the field when he was at work and carried to Mr. Waters' office. He was kept there, forenoon and afternoon, more than four hours, closely questioned and threatened; but he told nothing. Why did he not tell?

On the first trial he swore he remembered well enough, but he did not choose to tell. To be sure he swore both ways about it, but he finally said he did remember and would not tell; and on this statement a most ingenious argument was built by the counsel in his favor: "He would not betray his employer; improper as it was to deny what he knew, he had fidelity enough to refuse." But on this last trial he takes all that back; he swears positively he did not remember a word about it. Equally regardless of his own oath and the argument of counsel, he denies the whole. He says it all came into his mind about two days after his return to Wenham—the very words. What brought it to his mind he cannot tell. Now what credit can you give to this boy and his story?

But one of the most remarkable improbabilities of it is yet to come. He says he told the gentlemen at Mr. Waters' office that if they would come to Wenham the next day he would tell them all he could remember. That was on the twenty-second of July. Now do you believe if that were true they would not have gone? . . . And yet he tells you he heard nothing from them until ten days after that time. Then they came to Wenham and he told them about it.

Now, gentlemen, if you had seen as much as we have of the diligence of the committee and sub-committee in looking up testimony in this cause, you would not think this the least improbability in Leighton's story. Consider how important his testimony is. Without it, Palmer's and the whole evidence of the conspiracy would be useless. It is the very cornerstone of the prosecution. And yet it was not thought worth looking after for ten days immediately preceding the trial. Again, we shall be asked, what motive has Leighton to swear falsely? And we answer, fear, favor, and hope of reward.

He was told at Waters' office he should be made to remember; he said he was threatened with a warrant; and he knows of the immense rewards that have been offered. He remembers the pricking with the dagger, and he swears now to you that if Knapp escapes hanging, he expects he will kill him. Under all these circumstances, I put it to your consciences to say if you can take this boy's word against the life of the prisoner. If you disbelieve it, then you must wholly reject Palmer's testimony and all evidence of what was said and done by anyone but the prisoner or in his presence. There is absolutely no other evidence to connect the prisoner with Joseph or the Crowninshields in this matter.

But who is this Palmer, this mysterious stranger who has been the object of so much curiosity and speculation? He is a convicted thief. We produce to you the record of his conviction of shop-breaking in Maine. He is an unrepenting thief. . . . Mr. James Webster tells you his character among his neighbors in Belfast is as bad as it can be. He tells you himself that he has passed in his wanderings from tavern to tavern, sometimes by the name of Palmer . . . and sometimes that of George Crowninshield. The latter name he gave at Babb's house when he was called on to settle his bill; and whether he settled by a note he cannot remember, but Mr. Babb remembers that he did and signed that note George Crowninshield!

And how came Mr. Palmer a witness before you? He was arrested . . . committed to Belfast jail, brought up by land from Belfast in chains, put into a condemned cell in Salem, remained in jail two months, neither committed for trial nor ordered to [be recognized] as a witness, but kept for further examination at his own request until he is brought out and made a free man on the stand. Now what is this man's credibility? If his conviction had been in Massachusetts he would have been incompetent; he could not have opened his mouth in court. But the crime is the same, the law violated is the same, the infamy and punishment are the same in Maine as in Massachusetts, and his credibility is the same.

Add to that conviction, his subsequent . . . forgery, and you have left in him but a bare possibility that he may speak the truth. As to his temptation to testify against the prisoner, you see how he was brought here, under what liabilities he stands, and what is the price of his discharge. He tells you himself that, though a disinterested love of public justice first moved him to inquire into the matter, he thinks he deserves some little pecuniary reward for his exertions, and doubtless he thinks that reward will depend something in the success of them.

But what is his story? It is that being himself concealed at the house of the Crowninshields in Danvers, he saw Frank Knapp and Allen come there on Friday, April 2, about two o'clock; that Frank and George walked away together, and after their return Frank and Allen rode off; that the Crowninshields then came into the chamber where he was, and George detailed to him and Richard the whole design and motive of the murder as a matter then for the first time communicated.

Now perhaps there is nothing intrinsically very incredible about this story, except its too great particularity. If it be false, it is so artfully engrafted on the truth that Frank Knapp was there at that time and had an interview with George alone, that it would be almost impossible to detect it. Palmer, too, must be allowed the credit of ingenuity, whether his story be true or false. It is impossible for anyone in his situation to have testified with a more artful simplicity. And I admit too that he has had the good sense to tell no unnecessary falsehood. The only instance in which he has tripped is his saying that George Crowninshield told him on the ninth of April that he had melted the daggers the day after the murder for fear of the Committee of Vigilance, whereas the committee was not appointed until late in the evening of the ninth. . . .

But this conversation is too particular. Like Leighton's, it goes too much into all that the case requires. Why should the Crowninshields tell all this to Palmer without first sounding him? He says he rejected their offer immediately. Would they risk detailing the whole plan to him before securing any indication on his part of assent? Nay, after having communicated it to him and after he *had refused to have any part in it, would Richard have gone on to execute it? He is not a man to trust his life to the keeping of such a witness as Palmer, who had refused to become an accomplice. . . .*

Is Palmer corroborated? In the immaterial circumstances of his story in which he had the sense to tell the truth and no temptation to lie, he is confirmed by other witnesses. But on the only important point he stands alone and unconfirmed. The conversation between him and the Crowninshields rests, and must of necessity rest, on his single statement. But it has been said that his letter corroborates his story. How can that be? Would he be such a fool as to swear now to anything inconsistent with his letter of which we had a copy? . . .

But does that letter contain anything which he might not well have known, whether his story be true or false, and which is now confirmed by any other witness? Not a word. It states that he knew what J. Knapp's brother was doing for him on the second of April, that he was extravagant to give a thousand dollars for such a business, and that is all. The rest is but vague and unmeaning menace.

Now it is undoubtedly true that Frank Knapp was at Danvers on the second of April and had a private conversation with George, and that Palmer was at Danvers and saw him. And that single fact is the only one contained in the letter which is corroborated by any other witness. That he was there to engage the Crowninshields in this business and that they were to have a thousand dollars, comes from Palmer himself and from him alone.

Even Leighton's story, though intended to corroborate it, contradicts it by inconsistency in time and in the age of the plot. [Leighton] says nothing of the thousand dollars. But why should Palmer venture to mention a thousand dollars if that were not the sum offered? And why should he have written the letter at all if he knew nothing about Frank's business at Danvers?

The solution is easy. It supposes, indeed, some skill in Palmer, but we have seen enough of that. Consider when this letter was written. Not until after the arrest of the Crowninshields. If he had really heard this plot laid, why did he not give information of it immediately on hearing of Captain White's death, and of the immense rewards offered for the discovery of the murder?

He tells you he wrote that letter to bring the matter to light, from a pure love of public justice. Public justice has been a rather hard mistress to Palmer, but he is not the less faithful to her. Now why did not that love of public justice induce him to inform against the Crowninshields and Knapps before anybody else suspected them, and while public justice had some thousands of dollars to give him to obliterate the remembrance of her castigations?

He had the whole matter in his own breast. He had heard every word of the plot. If they were guilty, he had information enough to lead to their detection. Yet he waits five weeks after the murder and a fortnight after the arrest of the Crowninshields and then writes this letter to Knapp demanding money, but in fact, as he tells you, to get evidence against them. But what led him to suspect the Knapps? What was more easy? He probably knew that J. Knapp's mother-in-law was an heir of White; he saw Frank Knapp in private conversation with George Crowninshield four days before the murder, and he saw in the papers that the Crowninshields were arrested as the murderers. It required less than Palmer's shrewdness to put these things together.

As to the thousand dollars it may be his own pure invention; there is no other evidence of it. Or it may be that he heard the Crowninshields say after Frank left them that they expected a thousand dollars without saying from what source. His letter is therefore no corroboration at all. It does not contain a fact proved by anybody but himself except that Frank was at Danvers on the second. Nor is Palmer's story on the stand corroborated by any other witness in a single fact that had not been published in every newspaper in the State weeks before he testified.

This is the evidence of the conspiracy. I have but two remarks to make on it. If you could believe it on such evidence, the only effect of it would be to show that Frank Knapp was an accessory, and it makes nothing said or done by Joseph Knapp or the Crowninshields evidence against the prisoner. The very proof relied on to establish the fact of the conspiracy proves equally well all that of which such acts and declarations are legal evidence; that is, the design and object of the conspiracy.

The most, then, that can possibly be inferred from this evidence, bad as it is, is that the prisoner was an accessory before the fact; and that if he were in Brown Street at the moment of the murder, and in a situation in which he could give assistance, there would be a presumption that he was there for that purpose.

We are willing to meet the government on that ground. We deny that he was there and we deny that the man who was there could by possibility have given any assistance. Two men were seen in Brown Street at half-past ten, of whom one is alleged to have been the murderer and the prisoner the other. But what proof is there that the murder was committed at that hour?

If that fails, the whole case fails. Was there anything in the conduct of the men to show it? One was seen waiting half an hour in Brown Street. A little before eleven he was joined by another who came up either from the Common or from Newbury Street, and might as well have come from one as from the other as he was first seen in the middle of the street.

The man that came from the eastward did not run; he walked directly up to the other and held a short conference with him; they moved on together a few feet, stopped again, talked a few moments, and then parted—one stepping back out of sight and the other running down Howard Street. Of the two witnesses that saw them, Bray thought they were about to rob the graveyard; Southwick suspected, but what to suspect he did not know, and his wife suspected that he had better go out again to watch them.

A murder was committed that night in the next street, and this is all the proof that these were the murderers. A club, indeed, was afterwards found in Howard Street, but neither of these men had any visible weapons. What say the doctors? Dr. Johnson says he saw the body at six and then thought it had been dead between three and four hours. Dr. Hubbard now thinks longer, but says at the time he agreed with Johnson. There is pretty strong proof that the murder was in fact committed about three o'clock.

[One witness] saw a man, between three and four, come out of Captain White's yard and walk up Essex Street, but meeting the witness he turned about and ran down as far as Walnut Street. [Another witness] about the same time and near the lower end of Walnut Street, met probably the same man coming towards him. On seeing him, [the man] turned about and walked the other way. Now which was most likely to be the murderer—the man who might have come either from Newbury Street or from the Common at eleven, or the man who was actually seen to leave White's yard at half-past three, and twice turned back and once ran away to escape observation?

But here we are met with a dilemma on the second trial. What I have stated was the whole of [the first witness's] testimony on the first trial. He was then asked whether he had ever heard of that man since, and he said no. Now he is asked whether he has seen that man since, and to the utter amazement of everyone, after giggling like an idiot, he says he thinks it was the prisoner! And this is seriously taken up by the counsel for the prosecution. . . .

[The government now suggests, though it made no such suggestion in the first trial, that Frank entered the house after Dick Crowninshield's departure and

delivered more knife blows to Captain White.] But for what possible purpose, if Frank Knapp had met the murderer in Brown Street and heard that the deed was done at eleven, should he have gone into the house again and stabbed the dead body? Like another Falstaff did he envy the perpetrator the glory of the deed and mean to claim it as his own? Or was it for plunder? No, for the money was not taken. . . . This is but one of the many examples of the rapid growth of evidence in a popular cause. . . .

The government must satisfy you beyond reasonable doubt that either the murder was committed at half-past ten, or that the prisoner was the man who left the house at half-past three. You cannot believe both; and can you say that you are satisfied of either? Is there not a great, a very reasonable doubt of both? You must not convict the prisoner between the two. You must be as well satisfied of one as if the other did not exist. Which then will you take? . . .

Was the murder committed at half-past ten? What is the proof of it? And what was the man doing in White's yard at half-past three? And why did he run when he was seen? Which acted most like a murderer, the man that came into Brown Street or the man that ran from the yard? Which was the hour most appropriate to so horrible a deed? That at which a party was breaking up at Mr. Daland's, the next house to Mr. White's, or the still hour before daylight when no person was abroad but by accident?

And what is the fair result of the doctor's opinion on the view of the body? All these things concur to fix the murder on the man who left the yard in the morning. . . . There remains then, only the supposition that the murder was committed at half-past ten; and then the question is: Was the prisoner the man in Brown Street?

On this point we have the most deplorable examples of the fallibility of human testimony, and of the weak stand that even common integrity can make against the overwhelming current of popular opinion. The witnesses are four. [Peter] Webster and Southwick swore the same on both trials; Bray and Myrick have varied most essentially. As it now stands, Myrick and Webster are of little importance. Myrick saw a man in a frock coat, who he now thinks was the prisoner, standing on the corner of Brown and Newbury Streets from twenty minutes before to twenty minutes after nine. The man appeared to be waiting for someone, and when any person approached his post he walked away and then turned and met him. . . .

Now whether that was or was not the prisoner is not in itself of any impor-tance. It is hardly to be believed that a man who was to be engaged in a murder at half-past ten would be seen lingering near the spot for forty minutes at the early hour of nine. It would, if true, be no unfavorable circumstance. For what purpose connected with the murder was he there at that hour? Did the murder-ers take their measure so ill that one was on the watch for the other at a public corner near the scene of the murder an hour and a half before the time?

Besides, where are the persons whom Myrick saw meet the prisoner at the corner? He spoke to several. Why are they not found and produced? It is impos-sible they should not be found. We have been loudly and gravely called upon to produce the man in Brown Street if Frank Knapp was not he. It is thought very strange that if it were not he, some friend of justice should not come forward and own himself to be the man, at the risk of taking the prisoner's place at the bar as a principal in the murder.

So, too, it was asked, if Richard Crowninshield was not the man that joined him in Brown Street, why don't [sic] the prisoner show where Richard was? And yet we are told that the prisoner stood half an hour at a corner and was met by various persons, but not one of those persons is produced to prove it when it is the very question whether it was the prisoner or not, and Myrick tells you himself that others saw him where they certainly would have recognized him.

Now it is a principle of law that no evidence is good which of itself supposes better in existence, not produced. Myrick's evidence, then, is good for nothing until those who met the prisoner at the post are produced. Besides, how did Myrick recognize him? He had never known him; he never knew him until he was brought up for trial nearly four months after the night of the murder, and in a different dress. He was then told by a bystander which was Frank Knapp.

Being asked at the first trial who he thought the man at the corner was, he said he thought it was the prisoner, not from what he had observed alone, but partly from what he had heard about him. Now this was obviously no evidence at all. What a man thinks from what he hears is nothing. What he hears is no evidence; and still less what he thinks about it. But at this trial Mr. Myrick makes another step. He says he thinks it was the prisoner from his own observation alone, making allowance for the difference of dress.

Now, how much of an allowance that is depends on how much the appear-ance of a man, seen four or five rods off by a perfect stranger . . . consists in his dress. It can consist of nothing but dress, figure, and manner. Mr. Myrick's

*evidence, therefore, amounts to this and no more: "I think the prisoner's fig-
ure and manner the same as those of a man I saw four months ago, under
the circumstances above described." This is so slight that the difference in his
testimony is not worth mentioning, except to show the growing tendency of the
whole evidence.*

*About the time that Myrick leaves the prisoner in his frock at the corner,
Mr. [Peter] Webster overtakes him [the prisoner] in Howard Street in a wrapper.
He passed him without much observation; he did not see his face, but he thinks
it was the prisoner. The probability, from the change in dress, is that it was not.
And this reminds me of a remark made on the last trial, that such differences
and sudden changes of dress were to be expected for the purposes of disguise
when such business was on foot. With great deference to the learned counsel, it
seems to be highly improbable.*

*What is the evidence on this point? The prisoner is supposed to have had on
his usual frock and cap at the corner from a quarter before to a quarter after
nine; at half-past nine to have walked in Howard Street in the same cap and
wrapper; to have [sat] on the steps of the ropewalk in his own cap and camlet
cloak at half-past ten; and five minutes after to have been seen in the same
street in his frock.*

*Now I agree with the learned counsel that on such occasions disguise is to
be expected, and farther, that it is entirely incredible anyone should go undis-
guised. But what disguise is here? The wrapper does not, indeed, correspond
to any known dress of the prisoner; but in every other situation in which he is
seen, he is recognized by his usual dress and by that alone. Now it is incredible
enough that a man should, in a light evening, be out in his usual dress to commit murder in his native town; but that he should think to disguise himself by
putting on and off his own cloak, as well known as his own coat, and thus be
seen in two of his habitual dresses, is a little too much to ask you to believe. Why
not assume one effectual and complete disguise? Or, if he feared being seen too
often in one dress, why not put a strange cloak over a strange coat? And why
wear his own cap the whole evening?*

*The counsel has said that this was a murder, planned with great skill; noth-
ing could be more unskilled than the prisoner's part if he was there. But let
us come to the more material part of this testimony. Mr. Southwick swears
positively to having seen the prisoner on the ropewalk at half-past ten in his
own cap and cloak; that he passed him three times and watched him twenty*

minutes. He has known the prisoner from childhood. He did not speak though he felt very suspicious of him. He went into the house and took off his coat and came out again, and the man was gone. He met Mr. Bray, who pointed out a man standing at Shepard's post on the other side of the street in a frock and cap like [that of the prisoner].

Bray and he stopped and observed [the man] till he left Shepard's post, walked down the opposite side of the street, and passed them and stood at the post under Bray's window. They then crossed over and entered Bray's house, passing within twenty feet of him. Southwick says he did not recognize the man in the frock coat, but supposed him to be the same he had seen on the steps because there was no other person in the street, and because he had the same suspicions of him!

Now this testimony of Mr. Southwick is open to two or three important objections. In the first place, if Frank Knapp were on the steps to aid in a murder at that moment in execution, and expecting to be joined by the murderer, would he have permitted Southwick to pass him three times and watch him twenty minutes? He knew Southwick as well as Southwick knew him. Southwick says he dropped his head each time he passed him so that he could not see his face. So there is a foolish bird that puts its head in a hole and thinks itself safe if it cannot see its pursuers. Murderers are apt to be more cautious.

[Southwick] says he knew it then to be Frank Knapp, and told his wife so. But though he thought the man he and Bray saw was the same, and both wondered what mischief he could be about, he never told Mr. Bray who he thought it was. Is that possible? Yet both he and Bray agree in it. But the greatest impossibility of all is that he should not have recognized the prisoner, if it was he, in his usual dress, while walking down the opposite side of this narrow street. . . .

Now how inconsistent is this story with the supposition that that was the prisoner. [Southwick] knew Frank Knapp familiarly; he saw him and recognized him in his cloak on the steps; he saw a man on the opposite side of the street five minutes after, who he, for some reason not connected with his appearance, thought was the same. And yet, though that man wore the usual dress of the prisoner, and walked down the street by Southwick when it was light enough to distinguish persons across the street, and though Southwick passed within twenty feet of him to go into Bray's house, he did not recognize him as the prisoner.

Again, he thought the man in the frock was the same as the man in the cloak. He knew the man in the cloak was Frank Knapp, yet he and Bray wondered who the man in the frock could be; and Southwick never thought of telling Bray it was Frank Knapp. Now, if Southwick's testimony were believed, it not only would not prove that the prisoner was the man at the post, but it would prove almost conclusively that it was not.

It is impossible that Southwick should not have known him if it were he, and should not have told Bray if he knew him on the steps. Besides Southwick [has been placed on record in testimony under oath] that "for aught he knew the man in Brown Street might be Richard Crowninshield, and Frank Knapp the other—he could not tell who they were." . . .

But one word more with Mr. Southwick. When Chase and Selman were indicted for this murder, he went before the grand jury as a witness. . . . He there swore that the man he saw in Brown Street was about the size and height of Selman and said not one word about Frank Knapp! On this testimony, and that of Hatch, the convict, was Selman indicted and imprisoned as a felon eighty-five days, until another grand jury assembled and, as Hatch's oath was inadmissible and Southwick had turned his testimony against Knapp, Selman was discharged.

Now when was there anything more abominable than this, except in form? It is not, to be sure, within the reach of the law, but how is it in conscience? He swears now that he then knew it was Frank Knapp, and yet he indirectly swore then that it was Selman. And what is the contemptible evasion by which he tries to escape? Why, that it is true that he was about the size of Selman, and he was not asked whether it was Frank Knapp!

If he tells truth now, he knew then that by one word of truth he could clear Selman of all suspicion of being in Brown Street. He willfully suppressed that truth. Now why is he a more credible witness than if he had been convicted of perjury? It is said he told his wife it was Frank Knapp. She says so and it may be true, but it is not the very best corroboration. It is not of one half the weight of the fact that he did not tell it to Bray. Still that only goes to the identity of the man on the steps. It leaves the man at the post still nameless, and that is the important question. Southwick does not pretend to identify him.

Now this—with the addition of a statement from Bray that he could not tell who the man in Brown Street was, though he was about the size and shape of the prisoner and wore a cap and full skirted coat such as the hatters and tailors say Frank Knapp and a hundred others wear—was absolutely all the evidence on the first trial that the prisoner was in Brown Street. Two remarkable facts have happened since. One is that Mr. Bray, one of the most honest witnesses in the cause, has in this trial, to the same question, answered that he had no doubt the man he saw in Brown Street was the prisoner.

Now I have no disposition to accuse Mr. Bray of any intentional misstatement or overstatement, but here is a direct and flat contradiction. One week he says, "I have seen the prisoner in jail and in court, and I cannot say he was the man in Brown Street"; and the next week he says, "I have seen him in jail and in court, and I have no doubt he is the man." Nay more; though he said that he had thought more of it since the trial and become more certain—a strange way of correcting an opinion formed on what was seen four months ago—he said too that when he first saw the prisoner in jail he recognized him by his dress and motions.

Now there is no reconciling these things, let them be explained as they may. Both cannot be true. Which will you believe? That he does or does not recognize him? Mr. Bray is one of the Committee of Vigilance; let that go for what it is worth and no more. But which is more likely to be right—his first testimony, the result of the reflection of three months, before he knew what would be the event of the trial, or that result corrected by the revision of a week, when he knew that the first trial had failed on that very point? I repeat that I accuse Mr. Bray of no wrong, but I cannot acquit him of that subjection to the power of imagination which has brought others here, as honest as himself, to swear positively to things that never did and never could happen. . . .

Now take Bray and Southwick, the only material witnesses; make what allowances for error you think ought to be made, and can you say you are satisfied that the prisoner was in Brown Street? . . . But let us look for a few moments at the proof of the prisoner's alibi. It is applicable to two different times. The first between seven and ten, the second after ten. The first depends on the testimony of Page, Balch, Burchmore, and Forrester. Now Page says he knows it was Monday or Tuesday evening; he said on examination he knew it was not Saturday because he came home from college that day and spent the evening at home. Burchmore is positive it was on Tuesday; and though uncertain before, has since remembered that he told William Peirce so the day or day but one after the murder. We offer Peirce as a witness to the fact. Balch and Forrester both strongly believe that it was on Tuesday . . .

Now what is there against this? It is said they have expressed doubts and uncertainty heretofore. There is no contradiction; three of them give now only *their belief but it is a very strong one in all. Burchmore, however, is positive, and he gives a good reason for it and good proof of his correctness. . . .*

The other branch of the alibi is more important because it embraces the supposed time of the murder. Captain Knapp, the father, swears that he went home a few minutes before ten, and that Frank came in and went to bed a few minutes after. And there is a particularity about this account that marks it either as truth or as willful and cunning perjury; and Captain Knapp's character is enough to shield him from such a charge. He says he commended Frank's return at the prescribed hour; that Frank asked him if he should bolt the door, and he said no, that Phippen was out; that Frank, seeing him looking over his papers (for he failed the very night) asked him if he should help him, then threw his cap on the window seat near his own hat and went up to bed. Captain Knapp sat up till after one, and Phippen returned at that hour and sat up for the rest of the night. . . . [Frank] came down to breakfast as usual in the morning. . . .

But there is one piece of evidence that meets all the deficiencies of this case with a wonderful felicity, [that of Henry Colman, who swears he heard a direct confession from Frank Knapp, including a description of the location of the murder weapon]. The witness is a clergyman, and whatever credibility that office may claim for him, I am willing he should enjoy. In my mind it is no more than belongs to any man of honest reputation; and on one account something less, for I cannot think the clerical office so well fits a man to endure and resist the excitement to which the witness has been subjected, as a secular employment.

It is the experience of the world that clergymen, when they mingle in worldly business, are more powerfully acted upon by it than others. Now every material word of his testimony is contradicted by Mr. N. P. Knapp, the prisoner's brother. He went into [Frank's] cell with Mr. Colman and must have heard all that was said. . . . Now there stand two witnesses, equal in character, directly opposed to each other on a matter known only to themselves and to the prisoner. . . . Mr. Knapp cannot be mistaken about this matter. It is impossible that, after having employed counsel for the defense before the magistrate and being himself a lawyer and understanding the danger of such evidence, he could have heard Frank confess away his life without remarking and remembering it.

I say confess away his life; for though these confessions, if true, cannot harm him as a principal, he was then chargeable as an accessory, and on such a charge they would have been fatal. Mr. Colman, on the contrary, is most liable to be mistaken about it. Having had repeated conversations with Joseph, before and after on the same subject, it would be wonderful if he could accurately report, as he pretends to do, the very words of Frank. It would be wonderful if he could separate the substance of the interviews. He did not, as he says, expect to be called as a witness against Frank. [On the other hand,] Mr. Knapp did expect to be examined because he had early intimation of Mr. Colman's mistake about the club. . . .

Look at the intrinsic probability of the stories. The prisoner is a young but not a timid man. You have seen enough of his bearing at this trial to judge whether he would be likely to be surprised into a confession; and he was not surprised, for he had been examined and had counsel. Mr. Colman was a perfect stranger to him, not even known by sight. Now one of these witnesses tells you that the prisoner disclosed his whole guilt to a perfect stranger at first sight, without reluctance or hesitation, in direct answer to as many questions, and without threat, promise, or encouragement; while the other says he only said it was hard that Joseph should make any confession about him, but that he had nothing to confess and should stand his trial.

Which of these things is the more probable? And is it probable that N. P. Knapp, a lawyer, who was then providing for the defense of his brother, should have permitted him to make these confessions without interfering?

I have said that Mr. Colman heard confessions of the exact facts which the case required and no more. See how that is, and how probable it is. The prisoner makes no general confession, claims no right, and expresses no hope to be admitted State's evidence. But to four distinct questions respecting the details of murder, he [according to Colman] gave four distinct answers criminating himself.

Now what were those answers? That the murder was committed between ten and eleven, a fact as you have seen wholly without other sufficient evidence but all important to the case; that Richard Crowninshield was the actual murderer, a thing without the shadow of other proof except that [one witness believes he] saw him the evening before near White's house and looking away from it; that the club was hidden under a certain step of the [Howard Street] Branch Meeting House, the only proof that that club had anything to do with the murder; that the dirk was worked up at the factory; and lastly that Frank was absent from home at the time, to fortify the Brown Street evidence and destroy the alibi. . . .

Is it not remarkable that, finding Frank so communicative, Mr. Colman should not have gone on to verify Joseph's whole confession in the same way [as he did these few four questions]? He tells you he has Joseph's confession covering nine sheets of paper; and yet, though Frank answered so freely, [Colman] had the curiosity to ask him only these four questions. It is truly incredible.

Now what improbability is there in N. P. Knapp's account of this interview? Not the least. He agrees with Mr. Colman that Frank said it was hard that Joseph should confess, and he cannot positively swear that what Mr. Colman adds as to its being done for Joseph's benefit, did not follow, because he remembers the first part of the sentence and he may have forgotten the rest. But he swears that to the best of his belief, it was not so. And to the four questions and answers, he swears positively that no such things were said, because, if said, he must have remembered them. And is not this a perfectly proper distinction? . . .

But what is the amount of all these confessions? If true, they prove indeed that [Frank] knew too much of this guilty deed. But they imply no presence at it. All but his absence from home are facts that he might, and some that he must have learned afterwards from others. And what does the fact that he was absent from home prove? At most, it is but a circumstance corroborative of the Brown Street evidence. He may have been there or he may have been elsewhere. The form, indeed, in which we have the confession from Mr. Colman might imply that he was absent, knowing of the deed—"I went home afterward."

But, obviously, this all depends on the exactness with which the words are remembered. Suppose only a slight change, and the dialogue to run thus: "When was the murder committed?" "Between ten and eleven." "Were you at home then?" "No, I did not go home until after that time." Now this would contradict the alibi but would not contain any implication of his partaking in or knowing of the murder at the time. And when an implication depends on such slight differences, it is no evidence at all. And I repeat: What is the probability, if any confessions were made, that they were made in the words now delivered, when Mr. Colman has forgotten both words and substance of all the rest of the conversation?

One point only remains; but it is the great and important one. Believe the prisoner—if you will believe anything on such testimony as Leighton's and Palmer's—[to be] a conspirator and a procurer of the murder; believe him in Brown Street at half-past ten, and that the murder was committed at that hour— against the manifest weight of all the evidence but the confession; believe the confession, too, and the whole of it—improbable and contradicted as it is; and, whatever the prisoner may deserve in your moral judgment, he stands as clear *of this indictment as a principal, aiding and abetting, as Joseph Knapp does, who was in bed at Wenham.*

And here, gentlemen, if you ever come to this part of the case, you are to be tried as well as the prisoner. He is to be tried for his life, and you for a character which will last as long as life. The time will soon come when this trial will be coolly and impartially examined. . . .

Let us go back to the acknowledged law of the case. No matter what the prisoner has done or agreed to do, if he was not at the moment when the murder was committed in a place where he could give actual assistance, and there for that purpose, then he was not a principal in this murder. It has indeed been contended that it is enough that the parties thought the place a proper one for the purpose. Such is not the law; but here it is the same thing, for how can you judge that they thought it a fit place unless you yourselves think it so? . . .

Could the man in Brown Street give that help to the murderer, without the hope of which the murder would not have been committed? This is a question of fact for you to try on the evidence and the view. You must be satisfied of this beyond any reasonable doubt, or your verdict of guilty will be against yourselves. Now what assistance did the case admit? It was a secret assassination. If the prisoner had been actually present in the room or in the house, that alone would be enough. . . . But when you find but one accomplice, and him at a distance in another street, you must inquire why he was there. You must be satisfied that he was posted there with some power, and therefore with a purpose to aid.

It becomes material to inquire particularly what aid he could afford. The late lamented chief justice, in his charge which has been read to you, delivered with special reference to the facts in this case, says [that if Frank] was there to prevent relief to the victim, to give an alarm to the murderer, or to assist him to escape, then he was present, aiding and abetting. . . .

Was he there to intercept relief? If so, he would have taken a post where he could be aware of its approach. But did he do so? It is said the murderer entered the house at half-past ten. At that hour and for twenty minutes after, the prisoner is said to have been sitting wrapped in a cloak on the steps of the ropewalk, not watching others but hiding his own head from observation. From that time until five minutes before he was joined by the murderer, he was still farther off. . . . How could he know whether relief was approaching or not? He could not see the house from any one spot where he was seen that evening.

Anyone who passed him would have to turn two corners before he would be near White's house.

Now he could see nothing but Brown Street and nobody but those who passed through it. If anyone passed there, what was he to do? Was he to knock him down upon the possibility that he might be going to turn into Newbury Street, and then might turn into Essex Street, and then might go up that street toward White's house? On such a possibility was he to protect the murderer by an act that would infallibly create alarm to no purpose? The supposition is absurd. He could not intercept relief because he was not where he could be aware of it.

Could he give an alarm? An alarm of what? You see that he could not know of the approach of danger. If the enterprise had failed, Richard might have been discovered, overpowered, and removed before his accomplice could have been aware of any difficulty. But if it had been his object to intercept relief, or to give an alarm if he could not intercept it, where would he have been? At that point from which relief might be feared, and where early and certain intelligence of it might be had.

Where was that? Certainly, in Essex Street. Who would come to the relief? The inmates of Captain White's own house, or of the adjoining houses of Daland and Gardner, or of the opposite houses, or some casual passenger. Now against all these, the post of observation was in Essex Street and near the house. Or, if he wanted to watch the adjoining streets, why not stand at the corner of Newbury Street? Why not anywhere but at the places where he was seen during the whole time?

But one thing remains. Could he in Brown Street help the murderer to escape? If he had been waiting with a swift horse to convey him away, that might do. But one man on foot can no more help another to run away, than one can help another to keep a secret. One could only embarrass and expose the other. Was he then to defend him in his flight? Resistance was not to be depended on or expected; besides, the accomplice was unarmed, and of what avail would he have been in Brown Street where no force could be expected unless the alarm had become general.

Now we call on the prosecutor to satisfy you of [even] one mode in which aid could be afforded. On the former trial two ways only were suggested. First, that Richard might have gone into the garden early in the evening and waited for a signal from Frank in Brown Street to indicate the time when the lights were extinguished in Captain White's house. And, second, that Frank was in

Brown Street to see that the coast was clear in Howard Street, so that Richard might go there to hide the club.

Now these things, absurd as they seem, were really said and insisted on. And they are the best hypotheses that . . . counsel can make for the government. We want no better proof of the utter weakness of the point. If Richard was in the garden under the very windows, would he want Frank to tell him when the lights were put out? He could have watched every inmate of the house to his bed. He could have tracked every light up the stairs until they were extinguished in the chambers. He could have heard every noise and known when it ceased in the sleep of those within.

As to Frank's watching Howard Street, it would be enough to say that he was watched all the time and that he did not once look down Howard Street. Frank had been standing from five to ten minutes at Bray's post where he could not see a foot into Howard Street; and then Richard, having finished his conference, without any caution or examination, started and ran into that street with the speed of a deer. Did this look like watching? And for what purpose was Howard Street to be watched? That Richard might hide his club in a particular place selected, a club that nobody had ever seen and that could not be traced to him if found?

For what purpose then was the man in Brown Street? We are not bound to prove or to guess. But if it was the prisoner, and if the stories of the plot are true, he might have been there to know in season whether the enterprise had succeeded. Its failure might have been most material to be known to the contrivers before inquiry had gone far. If plunder was expected, he might have been there to share it. Neither of these things would make him a principal, for neither would be aiding at the time.

And now, gentlemen, as the last question in this cause, you are to say on your conscience: Are you satisfied beyond a reasonable doubt that the man in Brown Street, wherever he was, could have given any effectual aid in the actual commission of the murder, and selected that as the most proper place for that purpose? If you doubt about that upon the whole evidence, do your duty and acquit the prisoner. Such is the law; let it answer for its own deficiencies, if it be deficient, and trust that those who have that power will amend it if it needs amendment.

Gentlemen, of the jury, these are the prisoner's last words; his counsel have done and said all that they have found to do and say in his behalf. The rest is *for the government, the court, and for you. You are to be assailed with a power-ful argument by the learned counsel who is to follow me. Admire the eloquence, admire the reasoning; but yield nothing to it but admiration, unless it convinces your understanding that the evidence you have here heard, without regard to anything said or written elsewhere, ought to satisfy you of the fact that the pris-oner was where he could aid in this murder, and by such presence did aid in it.*

The prisoner is very young to be placed at the bar for such a crime. But, young as he is, I ask no mercy for him beyond the law. For every favorable consideration and sympathy consistent with the law, I would urge upon you his youth, his afflicted family, and the seduction of the evil example of others. By these, and all good motives, I would urge you not to sacrifice him against the law, that those more guilty than himself may be reached through him. His life is in your hands and in the hands of each one of you. May you, and each of you, give no verdict and consent to none but such as your hearts can approve now and forever.

23 | DANIEL WEBSTER'S SUMMATION AT THE SECOND TRIAL

SPEAKING OF WEBSTER'S SECOND SUMMATION, literary critic John Nichol has noted that the "terrible power of the speech and its main interest lie in the winding chain of evidence, link by link, coil by coil, round the murderer and his accomplices. One seems to hear the bones of the victim crack under the grasp of a boa-constrictor."[1] Charles Francis Richardson described the speech as "at once a masterpiece of English prose and of forensic argumentation."[2]

It appears that brevity jibes well with eloquence, as Webster's summation was overall just about seven thousand words as originally stated in court, before revision and expansion for print, as opposed to Dexter's original twenty-thousand-word remarks. The version of Webster's summation presented here comes from an original transcription made in court as Webster spoke. At the start of his remarks, Webster first expounded quite dramatically and graphically upon the narrative of the murder night, much as he had in his previous summation. Then he came to the evidence and testimony.

Whatever additional labor may be imposed on the committee of vigilance, or upon the court, or others connected with the criminal trial now proceeding on a second examination, it will not all be regretted, if this second examination should tend to establish the truth by fixing the guilt of the prisoner, if it should succeed in removing all doubts whether he is justly amenable to the law he is alleged to have broken. His learned counsel has said, with great propriety, that it is your single and individual duty to weigh the law and the testimony, and singly and individually to determine his guilt or innocence. If the discussion on the part of the defense had been conducted throughout in a spirit corresponding with that remark, I should proceed at once to an examination of the testimony in the case; but gentlemen, you have heard, by way of preliminary and concluding remarks, so many things not bearing on the evidence, so much wholly disconnected with the guilt or innocence of the prisoner, that I do not feel at liberty to proceed to the examination with this matter undisposed of.

It cannot have escaped your remark that a tone of complaint has prevailed in the defense, as if the prisoner was in danger of public feeling more than of pressing justice. You have been told of the getting up of the pursuit tending to the apprehension of the criminals, of the current of feeling bending against the prisoner, as it were, to destroy their last hopes of escape.

Is this a time to talk of hopes of escape, when the whole community is roused and startled by unparalleled iniquity, when every man's safety depends upon his personal exertions to discover the perpetrators of the outrage? You have heard of wicked combinations to overwhelm the guilty, of the time and adventitious circumstances under which he is brought to trial. You have heard of foul testimony; of a private prosecutor; and all in a tone of complaint, beginning at the beginning and ending at the end of the arguments for the defense.

Although all this is foreign to the case, it deserves notice—short notice—and shall receive it. I do not know that in all my practice, I have heard it made a subject of complaint what counsel were engaged in a cause. The efforts of the defendant's counsel have generally been directed to a defense and not to complaints that counsel was engaged. I recollect, in one of the last capital trials in this county, that I was concerned for the defense; and, in addition to the ordinary prosecuting officers, the respectable head of the Suffolk Bar, Mr. Prescott, was brought down from Boston to aid in behalf of the government. The counsel for the prisoner then contented themselves with answering his arguments, as they were able, and not with carping at his presence.

It is complained that rewards were offered. Does it ever happen otherwise when a secret crime, even theft, is perpetrated, that those interested do not offer rewards for the detection of the offenders? Rewards were offered in the case to which I alluded; handbills were issued from here to Virginia; and every means taken to lead to [the culprits]. The community was nearly as much excited as at present. But the height of the offending here is that a combination was formed, a committee appointed. There was also a committee appointed then. Is the human mind perverted; have we lost so much of moral sense as to be quiet under scenes like this? Has it come to this, that men cannot lift their hands without having it said they have combined? That they cannot stir without these remarks are boldly to be made to mark them with disgrace?

Again, it is said that the forms of ordinary justice were found too slow; and it is complained that a special session was appointed for these trials. The Legislature is drawn in as a part of the conspiracy against this prisoner; and because the private prosecutor was a member of the Senate, it is said to be all by his instigation! Does not everybody see that this session was absolutely necessary? Does not everybody know that in a capital trial the whole court must be present, and that the whole court can sit but one week in a year in this county?

Under the ordinary sessions these prisoners could not have been tried in three years. The act was passed from public necessity and was drawn by the late chief justice for the accommodation of his court. Who supposes that the extra session ought not to have been appointed, when the ordinary sessions in three years could not have dispensed justice in these cases?

This prosecution of the prisoner as a principal is said to have been an afterthought. When Richard Crowninshield died, neither had been indicted; and it is asserted without the slightest authority, that the idea of prosecuting the prisoner as a principal never arose till after the death of Richard. The prosecuting officers had not then determined on the course to be pursued.

The counsel say they are concerned for the law rather than for the defendant. The law is in no danger except from their interpretation. I rather rely on you, gentlemen, and on the court; and I doubt not that under your administration it will be fully and faithfully maintained. You are told, in a tone of admonition, that your verdict will be a precedent. I hope it will be a precedent; a precedent to show that a jury can justly and truly discharge their duty to the prisoner and firmly uphold the law.

It is truly said that the law is not established so much to punish the guilty as to protect the innocent. But who are the innocent? Who are they whom the law is framed to protect? They are the honest, the industrious, the peaceful, the innocent sleepers in their own houses. The law is established, that those who live quietly in the fear of God by day, may sleep quietly in His peace by night.

The gentleman can think of none who are innocent but those who are placed at that bar, yet unconvicted. And who are the guilty for whom the law provides its punishment? They are those who break in upon the silence of repose, and the helplessness of repose, to murder the innocent sleeper in his bed. It is of them that the law says, they are worthy of an ignominious death and must suffer its penalty.

You, gentlemen, are sworn to administer that law. You must do it without fear. If you, through mere unreasonable doubts and scruples, let the guilty escape, the law fails of its purpose; public security ceases, and men must rely on their own strength for their own safety. The jury must entertain no cavils, no studied evasions, no contrivances how they may suffer the escape of a prisoner; they must discharge their duty in saying whether he is guilty or innocent, and leave the consequences to another department of the government.

You will consider, gentlemen, how much consideration is due to the complaints about the manner in which the perpetrators of this murder have been [brought to the bar]; whether it makes any difference to the guilty, by what means his crime is brought to light; whether it is any cause of injury to be complained of, that he is found out.

The counsel, taking a lofty flight of sentimentality, complain that even Palmer has betrayed his bosom friends! They complain that Palmer has been seduced; and they thought it a great hardship that he had been produced as a witness for the government. But why don't they meet the case? If a fact is out—no matter whence it comes—why don't they meet that fact? Do they mean to deny that Captain White is dead? I thought it would come to that.

Is there proof of a conspiracy? If there is, it does not remove that fact that Palmer was knowing to it. It don't [sic] prove it, to be sure, but it does not remove it; and when established as a fact, the testimony bears with great cogency upon the case. Instead of stating that the thing is proved by such a witness, why not deny the fact? Why not assert that there was no conspiracy, instead of carping at the mode of proof? Over this point the counsel continually hover; they neither fly away nor light; they neither deny nor assent.

But they will find it necessary to come to somewhat closer quarters. The inquiry is into the truth of the fact. Instead of complaining that the prisoner had been detected by such means as Providence allotted, would it not have been better if they had asserted his entire innocence and denied all his guilt? Instead of complaining that he had been proved to be in Brown Street, would it not have been better to have shown that he was somewhere else?

This style of complaint has been carried to great extent against disinterested and respectable witnesses, as if it were as bad to have had a hand in the detection of the murderers as in the perpetration of the crime; as if to have known anything of the murderers were an act of the most flagitious and exquisite wickedness.

And it would seem that because the crime has been detected by extraordinary exertions, the man accused ought to be mildly and calmly judged.

Much has been said about prejudice against the prisoner. There is nobody that I know of who has a particle of wish to his injury further than may and ought to fall in the just dispensation of the laws. Nobody among those who conduct the prosecution feels a particle of displeasure with Frank Knapp; there is nothing of seeking revenge, nothing of persecution against him.

It is not to be endured that honest indignation should be turned from the criminal against those who have detected him. The community are unfit to live under protecting laws if, in a case like this, they would not rise unitedly to see them enforced. The members of the [Committee of Vigilance] were actuated by a desire to detect the murderers, not to fix the crime on A, B, C, or D. Every man felt an honest burst of feeling against the criminals; he would cease to be a man who did not; but no man labored to turn prejudice against the prisoner.

The public feeling of the community is misrepresented; it is represented as if it pursued its zeal for blood to the head of the defendant. This is entirely wrong; the only zeal felt on this occasion is that men may not be exposed to murder in their own houses unarmed, and that they should be quiet in the pursuit of their daily toil. And that feeling will exist to the end, until the law in its just interpretation has visited the perpetrators of this atrocious crime, whoever or wherever they may be.

I doubt not you will administer the law truly, as far as you have anything to do with it. The consequence of your verdict is not for your consideration. It is for you to say, in your own department, whether the prisoner is or is not guilty; and if it should appear, as has been represented, that on account of his youth or other circumstances, he may be deserving of a pardon, it is for others to say so.

In order to see what the evidence in the case does prove, we must ask if Captain White was murdered in pursuance of a conspiracy. This is the first question since the prisoner is charged in the indictment in three ways as a principal. He is charged as a principal; first, as having done the deed with his own hand; second, as an aider and abettor to Richard Crowninshield who did the deed; and third, as an aider and abettor to some person unknown.

You have already heard of two remarkable circumstances attending this trial. One is that Richard Crowninshield, generally supposed to have inflicted the blow, has gone, by the act of his own hand, from the tribunals of this world to the tribunals of eternal justice in another. He is called the perpetrator to distinguish him from those who were otherwise aiding to commit the murder, who are called principals in the second degree.

Another is that the main instigator of the murder, he at whose hiring and procurement and for whose benefit it was committed, who has made a confession of all the circumstances attending its commission, is not now a witness; he has refused to testify and, with the other accomplice, is yet within the reach of the law.

Your decision may, therefore, affect more than the life of the defendant. If he is not convicted as a principal, neither he nor anyone else can be convicted of any participation in the crime; such is the nature of the law, and the result will be on the community. This has no tendency to prove his guilt, and it is only mentioned to show you the full consequences of your verdict. The fate of the whole depends upon this verdict; and it is for you, gentlemen, to determine whether this and the other prisoners are guilty and should suffer according to the law.

Now let us begin at the beginning; let us see what we know, independent of any evidence—of any direct evidence. This case depends mainly upon circumstantial evidence; secret crimes ever do; midnight assassins take no witnesses. There are very important circumstances in the case wholly independent of any direct testimony. This has been called, by the learned counsel for the defense, circumstantial stuff. It is stuff; but not such stuff as dreams are made of! It shall be my business to weave this stuff into a web and see what may be made of it.

The circumstance of Palmer's letter from Belfast is more than stuff; the circumstance that Joseph Knapp Jr. wrote certain letters is more than stuff; the fact that the housekeeper was away is another circumstance and a piece of that same stuff; the facts that the doors were unbolted, the windows unbarred and opened, leading the way to the bed of the sleeping victim—this is stuff!

No, gentlemen, this is weighty matter; conclusive matter which comes, if unexplained, with terrible force against the prisoner at the bar. Let me invite your attention to those facts that tend to show how the murder was perpetrated . . .

The appearance of things the morning after the murder showed that it was the work of a conspiracy. No stranger had done the deed; no one unacquainted with the house and the habits of its inmates. This was not an act of violence in the open streets nor in the house; somebody within had opened for those without;

somebody who knew, had described to the murderer the situation in which all would be found; somebody who had access to the house had prepared it and made ready for the work.

This shows a band of men in execution of their purpose. And when the murder was perpetrated, the house was not alarmed. The assassin entered without fear or alarm; there was no riot, no violence. He found the way made plain before him. He found the window shutters unbarred and opened, the window fastening unscrewed, the sash thrown up. There was a lock on the chamber door but the key had been taken out and secreted, so that by no accident contrary to his usual custom could the victim preserve his life.

The path of the murderer to and from the house was marked. The plank by which he ascended the window was brought from the garden gate, and his retreat was shown by drops of blood and footprints in the earth. That is evidence of conspiracy, combination, and preconcerted arrangement. The house must have been prepared by somebody within to afford easy access to those without, or somebody must have gone to the perpetration blindly and in the face of difficulty and detection. These are circumstances independent of all direct evidence. Here was evidence of a prepared, concerted, conspired murder.

Can it be doubted who made this preparation? Can it be supposed that Richard Crowninshield went groping in ignorance, in the dark, to find his victim? Can it be doubted that this originated with Joseph Knapp Jr.? And when it is proved that the conspiracy was formed by the two Knapps and the two Crowninshields; when it is proved that the deed was to be done in the absence of the housekeeper; when it is proved that some of the conspirators were lurking suspiciously about the place at the time of the murder; when it is proved that Joseph Knapp Jr. was in the house in the afternoon before the murder, can it be doubted that they, or some of them, have been the murderers of Captain White?

The posture of the family affairs at the time: the old gentleman reputed to be rich, with no children nor any wife; no heirs but nephews and nieces, the wife of Joseph Knapp being the daughter of his niece and housekeeper and the granddaughter of his sister. Mr. Stephen White was the son of a brother of the deceased and, it was generally supposed, would be the principal inheritor of his property by a will. It became an object to the other heirs at law to destroy the will; for according to a very prevailing though erroneous belief, the property would, if Captain White died intestate, descend equally to the children of the sister and the children of the brother.

In this situation the murder was discovered. It alarmed everybody. Suspicion turned upon everybody interested in the death of Captain White. The enormity of the crime raised suspicions too horrible for utterance. If the object had been to steal the will, it did not succeed, for the will was found, a will that was good and complete. Suspicion turned at once from the heirs at law to the heirs under the will, as the only persons interested in the immediate death of the testator.

Here the counsel carry their argument to the extent of ridicule. There is evidence to show that the Knapps tried to fix the suspicion upon Stephen White; but the counsel insist that the Knapps found suspicion turned upon him and only tried to strengthen it. They say the Knapps are not very criminal in this matter because they only strengthen, they did not originate the suspicion.

Good God! What do the counsel mean? Did they not originate the suspicion when they killed Captain White? It is a good apology, indeed, that they only fomented a flagitious excitement which they had caused! It was not quite so wicked to write the letters—as if there had been no previous suspicions! Who made the original cause of suspicion but the murderers with their own poniards?

Gentlemen, if we are not right now regarding the perpetrators of this murder, then there is not the least thing known about it. The community is as ignorant as at the hour of its committal. The counsel thought they might admit that Richard Crowninshield was the perpetrator; and yet they say "let it be proved."

But the question is: Why did Richard Crowninshield kill Captain White? He did not murder without motive, without inducement. If he slew, who paid? He was not a gratuitous assassin. There is no going piecemeal in this case; you must come to the opinion that here is the truth, the whole truth, or that nothing whatever is known of the murderers. You must believe that you know the whole extent of the conspiracy. Let us inquire: What is the conspiracy?

Joseph Knapp Jr. was the discoverer and destroyer of a certain will; and if he could prevent Captain White from making another will, he would have a larger share of his fortune. He hired a ruffian; gave him aid to get into the house; the murder was committed. The two Knapps and the two Crowninshields were implicated by undeniable proof. Joseph Knapp had confessed but refused to testify. Of those four, one—the perpetrator—has gone to another account, and the prisoner is indicted as his aider and abettor in the commission of the fact.

This conspiracy began as far back, at least, as January. . . . Joseph [told a friend on the 7th of January] that Captain White had made a will and that Stephen White and Mr. Treadwell were executors. When asked how he knew, he said, "Black and white don't lie." He said it gave the bulk of the fortune to Stephen White, and when asked how he knew it, he repeated, "Black and white don't lie." When asked if the will was not kept in a trunk he said, "Yes, but there is such a thing as having two keys to the same lock." Here is evidence from J. Knapp's own intimations, that he had seen and could see the will whenever he chose. . . .

But the most important part of the evidence of the conspiracy is told by Palmer. He begins on the second of April. Palmer is said to be a totally incredible witness. I shall not attempt to purify his reputation or uphold his character either as a man or as a witness. He is before you, bad enough, gentlemen—as bad perhaps as they represent him—I am willing to leave it so. The prisoner's counsel say, and say truly, that such a witness is not to be believed without strong confirmation; but if his story is confirmed, you must believe him and must act accordingly. If he were an accomplice turned State's witness—a very discreditable situation—and standing supported in some parts of his testimony, you might believe him for the whole. If his story is credible and consistent, and wholly unsupported except by testimony to other circumstances you may even then believe him.

Much depends on circumstances, as to the credibility of such a witness. As to the complaints that the government have brought foul testimony, it is only to be said that the government do not select their own witnesses; they take such as have been chosen and furnished by the criminals. The defendant's counsel say Palmer was the bosom friend of some of the conspirators—surely it is not hard to judge a man by the testimony of his bosom friend!

The testimony of Palmer is competent for the government to use; it is before you and must pass for what it is worth. He stands, of all the witnesses in this case, the most entirely absolved from contradiction, either in his own story or by the testimony of other witnesses. His story is throughout consistent and credible; no one has attempted to detect any, the slightest, inconsistency in its details. Every part of his testimony to the conspiracy has been completely supported; they have not attempted with success to impeach him even in unimportant particulars. . . . So far as he is consistent with himself and credible in connection with the testimony of others, and so far as he is directly supported by others, so far he may be believed. The question is: Is his story true?

We did not make the witness; he is such as we found him, such as the conspirators had chosen to confide their secrets with; if he sees fit to reveal what he *learned in their company, he is fairly used for that purpose and is fairly believed so far as the jury see fit to believe him. Palmer's testimony is important in fixing the conspiracy if it is believed.*

He testifies to a ride of Frank Knapp to Danvers on Friday the second of April. At this time the project had been long in contemplation; this was not the first visit of Frank to the Crowninshields. Allen has testified to one in March. . . . He then goes on to state the conversations which took place between him and the Crowninshields after Frank came away. They told him of the proposal of the Knapps and offered him a partnership in the crime and the profit. . . .

Above all, the truth of Palmer's story is made manifest in the letter from Belfast. That letter is a most important piece of corroborative testimony. It was not written after the facts were known; it was not an afterthought got up to match the occasion. It was written long before the Knapps were suspected and bears internal and conclusive evidence of knowledge on the part of the writer. The letter begins, "You may be surprised to be addressed by a perfect stranger." And he was a stranger. There is no evidence that he had ever seen Joseph Knapp Jr.; and Frank had not seen him, for at the time of the visit he was secreted at the Crowninshields'. [The letter] then makes a demand of money—send me money. It is a threatening letter, and afterwards says, "I know your plans; I know your brother Frank and the business he was upon on the second of April."

How could Palmer, in Belfast, before the Knapps were suspected, have fixed upon the second of April if he had not possessed knowledge of what transpired on that day? Every line of it bears confirmation to the truth of his story.

Take [all this into account] and see if you doubt for a moment that Captain White was murdered according to the plan of a conspiracy; see if you doubt that these four were the conspirators.

Do you doubt Leighton? In manner he is a very bad witness; in some circumstances of his testimony he is a bad witness; all is against him in appearance; but do you think, notwithstanding all this, that he tells the truth? If you do, his testimony has a momentous weight in this case. It is not necessary, but it is of great importance. He tells you of a conversation which he says he overheard between the brothers Knapp at Wenham. . . . There is no doubt about the meaning of this [conversation]; it is all clear. If you believe the witness, you cannot doubt that "Dick" meant Richard Crowninshield, and "the old man" Captain White.

But do you believe him, gentlemen? He seems to have been dragged here a reluctant witness, unwilling to testify against his employers. The day after the murder he said that he knew something, but checked himself, thinking he might go too far. He tells you that he was fearful for his own safety if the prisoner should escape; what reason he had to fear, you will judge. Certain it is, from undoubted testimony, that he had felt the dagger's point of the murderer of Captain White. If his story be true, he had ample cause for fear.

But it is said to be extraordinary that the conversation should happen there, at the end of a lane, just in hearing of the witness. Gentlemen, it is extraordinary that such a conversation should happen anywhere. The time and place of all such facts seem extraordinary when they are made known. It is no more wonderful that such a conversation should happen where it did, than that it should happen anywhere else; and if the witness happened to be within hearing, it is not extraordinary that he should hear it. There is nothing incredible in the circumstance if you believe the witness.

It is said that it is dangerous to take a part of a conversation, when that part might be qualified by what preceded or followed it. You will perceive that this conversation might either stand alone or be connected with previous conversations on the same subject, and yet be wholly incapable of qualification. It is the same whether as a whole or a part and cannot be misunderstood. A different accent, which the witness could not give, would make it seem either distinct or connected with something else; but nothing could change its meaning.

The fact is the whole current of testimony bears with overwhelming force against the prisoner. When Palmer said that Dick was to kill the old man, and that Joseph Knapp Jr. was to give him a thousand dollars for it, a hundred facts disclosed themselves, before unnoticed. The story of Leighton is altogether true or altogether false; and you will consider if he had power to put together such a conversation even if he had the will. It is simple, clear, distinct. Nothing is so plain as truth; there is nothing that bears with so much cogency as truth, nothing that exposes itself like truth. It is not pretended that the story was made for him, and there is nothing so difficult in believing its truth, as in believing that he was its fabricator.

Let us now look at the acts of the parties themselves. Palmer's letter was directed to Joseph Knapp instead of Joseph Knapp Jr. By the way, that mistake about the name, though a slight circumstance, goes to establish the credibility of the witness. This letter, thus directed, fell into the hands of the father. Now let us keep a steady eye on this piece of circumstantial stuff and see what we can weave it into.

This letter fell into the hands of the father. He was utterly ignorant of its import and carried it to his sons at Wenham. . . . They had a hearty laugh about it. How could anyone on the Penobscot River know their plans and doings? They advised their father, unsuspecting man, to carry it to the committee of vigilance. He did so, and all hope of concealment for the guilty was lost.

Between the time of laughing at the letter on Saturday and Sunday morning, an occurrence took place to change the complexion of the letter. One of the Knapps had seen one of the Crowninshields and learned that one Palmer who had gone to the eastward did possess the knowledge of their guilty secrets. Then all was terror and alarm; and on the day following, Sunday, they wrote the letters to Stephen White and the committee of vigilance.

The letter to the committee, accusing Stephen White, was written by Joseph Knapp Jr., most certainly with the knowledge and concurrence of Frank. Was ever known a piece of more gratuitous, unqualified, inexcusable villainy? Merely to explain the apparent mysteries of that letter from Palmer, they engendered the basest suspicions of a man who, if they were innocent, they had no reason to believe guilty; and who, if they were guilty, they most certainly knew to be innocent. . . .

Now mark the destiny of crime! Every page, every word, every letter of that criminal attempt to conceal crime, is brilliant with the light of disclosure. Joseph Knapp Jr. wrote that letter to turn suspicion from himself and fix it upon Stephen White, and every line of it preaches that he was the murderer. If it were not rather the direction of an all-wise Providence, I should say it was the silliest piece of folly that ever possessed the head of a fugitive from justice.

Crime is ever obliged to resort to such subterfuges; it trembles in the broad light; its vision is distorted; it needs no springing tempest to shake it into disclosure; its evil genius adheres to it and leads it wherever it will. Who, for a moment, beholds this letter and doubts his guilt? The constitution of nature is made to inform against him. There is no corner dark enough to conceal him; there is no highway, no turnpike smooth enough and broad enough for him to bear along his guilty load. All occasions inform against him. Every step proclaims his secret to every passenger. His own acts come out to fix his guilt. In striving to turn away suspicion, the murderer writes his own confession; he declares the truth to every eye. In striving to place himself in the attitude of concealment, he bares his black bosom to the detestation of mankind. To do away with the effect of Palmer's letter, signed Grant, he writes his own condemnation, and affixes to it the name of Grant.

Do you doubt this? Who could have written that letter to the committee, signed Grant, but one who had seen this from Belfast, signed Grant? And who had seen this but the Knapps? The moment that letter was read, the whole truth was discovered.

Gentlemen, I shall detain you no longer. I think you can have no more doubt that the two Crowninshields and the two Knapps were conspirators for the murder of Joseph White. I think you cannot doubt that the murder was committed between ten and eleven on Tuesday evening of the sixth of April; that it was perpetrated by the hand of Richard Crowninshield; that somebody was in Brown Street to aid in the murder of Captain White; that that person must have been the defendant. The other two are accounted for; Joseph Knapp was at Wenham, George Crowninshield was with his companions at Salem.

Where were the defendant and Richard Crowninshield? I think you will believe the confessions; and if you do, there is no getting rid of the inference that arises. The confessions prove beyond all doubt that he was there. He could not have gone there to expose himself for any idle motive of curiosity. He went there to abet the murderer, by appointment and agreement. He did abet; he did follow his agreement; and thus has exposed himself to public justice.

Gentlemen, of all the evidence you are the judges. The law will be stated by the court, and you will feel bound by their decisions. No doubt you will judge the defendant fairly and reasonably, according to the evidence and the law. If any reasonable doubt of his guilt should arise, you will acquit him. You will judge individually and collectively. His life is in your hands. All our trust is that you will remember that, while you owe him a duty, you also owe the public a duty. There cannot be any more important truth to be disclosed relative to this crime; you cannot doubt that you now know all that will hereafter be known. You cannot fear that anything will arise to make you regret your verdict, neither can you fear that any mistake in testimony remains to be rectified.

No one rushed in to give proof of his guilt. The witnesses have been cautious and considerate. If he is convicted, and not pardoned, he must suffer death. You have sworn to administer the law, and you cannot take into your hands the prerogative of mercy. If his youth is in his favor, the power to pardon rests with the executive government of the commonwealth. Your duty is, if you find him guilty, to say so. I have no doubt your hearts will incline you to mercy; but you *will remember that you stand here for your country, and you cannot shut out the weight of testimony from your minds. The demand of public justice is—and it is ordained by Providence as well as by human law—that if a man is charged with the crime of murder, and found to be guilty, his life shall be forfeit to the community.*

We would all judge in mercy, but we must move steadily in the light of truth and justice. Doubts may arise in your deliberations, but you must not make them merely to let the prisoner escape. Very little can it matter to him, or to the rest of the unhappy men who are charged with participation in his crime, that the sentence of the law should be avoided. Poorly is he supported, poorly are they all supported, if the mere effort is to escape the penalty which separates them from the tribunal of another world. It is as if one should strive to avoid wetting his feet with the dewdrops of the morning, who had arrived at the brink of the whole ocean.

The kindest wish we can have for him is that he may have a devout sense that his only hope depends on the goodness of Almighty God, and that his prayers may reach the throne of Divine Mercy. The kindest wish we may have for you, gentlemen, is to wish that you may, by the assistance of God, be enabled to do your duty to the prisoner at the bar firmly and consistently; that you may do justice to him, and maintain the public law and the safety of the community.

————————

Fifty-three years later, in a biography that was otherwise highly critical of Webster, Henry Cabot Lodge would praise the summation in the highest terms:

> The opening of the speech comprising the account of the murder and the analysis of the workings of a mind seared with the remembrance of a horrid crime, must be placed among the very finest masterpieces of modern oratory. . . . The whole exhibits the highest imaginative excellence and displays the possession of an extraordinary dramatic force such as Mr. Webster rarely exercised. . . . I have studied this famous exordium with great care, and I have sought diligently in the works of all the great modern orators, and of some of the ancients as well, for similar passages of higher merit. My quest has been in vain. . . . [This speech] has never been surpassed in dramatic force by any speaker,

whether in debate or before a jury. . . . Before a jury Webster fell
behind [Thomas] Erskine as he did behind Choate, although neither
of them ever produced anything at all comparable to the speech on
the White murder. . . . Take him for all in all, he was not only the
greatest orator this country has ever known, but in the history of
eloquence his name will stand with those of Demosthenes and Cicero,
of Chatham and Burke.[3]

24 | THE EXECUTION OF FRANK KNAPP

> "How can human law inculcate benevolence and love, while it persists in setting up the *gallows* as its chief symbol?"
> —Nathaniel Hawthorne, "Earth's Holocaust" (1844)

IT TOOK THE JURY ONLY FIVE HOURS TO CONVICT, with the judges quickly thereafter sentencing Frank to death. Hawthorne was not happy with this. He saw Joe as the prime beneficiary of the conspiracy, and Frank as something of a dupe and tagalong. So too did Robert Rantoul Jr. The latter would maintain that the entirely circumstantial case against Frank had been long on oratory and short on actual evidence. Webster, he said, had used drama to obscure the absence of proven facts. But these points, although in larger measure valid, were also academic. The fact of Frank's intimate role in the crime simply could not be denied.

On September 1, Hawthorne wrote a cousin in Ohio (formerly a native of Salem), to relay the latest in the White murder case. Hawthorne said Salem had grown "rather more quiet" than it had been since the murder and Frank's trial, but he fully expected the excitement to pick up again as Frank's execution—scheduled for the twenty-eighth—approached, and when Joe Jr. and Crowninshield would be put on trial in November. According to Hawthorne, Frank Knapp's conviction and sentence seemed to have had "little or no impression on his mind." It was reported that the night after his sentence, the condemned man joked with his guards that he would rather be hung than remain a year in prison.

"He declares that he will not go to the gallows, unless two women go with him. Who these women are must be left to conjecture. Perhaps you have not heard that many people suspect Mrs. Beckford and her daughter, Joe Knapp's wife." Joe Knapp Sr., Hawthorne reported was "entirely broken . . . and almost crazy. . . . He and his Phippen have injured their reputation for truth, by the testimony they gave at the trial; but I have little doubt that they believed what they said; and if not, they had as much excuse as there can possibly be for perjury." There was, said Hawthorne, a general lack of pity for all members of the Knapp family. Everyone in town was eager to see justice done on the gallows. "For my part, I wish Joe to be punished, but I should not be very sorry if Frank were to escape." Word had it that Joe Jr. was totally dissipated. "He contrives to obtain spirituous liquors in his cell and is in a state of intoxication almost all the time. . . . I do not wonder that he feels unpleasantly, for he can have no hope of mercy, and it is absolutely certain that he will not be alive at the end of six months from this time."[1]

An unsigned item in the *Salem Gazette* of Tuesday, September 28—the day of Frank's execution—smacks of Hawthornian style:

The dread sentence of Death will this morning between the hours of 8 and 10 o'clock be executed on John Francis Knapp, for the Murder of Capt. White. The place of execution is at the north end of the Gaol [*sic*] and within the prison yard. The gallows was erected there yesterday afternoon under the direction of the Sheriff. The reflection that a fellow human being, now in perfect health, in the vigor of youth, not twenty-one years of age, will die within two short hours, and that his awful and ignominious doom is fixed and inevitable, fills the minds of all with awe and gloom. In most other cases there is some hope of life, however great the jeopardy or however imminent the danger of Death; the mariner floating on a fragment of a wreck, and the soldier mounting the deadly breach with the forlorn hope, are each cheered with the secret hope that their lives may be saved, though thousands of their comrades must perish around them. Knapp has no such chance of safety—no hope of escape—before the sun, that now shines, shall reach its meridian, his eyes will be sealed in death.

The two brothers, J. F. Knapp and J. J. Knapp Jr., had an interview on Saturday evening. They both requested it of the gaolor [*sic*] and were indulged; he conducted Joseph from his cell (in the third story of the prison) to the condemned cell of Frank on the lower floor. They spent some time together. It was the first time they had met since they were carried into Court together to be arraigned, about two months ago. Frank was calm and firm; Joseph is wasted and feeble in body and appears miserable and broken down in body and spirit, having little appetite for food, enjoying little rest, and with difficulty uttering articulate words. To the question from Joseph, whether Frank was really as well as he appeared to be, Frank replied, "Yes, I can sleep as sound now on the soft side of a plank as I ever could." Yesterday [Monday] they were indulged with another sad interview—their last in this world! They bade each other a last Farewell, under such circumstances, as must give poignancy to pain and sharpness to agony.[2]

Hawthorne attended the execution. Several thousand spectators gathered to witness the event. Frank Knapp had reportedly conversed freely with his jailers and a few visiting friends during the night. Regarding his coming fate, he expressed the hope that he might be able to meet it with firmness. He had dressed himself with great care in the early morning hours, as if preparing for any other type of social occasion. His wardrobe consisted of a dark green frock coat, white vest, dark pantaloons, and boots. After bidding a final farewell to his father and several siblings who'd gathered in his cell, at about 8:30 AM Frank allowed himself to be led out into the prison yard, accompanied by Joseph E. Spraque, Esq., high sheriff of Essex County, and four deputies. A clergyman, Salem's Episcopal rector Alexander Griswold, also walked by Frank's side, Bible in hand. An item in the *Salem Gazette* the following day reported the rest:

> He walked with a firm step, ascended the scaffold without assistance, and stood firmly, unsupported, while his feet were tied and the halter was placed about his neck. He did all that was possible in his confined state to facilitate the operations of the officer in laying his neck bare, and at that moment took from his own bosom a white pocket handkerchief, which continued in his hand till taken from it after death, his last movement in life being a spasmodic contraction of his fingers upon the handkerchief.[3]

From the high perch of the scaffold, Frank would have been able to see not only those assembled in the prison yard to witness his demise but also the estimated ten thousand men, women, and children gathered beyond the prison wall in honor of the occasion. He made no dying statement. When asked if he was ready, he simply nodded his head and said, "Yes." Just before the hangman's cap was draped over his eyes, he took one last look around and nodded to the crowd.

Then, promptly, Frank was falling. He died quickly, his neck broken, but was left to hang for an hour before finally being cut down and placed on a table, where Joe Jr. was allowed to come and see his brother in death.

Not long after, the shrouded Frank was taken next door to the Howard Street Cemetery and placed in a grave that to this day remains unmarked, but which one hopes is appropriately distant from the vault of Captain Joseph White. One imagines Joe Jr. watching out from his cell window as his brother went down into the earth for his eternal rest.

A small clipping from an unknown publication, evidently published not long after Frank's execution, sits with other clippings in a box of the Phillips Library of the Peabody Essex Museum:

> A writer in the *Newburyport Herald*, who is opposed to public executions, and pretends to have witnessed the recent one in this town, [was] evidently not present. . . . So far from being a scene of tumult, disorder and drunkenness, the melancholy transaction was strongly marked by the greatest decorum and solemnity. The incidents of the murder have developed enough to be deplored—without resorting to exaggeration and untruth. It is generally conceded, that executions conducted in as private a manner as possible would be more salutary.[4]

The entire scene of the execution had taken place well away from the legendary Gallows Hill of olden times. There was no superstition here at the foot of this scaffold. And there would be no residual shame for the prosecutors or spectators, no echoes of someone falsely accused and wantonly slain—nothing but the most basic justice, a murderer being murdered. The executioner did not even bother to hide his face. Some members of the crowd of watchers had come from as far away as Maine and Cape Cod—all to see Frank Knapp launched into eternity.

25 | EMPHATICALLY ENCOMPASSED BY A SEA OF BLOOD

"Suspicion always haunts the guilty mind; the thief
doth fear each bush an officer."
—Shakespeare, *Henry VI*

JOE JR.'S TRIAL BEGAN ON NOVEMBER 9. The prisoner, now charged
as a second-degree principal, came to the bar looking just as dissipated, dispir-
ited, and unwell as he had earlier. He seemed skeletal, and spoke only in a
hushed voice, with eyes cast down—unwilling to meet the gaze of the judges,
the attorneys, the jury, or the crowd that filled the overflowing courtroom. He
as well appeared disheveled, his dress random and uncaring, as if it just did
not matter. And it probably didn't. He was, to use a modern phrase, already
a dead man walking, with no hope of any form of salvation before him.

Webster had now returned and was ready to make efficient work of
the business of gaining conviction. Still, the proceeding would take three
days for testimony, even though the result seemed a foregone conclusion.
All the key facts—so far as were known—had been floating about in the
air since even before Frank's first trial, and for the most part had been solemnly proved and confirmed in the subsequent court proceedings. Frank had
already swung from a rope. Cold logic said that to exonerate Joe Jr. at this
point would be to put on record that an innocent man had most likely been
hung. Without Joe Jr.'s conviction, there would be no equilibrium. Indeed,
most—like Hawthorne—thought Joe Jr. far more guilty than Frank, given
their respective roles.

The same judges of the Supreme Judicial Court presided—Putnam, Wilde, and Morton. Once a jury was impaneled, the same script of opening statements, witnesses, arguments, and testimonies played out now as before, but in a much-condensed version. One major difference was that this time Joe Jr.'s entire written confession was allowed to be read in court. The attorney general himself read it—reportedly with great drama. On Wednesday morning, when Franklin Dexter gave his three-and-a-half-hour summation, he argued not so much on the facts as on the righteousness of Christian forgiveness, and for leniency—for charity to be given a family that had already suffered too much and had already sacrificed a life for a life. Did not the Bible speak of an eye for an eye? Indeed, had not two men already gone to uncertain Divine justice in payment for the single death of Captain Joseph White?

Webster, of course, saw things differently. Mercy, he said, was to be had in another realm, if at all. Joe Jr., as the father and instigator of the unholy enterprise, was "emphatically encompassed by a sea of blood." After all, he was not only responsible for the murder of Captain White but likewise ultimately responsible for the deaths of Dick Crowninshield and Frank Knapp. "In whatever light we view this murder, we can find no bright spot about it: all is dark, dismal, and bloody."[1]

The jury was quick to convict, returning with their verdict on Saturday morning, the thirteenth, and Judge Putnam quick to pronounce the sentence of death, setting the date for New Year's Eve. But first he had some remarks.

> Before we perform the duty of sentencing, we are desirous of preparing your mind, so far as it is in our power, to meet the tremendous doom which awaits you. It is not to aggravate your sufferings that we address you, for your present wretchedness excites feelings of compassion and not indignation. But we hope that by presenting to your review some of the horrible circumstances which have attended the crime for which you are to suffer, we may lead you to sincere contrition and repentance.
>
> The aged sufferer was a near relative of your wife. She was nurtured at his house and loved and cherished by him as a child. You were admitted to partake of his hospitality—you availed yourself of the opportunities to visit at the house of the deceased, to prepare the way for the entrance of your hired assassin to the bed chamber of the

victim. You were for months deliberately occupied in devising ways and means of his death. . . .

The execution of this awful conspiracy spread dismay, anxiety, and distrust throughout the country. Week after week passed away, and left the dreadful deed veiled in mystery. At length a discovery was made by means almost as extraordinary as was the crime. If such events had been set forth in a work of fiction, they would have been considered as too absurd and unnatural for public endurance. The story would have been treated a libel upon Man.[2]

George Crowninshield's brief trial for aiding and abetting took place on the afternoon of Friday, the twelfth, after Joe Jr.'s jury had retired to consider their verdict. The same judges sat on high, although the attorneys had changed. On the opposite side of the room, Solicitor General Davis and Attorney General Morton stood alone for the prosecution. Daniel Webster's fee from Stephen White had been meant to finance the sending of the Knapps to their deaths, not Crowninshield. Obviously, Webster's absence was a good thing for George, but so too was that a man equally as eloquent and nearly as prominent, not to mention expensive, was leading his defense team: Samuel Hoar.

The fifty-two-year-old Hoar brought a great deal of prestige to the defense table, where he was joined by junior Salem attorney Ebenezer Shillaber. Hoar had graduated from Harvard in 1802 and was married to Sarah Sherman, the daughter of Connecticut's Roger Sherman, who was a signer of both the Declaration of Independence and the Constitution. Hoar was a delegate to the Massachusetts Constitutional Convention of 1820, was elected to the American Academy of Arts and Sciences in 1824, and served the first of three terms in the Massachusetts State Senate in 1826 (a body to which he would return in 1832 and 1833). Hoar was known for his dismissive nature with regard to anything or anyone he thought absurd or stupid. In short, he did not suffer fools, either in court or out.

Both Hoar and his client were seen to smirk as Palmer—now prim and pious and, of course, the state's primary witness against George—told his story of being propositioned by George and Dick to become their accomplice in the murder. Crowninshield and Hoar appeared to be equally unconcerned as various other witnesses emerged with tales of sighting George here and there about Salem—on this street or that street, at one time or another—during the night in question. In George's defense, several people testified to receiving franc coins from him well before the murder, and before the time Joe Jr. was alleged to have given some of the coinage to Dick. Most important, a prostitute named Mary Weller, with whom George had spent the entire night of the murder, testified that he was with her from half past ten.

Hoar scoffed at rather than challenged the prosecution's marshaling of its case, telling the judges that it would be "absurd" for him to even bother "to defend a case made out like this. There is not a tittle of evidence to criminate the prisoner, except that given by Palmer, which is altogether unworthy of credit." Hoar insisted that it was not a case "weakly made out" but rather a case "not made out at all. Such a case ought not to be suffered to go to a jury."[3]

In his brief summation delivered on the morning of Monday, the fifteenth, Hoar continued to be absolutely disdainful of the charges against his client.

> Gentlemen, this case is an important one, and demands our deliberate consideration; but I can hardly speak with the gravity on the evidence that has been introduced, that the occasion requires.
>
> The government say George was in Salem on the night of the murder, but they take care not to call the witnesses who could describe his actions that night.
>
> But take Palmer's evidence in the strongest light, it does not make out the offense with which the prisoner is charged. . . . Nothing has appeared to show that he is guilty of this crime, that he took any part or lot in the matter.
>
> Taking for truth what Leighton says—is that anything against George Crowninshield? "When did you see Dick?" Not George. Would not something have been said of George had he been in the plot? Taking both Leighton and Palmer's testimony to be entirely true, my client is safe.
>
> I have taken too much time on this worthless man. Palmer. An insect, the smallest fly is not worthy of much regard; but if it forces itself into your eye, you must attend to it. I should have no confidence in our boasted trial by jury, if I thought it possible for a jury to convict a man on such evidence.[4]

After the charge, the jury took but an hour and a half to return a verdict of not guilty. A burst of applause indicated the sentiments of many of the onlookers before being sternly shut down by Judge Putnam. Neither Hoar nor Crowninshield seemed surprised. Nor did they seem relieved. They instead seemed simply pleased and satisfied with what they'd all along thought an inevitable result, and with themselves. Their manner implied that a nuisance of a matter had been dispensed with, and nothing more.

When the disappointed Morton offered up a charge of misprision of felony (concealment of one's knowledge of a felony), Hoar requested that the trial be taken up immediately: there and then. The court, however, thought a different jury should hear that case, which the judges now scheduled for November 25.

George's father was allowed to post a $500 bail, which the prosecutors thought far too small. Many believed that so low a bail amount (from the perspective of the Crowninshields) would permit George to flee prosecution. The low amount of George's bail "excited a great astonishment among many people, [and seemed designed] for the very purpose of enabling him to clear the coast."[5] But as Hoar undoubtedly assured his client, there was simply no need to flee. Without any living witness besides Palmer to testify as to what George knew and when he knew it, the government once again had no case at all.

Hoar was right to be confident. The trial lasted less than a day. The jury took just thirty minutes to return a verdict: innocent. George walked away a free man. His father retrieved the $500.

Through it all, George had seemed nothing less than amused. So far as the Crowninshields were concerned, the drama of the White murder had come to an end. Although the stigma of the crime would follow George for the rest of his long life, he'd never show any evidence of particularly giving a damn. He proceeded with his head held high.

26 | SHE MUST BE THE VERY DEVIL

> "No man, for any considerable period, can wear one
> face to himself and another to the multitude, with-
> out finally getting bewildered as to which may be
> the true."
>
> —Nathaniel Hawthorne, *The Scarlet Letter* (1850)

WEBSTER HAD, EARLY ON, expressed his own opinion of the conspiracy
to his friend and now employer Stephen White. It was Webster's belief—in
fact Webster's *certainty*—that Mary Beckford had been involved in the very
conception of the plan, inspiring and urging her son-in-law to act. This, as
Hawthorne observed, was not an uncommon view. Just as Stephen White
had become a topic of conversation when people asked, "Cui bono?" ("Who
benefits?"), so too had Mary Beckford's name come up just as loudly. Where
others speculated, Webster—in private—expressed no doubt. He believed it of
chief importance that it was Beckford who would have benefited more than
anyone else had the conspirators' theory of the will—that there was only one
copy, the one stored underneath Captain White's bed—proved true. And her
benefit would have been entirely to Stephen White's disadvantage. Her greatly
increased share of the estate would have come for the most part out of what
otherwise would be his. Webster was also troubled by the fact that Captain
White had, a month or two before his murder, suffered from an unexplained
illness that nearly killed him. Webster suspected an attempt at poisoning, with
Beckford behind it.

Stephen White had wasted no time scoffing at this idea when Webster first
mentioned it, in confidence. Beckford, he said, was devoted to their shared
uncle and adoptive father, and would no more cause the old captain harm

than would Stephen himself. Besides, as she would certainly have known, she was mentioned in the will with a sizable bequest, even if her daughter were now out of the will. Beckford's share of the legacy was no small amount. Still, Webster pointed out, it could not be overlooked that in the absence of a will Beckford's share would have been quite a bit larger, she and Stephen being the captain's only surviving adopted offspring. The difference was a multiple of approximately eight.

Stephen White soon enough had cause to reconsider Webster's opinion. Early in December, White was busily tending to the process of moving his household from Salem to Boston. At the same time, Phippen and his father and sister-in-law, together with Dexter and Gardiner, were working tire-lessly—albeit quite futilely—to win a pardon for Joe Jr., or at least to get him a commutation to life imprisonment. There was, indeed, a chance this might happen. Caleb Foote reported in the *Salem Gazette* a rumor that the governor was seriously considering the matter, as the governor believed that Joe Jr. was quite possibly not

> the prime mover of the murder, but that there is another person, not yet arrested, who plotted and originally instigated the commis-sion of the crime. Both Knapps have intimated as much; and all who are acquainted with them know it was not in character for them to have planned it; they were too passive and inert to have conceived or to have executed such an enterprise of their own heads. . . . Fur-ther prosecutions will undoubtedly take place, whatever may be the condition in life of the offender, whether high or low, rich or poor, if the prosecuting officers obtain sufficient evidence.[1]

It was Mary Beckford herself who gave Stephen White reason to revise his opinion about her involvement. He wrote to Webster on the seventeenth:

> Altho' we are in our household in the very hours of removal, being in the midst of band-boxes and bureaus, paper-hangings and paint, I cannot omit troubling you with a line to speak of the renewed excitement in Salem regarding the wretched woman Mrs. Mary Beckford. Suspicions, horrible as they are, have almost become certainty.

Yesterday she sent me a private message intimating her wish that I should not interfere to obtain a commutation for J. J. Knapp Jr. The message said she thought it better he should be hung. Now, I know she has been, with her daughter, Mrs. Knapp and Knapp's father, to Worcester to prevail on Governor Lincoln to grant a reprieve or commutation, though she herself kept in the background by remaining at the tavern incognito, doubtless with a view to induce [Joe Jr.] to believe she was interceding for him, while in truth she seeks his life to smother further investigation.

Dexter and Gardiner urged their request to the Governor and Council for commutation in Frank Knapp's case, chiefly on the ground that another person was at the bottom of the whole affair. . . . This, I know, will not take you by surprise, for I have long seen where your suspicions pointed, but it horrifies me, who have always thought her very weak but not wicked. She must be the very devil.[2]

Whatever the truth, Beckford could breathe easy. There was to be no pardon, nor was there to be a commutation. Joe Jr. made his scheduled date to die. The family—all except Beckford—spent a morbid Christmas within Salem Jail, keeping Joe Jr. company and trying desperately to achieve some measure of merriment: an attempt that utterly failed.

Joe Jr. had now given up the bottle. He'd also discovered Christianity in a new and passionate way, to the extent that he spoke of little else, especially Christian forgiveness: as if he were already negotiating for his entry into Grace after his fall from the gallows. He rehearsed his argument for St. Peter. The hope of Redemption with a capital *R*: this was his theme. It was a theme that had been helped along by the Reverend John P. Cleaveland, rector of Salem's Tabernacle Church, who'd been making nearly daily visits to the jail now that Henry Colman never went near the place.

Joe Jr. looked as if he were about to die even without the assistance of the noose: emaciated, aged by some twenty years at least, broken in both mind and body. On the morning of his execution, New Year's Eve, he dressed as best he could for his meeting with eternity, read his Bible, ate a small breakfast, and prayed with Cleaveland. Sprague and the deputies came for him at 9 AM. Upon the high gallows, Joe Jr. shivered in the winter cold while Sprague read the death warrant. Once again, just as it had been with Frank, a large crowd gawked—large, but just a bit smaller than the gathering Frank had inspired. Some attributed this to the frigid weather. Others thought it simply a fact that the public at large had become weary of the entire affair.

Joe Jr. died hard. The drop did not break his neck. Therefore, he dangled, struggling for breath, slowly suffocating over the course of five minutes, which must have seemed like five hours of torture both for Joe Jr. and for those who watched. Frank had been the luckier of the two: a quick snap, and he was done. Perhaps, some said, that was justice—for without Joe Jr., Frank would not have gotten into trouble in the first place.

Like Frank, Joe Jr. was quickly interred in the Howard Street Cemetery. It is supposed that both brothers lie side by side, and that they are in a spot quite close to the border of the cemetery and the jail, though no one knows for sure.

27 | THE COMPLAINT OF THE HUMAN HEART

"Other sins only speak; murder shrieks out."
—John Webster, *The Duchess of Malfi* (1623)

YEARS AFTER THE EVENT, Nathaniel Hawthorne would adopt aspects of the White murder in a number of works involving his frequently recurring themes of poisoned family fortunes and the tendency of the workings of the world to call for eventual retribution in the face of all sins. Not only had Dick Crowninshield and the Knapp brothers paid for their sins, but so too had Captain Joseph White been called to pay for his. Mary Beckford paid as well, if only through shame, infamy, innuendo, and isolation for the rest of her life—an object of deep suspicion. Likewise, Henry Colman paid: he whose fame had faded with the quickness of smoke, he whose relationship with his congregation wound up poisoned by his testimony and, it was thought, his betrayal of the Knapp brothers. There was, indeed, enough guilt to go around. And enough punishment. For Hawthorne, it was all just that much more proof of the spectacle of darkness that was the world.

Most scholars believe Webster's summations to the juries—especially his remarks regarding the uncontrollable need to confess—greatly influenced Hawthorne's sculpting of *The Scarlet Letter*'s Rev. Arthur Dimmesdale, the secret lover of the shunned outcast Hester Prynne (and the father of her illegitimate daughter, Pearl). In Dimmesdale's last sermon, Hester could hear "the complaint of the human heart, sorrow-laden, perchance guilty, telling its secret, whether of guilt or sorrow, to the great heart of mankind; beseeching its sympathy or forgiveness—at every moment—in each accent."[1]

190

Echoes of the White murder case also appear in Hawthorne's *The House of the Seven Gables*. As the late Harvard University scholar Francis Matthiessen noted, the "ghost of Webster's summation" haunts an extensive section of the novel in which Hawthorne's narrator castigates and condemns the corpse of the despotic Judge Jaffrey Pyncheon.[2] The fictional seven-gabled Salem home of the Pyncheon family (inspired by the famous Salem house that still stands) rested on land that—much like White's slavery-built fortune, and much like most of the finest slavery-financed homes of Salem—was wrongfully and sinfully acquired. In olden times, the ancestor who built the residence, Colonel Pyncheon, had caused the original owner of the land to be hung as a wizard in order to obtain the property. Therefore, the Pyncheons' ancestral residence is built upon a foundation of criminal, murderous lies: a guilt from which the family can never escape. This truth is what critic John Cyril Barton has called "the literary execution of Judge Pyncheon."[3]

In his short story "Mr. Higginbotham's Catastrophe," which was written not long after the Knapp trials, Hawthorne depicted a scene of an outraged citizenry denouncing a gossiper who has caused great turmoil in the community through his stories. When a young woman rises to defend the man, Hawthorne describes her eloquence thusly: "Daniel Webster never spoke nor looked so like an angel as Miss Higginbotham while defending [Dominicus] from the wrathful populace of Parker's Falls."[4]

The White murder also resonates in the work of Edgar Allan Poe. Webster had described for the jury the utmost coolness and self-possession with which Dick Crowninshield had gone about his work. This same attitude is to be found in Poe's fictional murderer of another old man in another bedchamber. The psychopathic killer in 1843's "The Tell-Tale Heart" brags about how "wisely [and] with such caution" he accomplished his task and how nightly he had gazed upon his victim as he slept, preparing and planning.[5]

But Poe also picked up on Webster's theme of the murderer's ultimate sense of guilt hammering within him like a drumbeat: inescapable. Webster had said of Dick Crowninshield: "The secret which he possesses, possesses him, and like the evil spirit spoken of in olden times leads him whithersoever it will. It is a vulture ever gnawing at his heart; he believes his very thoughts to be heard. His bosom's secret overmasters him, subdues him—he succumbs."[6] So too did Poe's antihero find himself unable to escape his guilt as it manifested: the sound of his victim's heart inexorably beating as it ticked away with "a low, dull, quick sound—much such a sound as a watch makes when enveloped in cotton."[7] The narrator dismembered the corpse and hid the pieces beneath the floorboards of the death room. But the sound of the beating heart neverthe-less became louder and louder, until he—unable to stand it anymore—ripped up the planks and revealed his crime to law enforcement.

Five years Hawthorne's junior, Poe was twenty-one at the time of the Knapp trials and could not have been insensible to them given their extensive publicity. So, the potential for the influence of Webster's much-commented-on remarks cannot be discounted.

Many of the principal participants in the White drama were still alive when the stories of Hawthorne and Poe were published, to broad notice. One wonders whether Phippen Knapp or Mary Beckford or George Crowninshield read *The House of the Seven Gables* and what any one of them may have thought about its broad themes of ancestral malfeasance, inherited guilt, and the timelessness of sin.

28 | GHOSTS

"My affection [for Salem] is probably assignable to the deep and ancient roots which my family has struck into the soil. It is now two centuries and a quarter since the original Briton, the earliest immigrant of my name, made his appearance [in what] has since become a city. And here his descendants have been born and died, and have mingled their early substance with the soil; until no small portion of it must necessarily be akin to the mortal frame wherewith, for a little while, I walk the streets."
—Nathaniel Hawthorne, *The Scarlet Letter* (1850)

THE OLD JAIL WHERE DICK CROWNINSHIELD killed himself and the Knapp brothers waited to die now houses luxury apartments such as the men just named could never have imagined. Nineteen apartments take up the main jail building, and three more are to be found in the old jailkeeper's brick house. The most expensive of the apartments directly overlook the Howard Street Cemetery, where both Knapp brothers lie along with Captain Joseph White, and where Giles Corey's ghost supposedly still walks on moonlit evenings. Harry Houdini staged an escape at the jail in 1906. Decades later, Albert DeSalvo, the Boston Strangler, called the building home. The main jail—which was never modernized and where inmates were forced to use chamber pots—finally closed in 1991, after prisoners filed a lawsuit over harsh treatment. There's a pricey prison-themed restaurant on the ground floor: the Great Escape. In fair weather, the old prison yard, where the Knapps and many others swung from the gallows, is now a beer garden. Some say the old jail is haunted by the more than fifty felons who were hung there through the years, but this does not seem to have caused any vacancies.

More than a mile away from the jail rests the spot that Hawthorne by tradition knew as the Gallows Hill of witch trial days. This overlooks what is now Gallows Hill Park. There's a small parking lot, a playground, and an open field for soccer and other sports. In Hawthorne's time, bonfires were lit at this location every year to commemorate those who died upon verdicts rendered by Judge Hathorne and his protégés. Only in 2016 would the enterprising researcher Emerson W. "Tad" Baker prove the actual site of the 1692 executions to be elsewhere, though not far away, at the obscure Proctor's Ledge, found off Pope Street, behind a Walgreens, amid a neighborhood of modern houses: a landscape of double driveways, basketball hoops, backyard pools, sundecks, tiki torches, and gas barbecue grills—modern consumerist America writ large.

Many generations of Hathornes and Mannings rest in Salem's Charter Street Burying Point graveyard. The grave of Judge John Hathorne and the presence of the nearby Witch Trials Memorial make this a popular stop on Salem's witch tours. Most of the witches, meanwhile, lie in unmarked graves near the recently discovered true site of their executions, behind the Walgreens, where another small memorial has been installed. As denizens of Satan, they were denied Christian rites and were left to rot near where they'd been executed. (It is said John Proctor Jr.'s corpse was reclaimed by his family under cover of night and buried on land he owned in Peabody. The families of Rebecca Nurse, George Jacobs, and some others did much the same.)

Hawthorne married Sophia Peabody, of a respectable Salem family, and eventually left town for good save for a brief five-year period spent there from 1845 through 1850. Though he removed himself from Salem in body, he never did so in spirit, for Salem was to be ever present in his fiction. In his 1850 preface to *The Scarlet Letter*, he savaged the place, by now but a shadow of its former self. Hawthorne described "a [once] bustling wharf . . . which is now burdened with decayed wooden warehouses, and exhibits few or no symptoms of commercial life; except, perhaps, a bark or brig, half-way down its melancholy length, discharging hides; or, nearer at hand, a Nova Scotia schooner, pitching out her cargo of firewood." He recalled when Salem was "a port by itself; not scorned, as she is now, by her own merchants and ship-owners, who permit her wharves to crumble to ruin while their ventures go to swell, need-lessly and imperceptibly, the mighty flood of commerce at New York or Bos-ton." Still, he conceded, "This old town of Salem—my native place, though I have dwelt much away from it both in boyhood and maturer years—possesses, or did possess, a hold on my affection, the force of which I have never realized during my seasons of actual residence here."[1] Only after leaving the place did he come to truly know it.

George Crowninshield went on to live a long and prosperous life. In Sep-tember 1831, little more than a year after the crime, Hawthorne told his cousin John Dikes Jr. that "George Crowninshield still lives at his father's and seems not at all cast down by what has taken place. I saw him walk by our house, arm-in-arm with a girl."[2] How George supported himself in the years before his father's 1844 death is not known, but thereafter he used his share of his father's estate to live a prolonged congenial retirement as a gentleman of leisure, albeit an eccentric gentleman of leisure. Crowninshield eventually married and moved to Roxbury, losing touch with most of his siblings.

The ill-used and largely abandoned Derby Wharf as it looked circa 1900, one hundred years after the peak of Salem's China and East India trade, a stark symbol of Salem's decline. *Photo by Frank Cousins from the Frank Cousins Collection of Glass Plate Negatives. Courtesy of Phillips Library, Peabody Essex Museum, Salem, MA*

This distance increased in 1852. The eldest of Richard Crowninshield Sr.'s sons, Edward, had been hospitalized in various lunatic asylums since about 1815. Shortly before Edward's death, which was known to be imminent, George visited Edward at what was then the McLean Asylum in Somerville and had him sign a will naming George as his executor and sole heir. Although Edward had been locked away for years, he possessed a significant trust that his father had set aside in the early 1840s in order to assure that Edward's medical and housing costs would be covered until the end of the son's days.

Upon Edward's passing, George presented the will—signed by Edward, being of "sound and disposing mind"—for probate. To this George and Edward's siblings firmly objected, bringing George to court. Edward was, at the time of his signing the will, under guardianship by order of a judge of probate "as an insane person being non compos mentis."[3] Therefore, the Crowninshield siblings had little problem in getting Edward's will thrown out and having his trust divided equally between them—with George getting his share but no more, just as he had when their father died in 1844.

The site of Richard Crowninshield Sr.'s Danvers mill is today, after the redrawing of lines, in Peabody rather than Danvers. During the 1890s, long after Richard's heirs had disposed of the property, the site was purchased by the A. C. Lawrence Leather Company. The firm knocked down Crowninshield's mill and built a massive tannery. The adjacent old mansion was first used as an adjunct factory and later as a "locker room" for tannery employees. Just like the old Salem Jail, the old tannery is now luxury apartments called cumulatively (and appropriately) the "Tannery Apartments." The brick mansion built by Richard Crowninshield Sr.—where Frank Knapp visited to scheme with Dick and George, and where Dick and George propositioned John Palmer to join them in homicide—is now the management office for the apartments, located at 18 Crowninshield Street. The name of the management company, Crowninshield Management Corporation, has nothing to do with the family and everything to do with the name of the street.

George Crowninshield died in July 1888 and was buried in Cambridge's Mount Auburn Cemetery. His obituary mentioned nothing about the crime. "Mr. George C. Crowninshield, for years a well-known resident of Roxbury and a member of the old and noted Crowninshield family of Salem, died yesterday. . . . He was always greatly interested in scientific matters and had several times made voyages around the world. He leaves no family other than a granddaughter."[4] It is said that George always lived modestly throughout his Roxbury years. Nevertheless, to his nineteen-year-old granddaughter Anna Stedman he left a fortune of $80,000 (more than $2 million in today's currency). George's daughter, Lucy Ann "Anna" Crowninshield Stedman (the wife of Joseph Stedman), predeceased him in 1874, at the age of forty. George's wife, another Lucy, had died very early in their marriage, perhaps during childbirth. The granddaughter married Gilman Parker. She died in 1913 at the age of fifty-one. The Parkers had one son, Frederick Gilman Parker, born 1882. Frederick, who died in 1965, married Martha S. Orcutt and had one daughter, Bernice Crowninshield Parker Warren, the wife of Robert Warren. Bernice died in 1979, at the age of seventy-five.

It is said that George's cousin George Caspar Crowninshield, a respected gentleman and the son of Navy Secretary Benjamin Crowninshield, never forgave George for what he'd done to their shared name. George Caspar died in 1857. His father, the former navy secretary, died in 1851. In the wake of the White murder, the Jacksonian four-term congressman had been defeated in his autumn 1830 bid for re-election by none other than the Committee of Vigilance veteran Rufus Choate, a Whig. Benjamin went to his grave believing that it was the disgrace brought to him by his nephews that had ended his political career. Like every one of the surviving siblings of Richard Crowninshield Sr., Benjamin made a point of having little or nothing to do with any of Richard's sons or daughters, or their descendants.

Various of the "respectable" Crowninshields married into several of the most prominent clans in Massachusetts and elsewhere, including the Adams and Endicott families. Yachtsmen Charles Francis Adams III, a descendant of Secretary of the Navy Crowninshield, served in the same post under Herbert Hoover. Arent S. Crowninshield achieved the rank of admiral in the US Navy and later commanded the navy's Bureau of Navigation during the McKinley administration. Frank Crowninshield served as the founding editor of *Vanity Fair* magazine. Benjamin Crowninshield Bradlee was editor at the *Washington Post* at the time the paper published the Pentagon Papers and investigated Watergate. Another descendant, Charles Francis Adams IV, was the first president, and later the chairman, of Raytheon.

Daniel Webster served as Whig senator from Massachusetts through 1841 and then again from 1845 to 1850. He also was secretary of state in the cabinets of Presidents Harrison (1841), Tyler (1841–43), and Fillmore (1850–52).

Webster's support for the Compromise of 1850, with the stringent Fugitive Slave Act as part of the package, made him widely unpopular in Massachusetts—denounced as a traitor to the antislavery cause. He died at his farm in Marshfield in 1852.

In 1831, a Knapp cousin and well-known biographer, Samuel Lorenzo Knapp (not to be confused with Samuel H. Knapp, the brother of Joe Jr. and Frank), wrote *A Memoir of the Life of Daniel Webster*. The book included an exposé of the life of Joseph White and a highly critical analysis of Webster's role in the trial of Frank Knapp, suggesting that Frank had been convicted not on the evidence, but on the basis of Webster's eloquence. Samuel L. Knapp was not a disinterested party—and not just because of his relation to the Knapp brothers. Knapp was also the husband of Mary Crowninshield, the eldest sister of Dick and George Crowninshield. His animus toward Webster should have taken no one by surprise.

But sometimes there is good money to be made with a strategic retreat. Shortly after the book appeared, Stephen White paid the publishers (Boston's Stimpson and Clapp) a hefty sum to recall all copies. Then he hired Knapp to edit and rewrite his manuscript with every mention of White, and the White trial, deleted. The revised work was published in 1835 by J. S. Redfield of New York.[5] Through the years, various members of the White family would continually exert steady influence wherever and whenever they could to minimize the historical memory of Joseph White, whose wealth they enjoyed having but whose means of acquiring it made them feel the type of shame Hawthorne had depicted with the Pyncheons. They wanted old Captain White to disappear from history. The Crowninshields were to be just as active in erasing the memory of the scandal.

Many years after both Webster and Stephen White were history, in 1936, the *Saturday Evening Post* published Stephen Vincent Benét's short story "The Devil and Daniel Webster," in which Webster represents a New Hampshire farmer who has made a Faustian bargain and sold his soul to Satan. When "Old Scratch" comes to collect his property, he finds Webster waiting for him, offering to challenge Satan's contract with the farmer before a judge and jury that he allows Satan to choose. As a result, Webster of course finds himself confronted by a judge and jury composed of Satan's own devoted minions from Hell. This is intended by Satan to be a Kangaroo Court, just as had been the Salem Witch Trials. And the presiding judge? None other than John

Hathorne. Despite having the deck stacked against him, Webster succeeds through the magnificence of his oratory to have the farmer's contract with the Devil annulled.

Nathaniel Hawthorne did not mind the Compromise of 1850. In fact, he cared nothing about the politics of slavery or abolition as a cause. Like his close friend from college Franklin Pierce (whose campaign biography he wrote in 1852), Hawthorne's sympathies were with the Democratic Party and states' rights. In general, Hawthorne thought all reformers—including some of his own Peabody in-laws—to be nothing but sanctimonious bores. In a sketch entitled "The Hall of Fantasy," he depicted an abolitionist who brandished "his one idea like an iron flail."[6] In this piece, as in others, Hawthorne mocked his abolitionist neighbors in his adopted hometown of Concord: men like Emerson, Thoreau, Bronson Alcott, and even George Crowninshield's defense attorney, Samuel Hoar.

Hawthorne understood their idealism but thought it pointless, for Hawthorne himself was nothing if not a pessimist: in fact, a fatalist. Men like White and his murderers, and institutions such as slavery, were—to Hawthorne's mind—inevitable. It had ever been so. The world was a dark and imperfect place, the only light an illusion. Reformers, for all their work and ambition, did nothing more than shovel sand against the tide and make themselves and others miserable in the process. (When the radical abolitionist John Brown went to the hangman's noose after his failed and rather preposterous 1859 raid at the federal arsenal in Harpers Ferry, Hawthorne's friend Emerson said that Brown's death would "make the gallows as glorious as the cross." Hawthorne's comment was quite different and probably worthy of old John Hathorne himself: "Nobody was ever more justly hanged.")[7]

As a corpse in the spring of 1864, Hawthorne did not return to Salem to sleep with his despised ancestors. Instead, he was laid to rest in Concord, at Sleepy Hollow Cemetery, where he reposes close by the graves of Emerson, Thoreau, and a number of others whom in life he'd criticized.[8]

Robert Rantoul Jr.—the young lawyer who'd helped defend each of the Knapps and who believed Webster's eloquence rather than the evidence had sent the Knapps to their ends—afterward found himself ostracized by many in Salem and his native Newburyport. He soon moved to South Reading and later, in 1833, to Gloucester. He served variously in the law offices of John Pickering and later Leverett Saltonstall before, in 1839, opening his own office in Boston and making his permanent home in Beverly. Rantoul was eventually elected to the legislature, where he demonstrated himself to be not only a dedicated abolitionist but also a leading champion for temperance and, notably, a tireless fighter against capital punishment in all its forms. Rantoul worked closely with William Lloyd Garrison and a Knapp cousin, newspaper publisher Isaac Knapp, when they together founded the New England Anti-Slavery Society and the abolitionist newspaper the *Liberator*. Rantoul did this despite the proslavery and states'-rights beliefs of many in his own Democratic Party. Rantoul also served variously as US attorney for Massachusetts, as a member of the Massachusetts School Board, and in Congress. He died in 1852.

As noted by Duane Hamilton Hurd in his *History of Essex County, Massachusetts*:

> The subject of capital punishment . . . was among those which he early and often urged on the attention of the Legislature. As chairman of committees he made three reports in as many successive years in favor of the abolition of the death-penalty, besides as many carefully prepared speeches, and not a few shorter ones in the program of debate. He afterward wrote "Letters on the Death-Penalty," addressed to the Governor and Legislature of Massachusetts, which were reprinted by order of the Legislature of New York. He also embraced every available opportunity for delivering lectures and addresses on this subject. His writings upon it probably contain all that has been or can be said in opposition to capital punishment, and they have been largely quoted wherever the question has been discussed on either side of the Atlantic.[9]

Franklin Dexter continued his very successful legal career after the White murder trials. He and his wife Catherine Elizabeth Prescott Dexter—of the notable Prescott clan of Boston and the North Shore—had several children and lived in Beverly. Although he served with distinction in the Massachusetts Bar, Dexter's main preoccupation eventually became writing—specifically, writing about the fine arts, to which he was dedicated. He published extensively in the *North American Review* and elsewhere. He was also quite interested in military matters and served as commander of the New England Guards. At the same time, he involved himself in antislavery causes. Dexter died in 1857, in his sixty-fourth year. His wife, Catherine, lived until 1891, dying just one day after her ninety-second birthday.

George Crowninshield's lead attorney, Samuel Hoar, went on to serve as an anti-Jacksonian member of Congress, to do a stint in the Massachusetts legislature, and, in 1854, to help found what became the modern Republican Party. His son Ebenezer Rockwood Hoar served as associate justice of the Massachusetts Supreme Court and as US attorney general during the Grant administration. Another son, Edward Sherman Hoar, became an attorney and was one of Henry David Thoreau's closest friends. A third son, George Frisbie Hoar, represented Massachusetts as a United States Senator for twenty-seven years. Hoar's eldest daughter, Elizabeth Sherman Hoar, was a member of Emerson's Transcendentalist Circle and figured largely in editing its publication, the *Dial*. Samuel Hoar died in 1856 and is buried at Sleepy Hollow Cemetery, Concord, as are many of his descendants, not a few of them named Samuel, and not a few of them attorneys.

Joseph Knapp Sr. remained in Salem for the rest of his life, remarried, and conducted a small business making cigars. However, he was largely shunned and thus became an involuntary recluse. He died in 1847 and is buried with his wives at Salem's Harmony Grove Cemetery.[10]

Nathaniel Phippen Knapp left the legal profession behind him, became an Episcopalian priest, and married one of the aristocratic Lees of Virginia. Phippen's wife, Ellen McMacken Lee Bedford, was a cousin of Robert E. Lee and the granddaughter of Richard Henry Lee, a signer of the Declaration of Independence. Phippen fathered two children with Ellen and, after a variety of other assignments in Alabama, spent the bulk of his career overseeing Christ Church in Mobile until his death in 1854.[11] He never returned to Salem.

While Phippen abandoned law for the Episcopal priesthood, the Rev. Henry Colman went the opposite direction. He abandoned his ministry a year after the Knapp and Crowninshield trials, opting instead to pursue what became a successful career as an expert writer, editor, and researcher on agricultural topics. In his farewell sermon, he spoke about all manner of death: the deaths of the innocent, the deaths of the guilty, and the slow demise of Salem itself.

"Misfortune and death have been busily at work among us," he told his flock. "The removal of families from the town, who were once connected with us, has been almost unprecedented. The bereavements of death have been numerous and most afflictive.... The future is veiled in darkness. The connections of life at the longest must be short. Time places his rough hand upon us all.... Time permits no man to pause or linger, but continually impels us forward."[12] The great merchant families were all moving away and taking their commerce with them. Salem's death struggle was entering its final phase. Colman himself was to pass in 1849.

Mary Beckford lived on at the farm in Wenham until her death in 1851 at age eighty-two.[13] Throughout all the long years, she continued to be widely suspected as an accomplice, and quite possibly the real instigator, in the White murder. The gossip never ceased, nor did Mary's isolation. Infamy has a way of sticking. Some also suspected her daughter, though these were a distinct minority. Four years after Joe Jr.'s execution, Mary Beckford Knapp married Boston attorney and Harvard graduate Edmund Kimball, of an old founding family of Wenham, and bore eight children. Mary Beckford Kimball died in 1888. Both Marys, along with Edmund and scores of other Kimballs, are buried in Wenham Cemetery.

As has been noted, Stephen White left Salem for good not long after the trials and executions, settling for a time in Boston. White had already planned his move before the murder of his uncle, as part of the process of shifting his business interests out of the failing town. Having inherited the Knapp home from Captain Joseph White, Stephen evicted the Knapps and sold the building. He also sold his own home and White's Wharf but kept a farm Captain White had owned in Wenham, not far from the Beckford farm, called Cherry Hill Farm.[14] White leased the farm for several years before selling. He also kept Captain White's mansion for about four years, renting it out.

Stephen and several partners established the East Boston Shipyard, where they began building clipper ships of a heft that shallow Salem Harbor could not accommodate. This enabled the first stage of the rise of East Boston's prominence as a ship-building center. He also still continued with international trade, with his vessels now sailing for the most part out of Boston rather than Salem, although some of his smaller ships still made their home at Salem, on wharves owned by others. At the same time, Stephen worked to expand his mills in New Hampshire and Maine. Additionally, he did rather well, at least at first, with significant investments he made in the timber business of western New York, cutting giant white oaks and sending the enormous timbers down the Erie Canal and then the Hudson to Manhattan, and from there dispatching them on coastal vessels for use in the Boston shipyards. Arthur H. Clark wrote the following:

> Sawmills were erected on [Grand Island, in the Niagara River just a bit to the south of Niagara Falls], and a supply of the finest quality of ship timber was created, and brought by the Erie Canal to tidewater [the Hudson], thence by coasting vessels to East Boston. This attracted ship builders from other towns, and eventually made Boston a famous shipbuilding centre [sic]. Stephen White owned the first ship built in East Boston, the *Niagara*, of 460 tons, appropriately named after the river from which the timber used in her construction had come. She was built in 1834.[15]

Stephen established a settlement and sawmill on Grand Island, which he christened "Whitehaven."

The financial panic of 1837 seems to have put something of a dent into Stephen White's business affairs. He remained, however, quite a wealthy man. Having been a widower since 1827, White in 1837 remarried to a local New York woman, Mary Matthews, the widow of a Niagara River steamboat skipper. Out near Niagara Falls, not far from the timberlands owned by his East Boston company, White had already built a magnificent home, Beechwater, on a Niagara River island he'd purchased and came to call White's Island (now known as Tonawanda Island).[16] Daniel Webster, who held an interest in White's enterprise, was a frequent guest here, and it was in this newly built home that in 1835 Webster's son Daniel Fletcher Webster (known as Fletcher) became the husband of White's daughter Caroline. The mansion was abandoned after Stephen White's widow passed away and became known by local children as the "ghost house." It was finally torn down in 1906.

Stephen White died in 1841, in his fifty-fourth year, during a visit to Manhattan. At his passing, he left many unpaid debts in Massachusetts. Fortuitously, and certainly not accidentally, White had removed most of his assets to New York and New Hampshire, out of the reach of Massachusetts creditors. Thus, he left an estate that was still sizable for the time and that endured for his heirs, despite recent financial reverses. The sole assets of his estate left behind in Massachusetts represented just $55: the value of more than one thousand unbound copies of the suppressed first edition of Samuel L. Knapp's *A Memoir of the Life of Daniel Webster.*

His family prospered, for the most part. A granddaughter of Stephen's married Abbott Lawrence, son of the industrialist and financier of the same name, the man who had founded the mill town of Lawrence, Massachusetts. Another granddaughter married into the Peabody family. (Sadly, Stephen's one and only son, the namesake of Captain Joseph White and an 1833 graduate of Harvard, suffered from depression and committed suicide at the McLean Asylum, Somerville, three years before Stephen's death.) In his will, Stephen made sure to pay homage to his uncle and benefactor, directing that not less than $500 be used to erect a monument to Captain Joseph White's memory at Mount Auburn Cemetery, Cambridge.

In Salem, Hawthorne's birthplace remains in good order, but not at its original location on Union Street. During the late 1950s, it was moved to the same campus on which rests the House of the Seven Gables. Both are open to the public and maintained by the Peabody Essex Museum. The home of Joseph Knapp Sr. likewise still stands, albeit not at its original location. It is said that Knapp's two executed sons haunt the place. A latter-day owner went so far as to move the house from 85 Essex Street to a location not far away on Curtis Street in hope that the spirits would stay with the land and not the domicile. (This experiment reportedly failed.)

One of Salem's several Crowninshield homes, the original circa 1727 Crowninshield-Bentley House built by John Crowninshield, great-grandfather to Dick and George Crowninshield, is also well preserved—another item in the Peabody Essex collection. This too has been moved: dragged down the block from its original location at 106 Essex Street to 126 Essex Street, ironically next door to the old home of Captain Joseph White, this also maintained by the museum. The Crowninshield home is referred to as the Crowninshield-Bentley House in recognition of the fact that Reverend William Bentley lived here as a boarder for a considerable amount of time, from 1791 to 1819.

As heir to the East India Marine Society, the Peabody Essex Museum oversees that society's complete collection of artifacts and maintains the society's still grand Marine Hall, along with the many other buildings under its umbrella—all of them shipwrecked in the modern era, held in suspended animation as museum pieces amid modern sprawl and kitschy commercialization tied to witch-trial tourism. (Only in this country can the site of a great catastrophe of intolerance, mayhem, and suffering—such as was the witch hysteria of 1692—become the equivalent of a theme park exploiting that dark legacy.)

Captain White's mansion has been renamed the Gardner-Pingree House, paying homage to the first (Gardner) and last (Pingree) owners of the property and not accidentally ignoring White. For many years, the volunteer docents—for the most part amiable retirees—knew little or nothing about the White murder. The house has been preserved and presented primarily as an example of the way of life enjoyed by wealthy shipping families in the early 1800s, not as a crime scene, although in more recent years the legacy of the White murder has been added to the house-tour script. This addition would have been an anathema to museum benefactor and noted preservationist Louise du Pont Crowninshield, heiress to du Pont wealth and the wife of yachtsman Francis Boardman Crowninshield. (F. B. Crowninshield had fought with Theodore Roosevelt's Rough Riders in Cuba and, in 1912, financed the building of a

Salem's East India Marine Hall as it stands today, 161 Essex Street. The building is owned and managed by the Peabody Essex Museum.
Photo by the author

schooner yacht he named *Cleopatra's Barge II.*) In her time, Louise not only made sure the interpretation offered at the Gardner-Pingree House made no mention of Captain White or the circumstances of his demise but also did her best to in other ways quash or at least limit serious research into the murder and trial. Louise died in 1958. The apparition of the White murder survived her.

Wharves too have ghosts. Officially, only four Salem wharves survive: the Derby Wharf, Central Wharf, Hatch's Wharf, and elements of Tucker Wharf. But the remains of many others still linger and still haunt if one knows where to look. Of particular interest, the remnants of the old *L*-shaped wharf of the White family—White's Wharf, which once extended some 150 feet from Derby Street into Salem's South River—are now encompassed within the northeast section of Central Wharf and the north edge of Hatch's Wharf.[17] Other wharves lurk as well but are indiscernible, the waters between them having been filled to extend and expand the general waterfront. Such is the case, for example, with the Pickering Wharf. Elsewhere, the remains of Crowninshield's Wharf (a.k.a. India Wharf) and Orne's Wharf host the southern border of today's Safe Harbor Station power plant property. In other words, the old Salem waterfront hides in plain sight.

There has been only one modern book-length work dealing explicitly and exclusively with the White murder: a 1956 volume entitled *Daniel Webster and the Salem Murder* (Columbia, MO: Artcraft Press), written by Dartmouth professors Howard Bradley and James Winans. (Robert Booth's superb and essential *Death of an Empire* includes discussion of the murder and trials but has a far wider scope, being a full-fledged history of the rise and fall of Salem as a merchant port, with special emphasis on the life, fortunes, and misfortunes of Stephen White.) As the title of the Bradley and Winans book suggests, the publication focuses on Daniel Webster's role and, more to the point, his rhetoric. (Bradley was a professor of speech and Winans a professor of public speaking.) Interestingly, when Bradley and Winans were researching their book in the early 1950s, they had a hard time extracting cooperation from the Peabody Essex Museum, this in large measure—they believed—because museum benefactor Louise du Pont Crowninshield wanted it that way.

Things are much easier these days. At the museum's library, the full range of papers and artifacts related to the White murder and the subsequent trials are readily available for study. Whether the long-vanished spirit of Louise du Pont Crowninshield likes it or not, some ghosts—just like those of the two executed Knapps who haunt the old Knapp home, not to mention the ghosts of Salem's dark slaving history and the even darker ghosts of the witch trials—are ultimately impossible to repress or exorcise. The same goes for the ghost that is this tale.

Salem's Derby Wharf in 2020, the old counting houses and warehouses long gone and sea rise threatening eventual destruction. Now a part of the Salem Maritime National Historic Site. *Photo by the author*

ACKNOWLEDGMENTS

I AM GREATLY INDEBTED to the staff of the Phillips Library and the Peabody Essex Museum, for their courtesy and efficiency in making resources available even amid the crisis of the COVID-19 pandemic. In this regard, I wish to especially thank Suzanne Inge for her help with illustrations. I am also grateful to the staffs at the Yale Law School's Lillian Goldman Library and the good people at the Dartmouth College Library, where the Bradley and Winans papers are held. My ace agent Kathy Green was enthusiastic about this project from the start, as was Chicago Review Press senior editor Jerome Pohlen. Chicago Review Press managing editor Devon Freeny has been a pleasure to work with, and copyeditor/fact-checker Joseph Webb has been a lifesaver on more than one occasion. The same goes for proofreader Jason Mortensen and ace indexer Jean Skipp. During my research, I was gratified to run across a very useful 1956 essay regarding Hawthorne's *The House of the Seven Gables* by my old friend, mentor, and teacher Alfred H. Marks of the State University of New York at New Paltz—a remarkable man of whom it was a good and wonderful thing to be reminded.

A P P E N D I X

The Last Will and Testament of Captain Joseph White

WILL OF JOSEPH WHITE, Essex Co., Mass., 8 Jan 1830.[1]

<u>I Joseph White, of Salem</u> in the county of Essex, merchant, do make this my last will and testament, in manner following, that is to say:

In the first place, I order my executor herein after named to pay all my debts and funeral charges.

Item. I give and devise to my nephew <u>Stephen White</u> and to <u>John White Treadwell</u>, of Salem, and the survivor of them and the heirs of such survivor, one half of the real estate I have lately bought in the city of Boston, consisting of dwelling houses and the land under and belonging to the same, situate in "Legrange Place," so called, to wit, the house or building numbered four, the building numbered thirteen, and the land under and belonging to the same, and one undivided half of the building numbered twenty two, and the land under and belonging to the same, together with the privileges and appurtenances to the said real estate belonging: Upon the special trust and confidence here following, that is to say; that they and the survivor of them, and the heirs of such survivor, do and shall hold the same for the use and benefit of my niece <u>Mary B. West</u>, wife of Nathaniel West junior, of Salem, merchant; and do and shall pay to or otherwise authorize and empower the said Mary to receive and to take all the rent and income of the said real estate, as the same shall become due and payable, for and during the term of her natural life; for her own sole and separate use and benefit. And I do hereby direct and declare, that the receipts of the said Mary, under her hand, shall, notwithstanding her coverture, be good and sufficient releases and discharges for said rent and income. And upon trust *further, that from and after the decease of the said Mary B. West, they the said trustees, and the survivor of them, or the heirs of such survivor, do and shall, as soon as conveniently may be, assign and convey all the said real estate unto all and every lawful child or children of said Mary, living at the time of her decease, and the child or children of any deceased child of said Mary (by right of representation) equally to be divided among them; and if there shall be but one child of said Mary then living, and no child or children of any deceased child, then the whole of said real estate shall be conveyed and assigned to such one child.*

Item. I give devise to <u>the said Stephen White and John W. Treadwell</u>, and the survivor of them, and the heirs of such survivors, the other moiety of half of the said real estate I have lately bought in the city of Boston, consisting of dwelling houses, and the land under and belonging to the same, and the privileges and appurtenances to the same belonging, situate in said "Legrange Place," to wit, the house numbered six, the house numbered sixteen, and one undivided half of the house numbered twenty two, with the land under and belonging to the same: Upon the special trust and confidence here following, that is to say; that they and the survivor of them, and the heirs of such survivor, do and shall hold the same for the use and benefit of my niece <u>Abigail Elizabeth Hodges</u>, wife of George A. Hodges, of said Boston, merchant; and do and shall pay, or otherwise sufficient I authorize the said Abigail Elizabeth to receive and take all the rent and income of the said real estate, as the same shall become due and payable, for and during the term of her natural life, for her own sole and separate use and benefit. And I do hereby direct and declare, that the receipts of said Abigail Elizabeth under her hand, shall, notwithstanding her coverture, be good and sufficient releases and discharges for the said rent and income. And upon trust further, that, from and after the decease of said Abigail Elizabeth Hodges, they the said trustees, and the survivor of them, or the heirs of such survivors, do and shall, as soon as conveniently may be, assign and convey all the said real estate unto all and every lawful child or children of said Abigail Elizabeth, living at the time of her decease, and the child or children of any deceased child of said Abigail Elizabeth (by right of representation) equally be divided among them; and, if there shall be but one child of said Abigail Elizabeth then living, and no child or children of any deceased child, the whole shall be conveyed and assigned to such one child.

Item. I give, devise and bequeath to <u>the said Stephen White</u>, my executor herein after named, and his heirs, executors and administrators, my real estate in Lynn in said county of Essex, consisting of my Farrington farm, so called, *which was conveyed to me by* <u>Mr. Newell</u>; *also, the sum of eight thousand dollars: Upon the special trust and confidence here following, that is to say; that he the said Stephen, his heirs, executors and administrators, do and shall hold the same for the use and benefit of my nephew* <u>John White</u>; *and do and shall, as soon as conveniently may be after my decease, invest the said sum of eight thousand dollars, and keep the same invested, in such productive stocks or funds, or upon such other securities, whether real or personal, as he or they shall think most beneficial to the said John White; and do and shall vary alter and transpose such stocks, funds or securities, for any others, when and so often, as it shall to the said Stephen White, his executors or administrators seem advantageous; and do and shall pay to the said John White, or otherwise sufficiently authorize and empower him to receive, the income, dividends and interest of the said farm and of the said principal sum of eight thousand dollars, for and during the term of the said John's natural life. And upon the trust further, that, from and after the decease of the said John White, he the said Stephen White, his heirs, executors or administrators, do and shall, as soon as it may be conveniently done, convey, transfer, assign and pay over, the said estate in Lynn aforesaid, and all the principal monies, stocks, funds and securities, unto all and every the lawful child or children of any deceased child of his, then the whole shall be conveyed, transferred, assigned and paid over, to such one child.*

Item. I give and bequeath to my niece <u>Mary Bickford</u> *[sic], widow of the late John Bickford, and her executors, administrators and assigns, the sum of fifteen thousand dollars.*

Item. I give to <u>Robert Stone, of Salem, merchant</u>, *and his executors, administrators and assigns, the sum of five thousand dollars.*

Item. I give and bequeath to <u>Anstis Dunlap, sister of the said Robert Stone</u>, *and her executors, administrators and assigns, the sum of five thousand dollars.*

Item. I give and bequeath to <u>Joseph White junior, son of my nephew Stephen White</u>, *and his executors, administrators and assigns, the sum of eight thousand dollars.*

Item. I give and bequeath to <u>Elizabeth Stone Gray, daughter of my nephew Joseph White deceased, the wife of Samuel C. Gray, of Boston</u>, *and her executors, administrators and assigns, the sum of twenty five thousand dollars.*

Item. I give and bequeath to <u>Mary Barrow White, daughter of my nephew Joseph White deceased</u>, *and her executors, administrators and assigns, the sum of twenty five thousand dollars.*

Item. I give and bequeath to <u>Charlotte Sophia White, daughter of my said nephew Joseph</u>, and her executors, administrators and assigns, the sum of twenty-five thousand dollars.

And my will is, and I accordingly direct, that all legacies herein before given and bequeathed, shall be paid by my executor herein after named in three equal payments in six, twelve and eighteen months, from and after my decease.

Item. I give and bequeath to <u>my nephew Francis White</u> the sum of two hundred and seventy dollars annually during his life. And I direct my executor to apply that sum annually, at his discretion, for the support and maintenance of the said Francis during the term of his natural life. And I authorize my said executor to purchase an annuity of that amount at the Massachusetts hospital life insurance company, or at some other similar incorporated institution, the said annuity to be paid to the said Stephen, his executors and administrators, in trust, to be appropriated and applied for the support and maintenance of the said Francis White during his life. And, in default of the said Stephen my said executor's purchasing an annuity as aforesaid, then I hereby expressly change my real estate, which is herein after devised to the said Stephen, with and for the payment of the said sum of two hundred and seventy dollars annually for the support of the said Francis White as aforesaid.

And, as to all the rest, residue and remainder of my estate, real, personal and mixed, not herein before devised or bequeathed, wheresoever the same may be situated, I give, devise and bequeath the same to <u>my nephew Stephen White</u>; to have and to hold the same to him, his heirs, executors, administrators and assigns, to his and their proper use and benefit forever. And I do hereby constitute and appoint the said Stephen White sole executor of this my last will and testament. And I do revoke all former wills, by me at any time made.

In witness whereof, I the said Joseph White have hereunto set my hand and seal, this January 8th day of January in the year of our lord one thousand eight hundred and thirty.

Joseph White

Signed, sealed, published and declared by the said Joseph White as his last will and testament, in the presence of us, who in his presence and at his request have hereunto set our names as witnesses.

Elijah Porter, William Ives, J. Ward

NOTES

Prologue

1. Pearson, *Murder at Smutty Nose*, 250.
2. Lawson, *American State Trials*, 636.

1. Old Salem by Moonlight

1. The mansion at 128 Essex Street was purchased by White in 1814. He bought it from Nathaniel West, who'd acquired it from the original owner, John Gardner. David Pingree purchased the house from the White estate in 1834. The Pingree family kept the mansion for ninety-nine years, eventually in 1933 donating it to the Essex Institute, forerunner of the Peabody Essex Museum, which now maintains the residence.

2. An Inconvenient Apparition

1. See accounts relating to Benjamin's character and habits in box 1, folder 3, testimonies, confessions, and statements of Mary W. Knapp, Nathaniel P. Knapp, John Francis Knapp, Joseph J. Knapp Jr., 1830, in Joseph White (1748–1830) Murder Trial Papers, Series I, Phillips Library, Peabody Essex Museum.
2. Wigmore, *Principles of Judicial Truth*, 1082–1084. Note that all testimony from Benjamin White, Lydia Kimball, and Dr. Samuel Johnson in this chapter comes from this same source.
3. Mary bought the place in 1829 from the estate of former US secretary of state Timothy Pickering.
4. Thomas Needham III (1780–1858), who lived at 205 Essex Street, came from a line of distinguished cabinetmakers of the same name whose works remain much in demand at auctions.
5. Abigail was born circa 1707 and died in 1800, having spent the last two decades living in the Salem home of her son Captain Joseph White. She had married Joseph White Sr. on January 13, 1745.

3. Wharves and Decline

1. Paine, *Ships and Sailors of Old Salem*, 10. Note that a *supercargo* is the formal representative of a vessel's owner traveling aboard the vessel and charged with the fiduciary responsibility of looking after cargo and cash, overseeing all related transactions. In other words, the supercargo is on board in order to keep everybody honest. A *factor* serves much the same purpose, but instead of traveling with a vessel he is generally stationed at one particular port.

2. One spurious and anonymous "memoir" relating to White murder conspirator John Francis "Frank" Knapp claims that Knapp visited Napoleon on St. Helena shortly before the deposed emperor's death during a voyage as skipper of the *General Endicott* in 1821. However, Knapp was just ten years old when Napoleon died. The entire "memoir" was merely an attempt by the anonymous writer to create a spectacular story and ride the wave of interest in the White murder at the time of the trials and executions. See J.W.S. [pseud.], *Wild Achievements and Romantic Voyages of Captain John Francis Knapp (One of the Salem Murderers), While Commander of the Ship* General Endicott: *With an Account of His Seeing the Celebrated Magellan Clouds, and Visit to Bonaparte at St. Helena*, Publisher Unknown, 1830. Copy in the Lillian Goldman Law Library, Yale University.

3. Booth, *Death of an Empire*, 152.

4. Bentley, *Diary of William Bentley*, 1:104. Minister and polymath William Bentley (1759–1819) reportedly possessed the second-most-extensive private library in the United States, with only Thomas Jefferson's library outranking his. He declined in 1805 an offer from Jefferson to become president of the University of Virginia and also a subsequent offer to become chaplain to the Congress of the United States. In his ministry, he was noted for emphasizing good works over doctrine.

4. A Melancholy Process of Decay

1. After residing in a number of other dwellings about town, from 1825 through 1827, Hawthorne and his mother and sisters lived in the old Manning family home located at 10½ Herbert Street, built by Richard Jr. in 1793. This large house has long since been subdivided into condo units. The house at 31 Dearborn Street is today at 26 Dearborn Street, having been moved down the block and across the street during the 1850s. Hawthorne lived in the Dearborn Street home from 1828 (the year Robert Manning had the place built) to 1832. In addition to owning 31 Dearborn, Hawthorne's uncle owned and lived in the residence next door (at that time), 33 Dearborn Street, built in 1824. What is now 26 Dearborn remains a private family home, as does 33 Dearborn. Along with helping run the family's

stagecoach business, Robert was also a noted pomologist who cultivated extensive gardens about his Salem home. (In addition to the considerable time he spent in Salem, Hawthorne spent several years of his boyhood residing at the home of another uncle, Richard Manning III, in South Casco, Maine.)

2. Mouffe, *Hawthorne's Lost Notebook*, 67–68.
3. Paine, *Ships and Sailors of Old Salem*, 6.
4. Hawthorne, *Scarlet Letter*, 8.
5. Miller, *Salem Is My Dwelling Place*, 24.
6. Bridge, *Personal Recollections of Nathaniel Hawthorne*, 36–37.
7. Fogle, "Weird Mockery," 192.
8. Lowell, *Literary Essays*, 21.

5. Great the Pain This Monster Must Be In

1. Now 31 Washington Square North.
2. Joseph White Jr.'s mansion, known today as the White-Silsbee/Hodges-Mott House, stands at 33 Washington Square North, which was formerly 8 Oliver Street before renumbering. Note that another Story sister, Charlotte, married to John Forrester Sr., lived in yet another adjacent mansion. Supreme Court Associate Justice Story, meanwhile, maintained a residence just around the corner. John Forrester Sr. was Nathaniel Hawthorne's first cousin, once removed.
3. Lewis, "Murder of Captain Joseph White," 461.
4. "Murder of Joseph White: The Following Lines Were Written on the Death of Joseph White of Salem, Who Was Found Murdered in His Bed on the Morning of the 7th of April 1830, Aged 82 Years," Broadside, L. Deming, 1830, box KF223. W45 M873 1830, Phillips Library, Peabody Essex Museum.
5. Warren, *History of Harvard Law School*, 444.
6. Bradley and Winans, *Daniel Webster and the Salem Murder*, 19.

6. Murder as One of the Fine Arts

1. The essay is included in *Miscellaneous Essays* by Thomas De Quincey, which is most easily found in its complete text on Project Gutenberg, at gutenberg.org.
2. Wigmore, *Principles of Judicial Truth*, 1085. See also box 1, folder 19, White's autopsy and newspaper account of same, 1830, Joseph White (1748–1830) Murder Trial Papers.
3. "Murder of Captain Joseph White of Salem." *Republican*, April 13, 1830.
4. Newspaper clippings about the White murder, E W585 1830 15, Essex County Collection, Phillips Library, Peabody Essex Museum.

7. The Knapps of Salem

1. Bradley and Winans, *Daniel Webster and the Salem Murder*, 14.
2. Bennett, "Portraits of the Salem Prisoners."

8. The Crowninshields of Salem

1. Ferguson, *Cleopatra's Barge*, 11.
2. H. P. Lovecraft's story "The Thing on the Doorstep" was published in the January 1937 issue of *Weird Tales*. Lovecraft made extended visits to Salem in 1923 and 1929.
3. Goodwin, "First Living Elephant in America," 256–263.
4. Crowninshield, *Story of George Crowninshield's Yacht*, 12.
5. Phillips, *Salem and the Indies*, 382.
6. The Jacobean/Medieval Revival–style Retire Beckett House is owned and maintained by the Peabody Essex Museum and is easily the oldest standing structure in the entire town of Salem, having been built circa 1665 for John Beckett. It formerly stood, appropriately, on Beckett Street but was moved to the Peabody Essex campus in 1924. The museum store takes up the first floor.
7. Saville, *Hidden History of Salem*, 27.
8. Ferguson, *Cleopatra's Barge*, 94–95.
9. Crowninshield, *Story of George Crowninshield's Yacht*, 25.
10. During the mid-1990s the Smithsonian's Paul Forsythe Johnston (a former curator at the Peabody Essex Museum) excavated the yacht's final resting place in in Hanalei Bay, on the north coast of Kaua'i Island. His research team gathered numerous artifacts. It also uncovered a significant portion of the stern of the vessel, which it photographed and measured before reburying it. The artifacts recovered in the 1990s are all from the vessel's Hawaiian period and are housed at Hawaii's Kaua'i Museum.
11. The children were Edward (born 1800), Mary (1803), Richard Jr., "Dick" (1804), George (1806), Ann (1807), John (1808, died as an infant), Margaret (1809), Sarah (1813), Elisabeth (1818), and Jacob (1818, died as an infant).
12. Peabody's Farnham Park, 29 Endicott Street, sits on what was once a part of the Elias Hasket Derby farm.
13. Bentley, *Diary of William Bentley*, 4:402. Today, Buxton's Hill is commonly referred to as Buxton Hill rather than Buxton's. Richard Crowninshield's mill sat on what is known to this day as Crowninshield Pond, fed by Proctor Brook.
14. Bentley, 4:586.
15. Bacon, *Reminiscences*, 7. Louisa is perhaps a bit too damning in her assessment of Richard Sr.'s offspring. They were not all train wrecks. Sarah Crowninshield

married a Joseph Potter and led a respectable life in Salem, dying in 1863. Her son, Joseph Alonzo Potter, an invalid who only lived to the age of twenty-two, became a noted scholar and practitioner of the game of chess, wrote a weekly chess column for the *American Union* newspaper of Boston, corresponded extensively with other experts (to the tune of over one thousand letters), and left one hundred original chess problems for others to solve. He died in 1859. Mary Crowninshield somewhat ironically married a Knapp cousin, Dartmouth graduate Samuel Lorenzo Knapp, an attorney and writer twenty years her senior who'd served as a commander in coastal defense during the War of 1812, been elected to the Massachusetts legislature, and wrote many books. Mary died in 1855. The couple had a daughter whom they named Cleopatra, after the grand yacht of Mary's uncle George Crowninshield Jr. Cleopatra Knapp (1832–1909) remained in the Boston area, married George Munroe Farrington, and had four children with him.

16. Ferguson, *Cleopatra's Barge*, 135.

9. Vigilance

1. Hawthorne, *House of the Seven Gables*, 333.

10. A Damned Eternal Fortune

1. Palmer, *Explanation*, 14. Copy in the Lillian Goldman Law Library of the Yale Law School.
2. See Dwight's obituary in the *New York Times* of July 27, 1854.

11. Forever Stained with Blood, Blood, Blood

1. West, *Arbiters of Reality*, 23.
2. Bradley and Winans, *Daniel Webster and the Salem Murder*, 21.
3. *Trial of John Francis Knapp*, 60. Copy in the Phillips Library, Peabody Essex Museum.
4. See original indictment in box 1, folder 1, Joseph White (1748–1830) Murder Trial Papers.
5. Booth, *Death of an Empire*, 211.
6. Ferguson, *Cleopatra's Barge*, 140.
7. The original of this letter is to be found in box 1, folder 7, Joseph White (1748–1830) Murder Trial Papers.
8. The original of this letter is to be found in box 1, folder 7, Joseph White (1748–1830) Murder Trial Papers.
9. Bradley and Winans, *Daniel Webster and the Salem Murder*, 22.

10. Bradley and Winans, 23.
11. Palmer, *Explanation*, 105.
12. Wigmore, *Principles of Judicial Truth*, 1091.

12. In the Hands of an Angry God

1. Batchelor, "Oriental Religions and Unitarianism," 6.
2. Marti, "Reverend Henry Colman's Agricultural Ministry," 525.
3. *Trials of Capt. Joseph J. Knapp, Jr. and George Crowninshield*, 5. A copy may be found in the Widener Library, Harvard.
4. *Trials of Capt. Joseph J. Knapp, Jr. and George Crowninshield*, 6.
5. *Trial of John Francis Knapp*, 11.
6. Bradley and Winans, *Daniel Webster and the Salem Murder*, 25.

13. Joseph Knapp Jr.'s Confession as Transcribed by Henry Colman

1. *Trials of Capt. Joseph J. Knapp, Jr. and George Crowninshield*, 27–30. Also see related additional documents in box 1, folder 3, Testimonies, confessions, and statements of Mary W. Knapp, Nathaniel P. Knapp, John Francis Knapp, Joseph J. Knapp Jr., 1830, Joseph White (1748–1830) Murder Trial Papers.
2. In response to direct questions from Committee of Vigilance members Barstow and Phillips, Joe Knapp Jr. made a second supplementary confession two days later, on May 31, in which none of the material facts were altered but simply expanded upon slightly.

14. The Fiend Has Robbed Justice of Its Victim

1. The Bunker Hill home in which Franklin Dexter was raised—a late Georgian-Federal mansion built for his father in 1791—still stands at 14 Green Street, Charlestown, Massachusetts. It is today Memorial Hall of the Abraham Lincoln Post of the Grand Army of the Republic. Once surrounded by sprawling, carefully manicured grounds, it is now tightly packed into a dense urban neighborhood, and in much need of repair.
2. Various accounts have presented Franklin Dexter as being Dick Crowninshield's own attorney, which he was not, and have speculated about detailed conversations between Dick and Dexter concerning the laws of principals and accessories. There is no evidence for this. The description given here is what was vouched for by defense attorney Robert Rantoul Jr. See Rantoul's comment in box 1, folder 9, notebook, 2nd trial of John Francis Knapp (Aug. 14, 1830), 1830–1831, Joseph White (1748–1830) Murder Trial Papers.

3. Bell, *We Shall Be No More*, 141.
4. "Death of Crowninshield," *Salem Register*, June 16, 1830.
5. Bell, *We Shall Be No More*, 142.

15. An Elaborate Game of Chess

1. Bradley and Winans, *Daniel Webster and the Salem Murder*, 28.
2. Bradley and Winans, 29.
3. Pearson, *Murder at Smutty Nose and Other Murders*, 37.

16. Black Dan

1. Martineau, *Retrospect of Western Travel*, 280.
2. Martineau, *Society in America*, 42.
3. Crouthamel, *Bennett's New York Herald*, ix.
4. Halttunen, *Murder Most Foul*, 3.
5. Farrell, "Pretrial Publicity in 1830 Salem," 232.
6. Bradley and Winans, *Daniel Webster and the Salem Murder*, 219.
7. Bell, *We Shall Be No More*, 147.

17. A Murder of No Ordinary Character

1. Nevins, *Ordeal of the Union*, 288.
2. Bradley and Winans, *Daniel Webster and the Salem Murder*, 33.
3. Bradley and Winans, 35.
4. Newspaper clippings about the White murder, E W585 1830 15, Essex County Collection.
5. "Knapp Trial Begins in Salem," *New Hampshire Sentinel*, August 4, 1830.
6. Hamilton, *Memoirs, Speeches, and Writings of Robert Rantoul Jr.*, 18.
7. Box 1, folder 10, list of jurors; all those sworn to testify, undated, Joseph White (1748–1830) Murder Trial Papers.
8. Lawson, *American State Trials*, 416.
9. Lawson, 419.
10. Lawson, 417.
11. Lawson, 419–420.
12. *Report of the Evidence*, 8. See also box 2, folder 2, Testimonies of the trial, undated, Joseph White (1748–1830) Murder Trial Papers.
13. *Report of the Evidence*, 9–10.
14. *Report of the Evidence*, 13.

15. Box 1, folder 14, Testimonies of Southwick and Bray, undated, Joseph White (1748–1830) Murder Trial Papers. A *ropewalk* was a place where ropes could be made by laborers who walked out the twists in the strands. Most seaport towns had these, as rope manufacture was essential to the operations of ships and ports.

16. *Report of the Evidence*, 23. The irony here is that Burns never claimed to have seen anything on the night of the murder, nor did he ever even confirm being out on the streets on the evening in question.

17. *Report of the Evidence*, 66.

18. The Cry of the People Is for Blood

1. Transcript in box 1, folder 13, statements, undated, Joseph White (1748–1830) Murder Trial Papers.

19. Refuting the Truth

1. *Report of the Evidence*, 58. See also box 2, folder 2, Testimonies of the trial, undated, Joseph White (1748–1830) Murder Trial Papers.

2. *Report of the Evidence*, 66. See also box 2, folder 2, Testimonies of the trial, undated, Joseph White (1748–1830) Murder Trial Papers.

3. Rachel Hathorne's husband, Simon Forrester, was an Irish immigrant who came to Salem aboard a ship owned by Captain Daniel Hathorne—Nathaniel Hawthorne's paternal uncle and Rachel's father—in 1776.

4. John Remond and his wife Nancy Lenox Remond were the parents of the noted abolitionist and orator Charles Lenox Remond. The elder Remond was a highly successful Salem entrepreneur on a range of fronts, operating not only his shop in Derby Square but also a prosperous catering business in Hamilton Hall, which still stands at 9 Chestnut Street.

5. *Report of the Evidence*, 66. See also box 2, folder 2, Testimonies of the trial, undated, Joseph White (1748–1830) Murder Trial Papers, Series I.

6. Bradley and Winans, *Daniel Webster and the Salem Murder*, 95.

20. The Conclusion of Webster's Summation in the First Trial: *"Suicide Is Confession"*

The text of Webster's summation is taken from the *Boston Courier*, August 13, 1830.

21. A Contagion of Unexampled Popular Frenzy

1. Bradley and Winans, *Daniel Webster and the Salem Murder*, 98.
2. *Report of the Evidence*, 26.

22. Franklin Dexter's Summation at the Second Trial

1. *Report of the Evidence*, 9–31.

23. Daniel Webster's Summation at the Second Trial

The author gives here the version of the summation transcribed in the courtroom by Lynde M. Walter, editor of the *Boston Evening Transcript*, and subsequently published by that paper, thence in *Report of the Evidence*, 31–62. A much expanded and revised version of the speech, based on Walter's original transcription, was subsequently produced and published by Webster himself and appears in the standard editions of Webster's works. However, what's presented here most closely resembles what was originally uttered in court. The author has made a very few cuts to Webster's remarks, only for the sake of eliminating redundant details of testimony and evidence with which the reader will, by this time, already be well acquainted.

1. Bradley and Winans, *Daniel Webster and the Salem Murder*, 219.
2. Richardson, *Daniel Webster for Young Americans*, xxx.
3. Lodge, *Daniel Webster*, 198–199.

24. The Execution of Frank Knapp

1. Hungerford, "Hawthorne Gossips About Salem," 455–469.
2. "Knapp Execution Today," *Salem Gazette*, September 28, 1830.
3. "Knapp Executed," *Salem Gazette*, September 29, 1830.
4. Newspaper clippings about the White murder, E W585 1830 15, Essex County Collection.

25. Emphatically Encompassed by a Sea of Blood

1. *Trials of Capt. Joseph J. Knapp, Jr. and George Crowninshield*, 18.
2. Lawson, *American State Trials*, 636. See also *Trials of Capt. Joseph J. Knapp, Jr. and George Crowninshield*, 31.
3. *Trials of Capt. Joseph J. Knapp, Jr. and George Crowninshield*, 25.
4. Bradley and Winans, *Daniel Webster and the Salem Murder*, 225–226.
5. Brown, *Self-Evident Truths*, 268.

26. She Must Be the Very Devil

1. "Salem Murder," *Salem Gazette*, December 21, 1830.
2. Webster, *Works of Daniel Webster*, 90–91.

27. The Complaint of the Human Heart

1. Hawthorne, *Scarlet Letter*, 243.
2. Matthiessen, *American Renaissance*, 214–215. See also Marks, "Who Killed Judge Pyncheon?," 362.
3. Barton, *Literary Executions*, 24.
4. Hawthorne, *Twice-Told Tales*, 81.
5. Poe, *Dover Reader*, 196.
6. Taken from the *Boston Courier*, August 13, 1830.
7. Poe, *Dover Reader*, 197. For an exhaustive consideration of Hawthorne, Poe, and the literary relationship of both to the White murder, see chapter 1 of Kopley, *Threads of the Scarlet Letter*.

28. Ghosts

1. Hawthorne, *Scarlet Letter*, 7–9.
2. Hungerford, "Hawthorne Gossips About Salem," 462.
3. Gray, *Reports of Cases*, 524.
4. "Death of George C. Crowninshield," *Boston Evening Transcript*, July 26, 1888. The obituary misstates Crowninshield's age at the time of his death as eighty-five. He was actually eighty-two. Some genealogical sources misstate George's death year as 1889; however, the July 1888 publication in the *Transcript* seems conclusive. Anna Stedman, the granddaughter, was born in 1861 and died in 1913.
5. Thanks to the exertions of Stephen White, no copies of the first edition of this book are to be found anywhere—at least none that this author could uncover.
6. Hawthorne, *Mosses from an Old Manse*, 166.
7. Miller, *Salem Is My Dwelling Place*, 473.
8. Nathaniel and Sophia's three children led strange and troubled lives. Their eldest, Una, spent time in asylums and died young, in 1877, at the age of thirty-three, without ever marrying. Their youngest, Rose, endured an unhappy marriage to the talented but alcoholic editor and writer George Lathrop, suffered the death of a child, and eventually—with Lathrop—converted to Catholicism. After George died in 1898, Rose entered a convent and became a nun. She established St. Rose's Free Home for Incurable Cancer in Manhattan, and also the Rosary Hill Home in—ironically—Hawthorne, New York. Rose published *Memories of Hawthorne*

in 1923 and died in 1926. The Hawthornes' son, Julian, became a writer of weird tales—fantasies and mysteries of ghosts and hauntings. He also served time in prison for embezzlement and died in California in 1934.

9. Hurd, *History of Essex County*, xlii.

10. Joseph Jenkins Knapp Sr.'s second wife was Lydia Fisk King.

11. For an exhaustive account of Nathaniel Phippen Knapp's theological career, see Sprague, *Annals of the American Episcopalian Pulpit*, 742–745. Phippen's wife was Ellen McMacken Lee Bedford. (Ellen's maiden name was Lee. She'd previously been married to a Thomas Bedford, of Kentucky.) Phippen and Ellen's son, Ludwell Lee Knapp, born 1845, fought for the Confederacy during the Civil War. He died by suicide at Waco, Texas, in February 1883, at age thirty-seven, without having married. Phippen's daughter, Caroline Francis Knapp (1847–1926) married the Rev. John Richard Joyner. (Note Caroline's middle name honoring her executed uncle.) The Joyners had five children: Ludwell Lee Joyner (1874, died an infant), Wilmer Joyner (1875–1951), Reginald Joyner (1879-1947), Richard Lucien Joyner (1883-?), and Emily Williams Joyner (1887-1959). See Wilmer Joyner's obituary in the *Washington Evening Star*, August 17, 1951.

12. Booth, *Death of an Empire*, 274.

13. Today known as Larch Farm, Mary Beckford's property in Wenham is located at 38 Larch Road. The house there, known as the Goldsmith-Pickering House after the two owners before Beckford, is a classic First Period structure expanded through the years and remodeled in the 1780s to give it the look of the Federal era. The house is on the National Register of Historic Places and is in private hands.

14. Cherry Hill Farm was located on what is today Wenham's Cherry Street. The lands of the former farm now overlook the Indian Hill Reservoir.

15. Clark, *Shipping Era*, 50.

16. Before Stephen White owned the island, it was known as Canary Island and then Leggate's Island. Beechwater was designed by Boston architect Samuel Perkins.

17. See detailed archaeological information contained in the February 2014 Department of the Interior, National Park Service, documentation related to the Salem National Maritime Site's recognition in the National Registry of Historic Places, at https://www.nps.gov/nr/feature/places/pdfs/ad_66000048_04_08_2014.pdf.

Appendix: The Last Will and Testament of Captain Joseph White

1. Joseph White, will dated January 8, 1830, Film Roll—"Probate Records, Vol 407–408, Book 107–108, 1829–1833," Img. 209–211, Massachusetts, Wills and Probate Records, 1635–1991, Essex County, MA.

BIBLIOGRAPHY

Bacon, Louisa Crowninshield. *Reminiscences*. Salem, MA: Privately published by New-comb & Gauss, 1922.

Barton, John Cyril. *Literary Executions: Capital Punishment and American Culture, 1920–1925*. Baltimore, MD: Johns Hopkins University Press, 2014.

Batchelor, George. "Oriental Religions and Unitarianism." *The Christian Register*, December 23, 1915.

Bell, Millicent. *Hawthorne's View of the Artist*. Albany, NY: State University of New York Press, 1962.

Bell, Richard. *We Shall Be No More: Suicide and Self Government in the Newly United States*. Cambridge, MA: Harvard University Press, 2012.

Bennett, James Gordon. "Portraits of the Salem Prisoners." *Marblehead Register*, August 21, 1830.

Bentham, Jeremy. *A Treatise on Judicial Evidence, Extracted from the Manuscripts of Jeremy Bentham, Esq. by M. Dumont*. London: Baldwin, Cradock, and Joy, 1825.

Bentley, William. *The Diary of William Bentley, DD, Pastor of the East Church, Salem, Massachusetts*. Vol. 1: April 1784–December 1792. Salem, MA: The Essex Institute, 1905.

———. *The Diary of William Bentley, DD, Pastor of the East Church, Salem, Massachusetts*. Vol. 4: January 1811–December 1819. Salem, MA: The Essex Institute, 1914.

Booth, Robert. *Death of an Empire*. New York: St. Martin's Press, 2011.

Bradley, Howard A., and James A. Winans. *Daniel Webster and the Salem Murder*. Columbia, MO: Artcraft Press, 1956.

Bridge, Horatio. *Personal Recollections of Nathaniel Hawthorne*. New York: Harper & Brothers, 1893.

Brown, Richard. *Self-Evident Truths: Contesting Equal Rights from the Revolution to the Civil War*. New Haven, CT: Yale University Press, 2017.

Clark, Arthur H. *The Shipping Era: An Epitome of Famous British and American Clipper Ships, Their Owners, Builders, Commanders, and Crews, 1843–1869*. New York: G. P. Putnam's Sons, 1911.

Clarke, Helen. *Hawthorne's Country*. New York: Baker and Taylor, 1910.

Crouthamel, James L. *Bennett's New York Herald and the Rise of the Popular Press*. Syracuse, NY: Syracuse University Press, 1989.

Crowninshield, George. *The Story of George Crowninshield's Yacht* Cleopatra's Barge. Boston: Privately published, 1913.

Farrell, James M. "Pretrial Publicity in 1830 Salem: Daniel Webster, New England News, and the Knapp-White Trial." *Journalism History* 44, no. 4 (Winter 2019): 232–240.

Ferguson, David L. *Cleopatra's Barge: The Crowninshield Story*. Boston: Little, Brown and Company, 1976.

Fogle, Richard Harter. "Weird Mockery: An Element of Hawthorne's Style." *Style* 2, no. 3 (Fall 1968): 191–202.

Goodwin, George G. "The First Living Elephant in America." *Journal of Mammalogy* 6, no. 4 (November 1925): 256–263.

Gray, Horace, Jr. *Reports of Cases Argued and Determined of the Supreme Judicial Court of Massachusetts*. Vol. 2. Boston: Little, Brown and Company, 1863.

Halttunen, Karen. *Murder Most Foul: The Killer and the American Gothic Imagination*. Cambridge, MA: Harvard University Press, 1998.

Hamilton, Luther, ed. *Memoirs, Speeches, and Writings of Robert Rantoul, Jr.* Boston: John P. Jewett & Company, 1854.

Hawthorne, Nathaniel. *The House of the Seven Gables*. Boston: Ticknor & Fields, 1851.

———. *Mosses from an Old Manse*. Vol. 1. London: Wiley & Putnam, 1841.

———. *The Scarlet Letter: A Romance*. Boston: Ticknor & Fields, 1850.

———. *Twice-Told Tales*. New York: Dent, 1917.

Hungerford, Edward B. "Hawthorne Gossips About Salem." *The New England Quarterly* 6, no. 3 (September 1933): 445–469.

Hurd, D. Hamilton. *History of Essex County, Massachusetts, with Biographical Sketches of Many of Its Pioneers and Prominent Men*. Vol. 2. Philadelphia: J. W. Lewis & Company, 1888.

Knapp, Samuel L. *A Memoir of the Life of Daniel Webster*. Rev. 2nd ed., New York: J. S. Redfield, 1835.

Kopley, Richard. *The Threads of the Scarlet Letter: A Study of Hawthorne's Transformative Art*. Newark: University of Delaware Press, 2003.

Lawson, John Davison. *American State Trials*. Vol. 7. St. Louis, MO: Thomas Law Books, 1917.

Lewis, Walker. "The Murder of Captain Joseph White: Salem, Massachusetts, 1830." *The American Bar Association Journal* 54 (May 1968): 460–466.

Lodge, Henry Cabot. *Daniel Webster*. Boston: Houghton Mifflin, 1883.

Lowell, James Russell. *Literary Essays*. Vol. 2. Boston: Houghton Mifflin, 1890.

Marks, Alfred H. "Who Killed Judge Pyncheon?—The Role of the Imagination in *The House of the Seven Gables*," *PMLA* 71, no. 3 (June 1956): 355–369.

Marti, Donald B. "The Reverend Henry Colman's Agricultural Ministry." *Agricultural History* 51, no. 3 (July 1977): 524–539.

Martineau, Harriet. *Retrospect of Western Travel*. Vol. 1. London: Saunders & Otley, 1838.

———. *Society in America*. Vol. 2. Paris: Baudry's European Library, 1837.

Matthiessen, F. O. *The American Renaissance: Art and Expression in the Age of Emerson and Whitman*. London: Oxford University Press, 1941.

Miller, Edwin Haviland. *Salem Is My Dwelling Place: A Life of Nathaniel Hawthorne*. Iowa City: University of Iowa Press, 1991.

Moore, Margaret B. *The Salem World of Nathaniel Hawthorne*. Columbia, MO: University of Missouri Press, 1998.

Mouffe, Barbara S., ed. *Hawthorne's Lost Notebook, 1835–1841*. University Park: Pennsylvania University Press, 1978.

Nevins, Allan. *The Ordeal of the Union*. Vol. 1. New York: Collier Books, 1992.

Paine, Ralph Delahaye. *The Ships and Sailors of Old Salem: The Record of a Brilliant Era of American Achievement*. Boston: Charles E. Lauriat Co., 1923.

Palmer, John C. R. Jr. *Explanation, or, Eighteen Hundred and Thirty: Being a Series of Facts Connected with the Life of the Author, From Eighteen Hundred and Twenty-Five to the Present Day*. Boston: Privately published by S. N. Dickinson, 1831.

Pearson, Edmund. *Murder at Smutty Nose and Other Murders*. New York: Charles Scribner's Sons, 1938.

Phillips, James Duncan. *Salem and the Indies: The Story of the Great Commercial Era of the City*. Boston: Houghton Mifflin, 1947.

Poe, Edgar Allan. *Edgar Allan Poe: The Dover Reader*. New York: Dover, 2014.

A Report of the Evidence and Points of Law, Arising from the Trial of John Francis Knapp, for the Murder of Joseph White, Esquire. Boston: W. & S. B. Ives, 1830.

Richardson, Charles Francis, ed. *Daniel Webster for Young Americans*. Boston: Little, Brown and Company, 1903.

Saville, Susanne. *Hidden History of Salem*. Charleston, SC: The History Press, 2010.

Sprague, William Buell. *Annals of the American Episcopalian Pulpit*. Vol. 5. New York: Robert Carter & Brothers, 1861.

Trial and Conviction of John Francis Knapp as Principal in the Second Degree for the Murder of Capt. Joseph White, Before the Supreme Judicial Court of the Commonwealth of Massachusetts, at a Special Session, Commenced at Salem, July 20, 1830. Boston: Dutton and Wentworth, 1830.

The Trials of Capt. Joseph J. Knapp, Jr. and George Crowninshield, Esq., for the Murder of Capt. Joseph White of Salem on the Night of the 6th of April 1830. Boston: Charles Ellms, 1830.

Warren, Charles. *History of the Harvard Law School and of the Early Legal Conditions of America.* Vol. 1. New York: Lewis Publishing Company, 1908.

Webster, Daniel. *Works of Daniel Webster.* Boston: Little, Brown and Company, 1857.

West, Peter. *The Arbiters of Reality: Hawthorne, Melville, and the Rise of Mass Information Culture.* Columbus: Ohio State University Press, 2008.

Wigmore, John Henry, ed. *The Principles of Judicial Truth.* Vol. 1. Boston: Little, Brown and Company, 1913.

INDEX